Revolution in Texas

Revolution in

Texas

How a Forgotten Rebellion and Its Bloody Suppression Turned Mexicans into Americans

Benjamin Heber Johnson

Yale University Press

NEW HAVEN AND LONDON

Published with assistance from the income of the Frederick John Kingsbury
Memorial Fund, and with assistance from the Louis Stern Memorial Fund.

Designed by Gregg Chase
Set in Monotype Bulmer type by Duke & Company
Printed in the United States of America by R. R. Donnelley & Sons.

Library of Congress Cataloging-in-Publication Data
Johnson, Benjamin Heber.
    Revolution in Texas : how a forgotten rebellion and
its bloody suppression turned Mexicans into Americans /
Benjamin Heber Johnson.
    p. cm. — (Western Americana series)
Includes bibliographical references and index.
ISBN 0-300-09425-6 (cloth : alk. paper)
1. Texas—History—1846–1950. 2. Texas—Politics and
government—1865–1950. 3. Texas, South—History—
20th century. 4. Revolutions—Texas, South—History—
20th century. 5. Violence—Texas, South—History—20th
century. 6. Texas, South—Ethnic relations. 7. Mexican
Americans—Texas, South—History—20th century.
8. Mexican Americans—Texas, South—Politics and
government—20th century. 9. Mexican-American Border
Region—History—20th century. I. Title. II. Series.
F391.J64 2003
976.4'4061—dc21

                                      2003009133

A catalogue record for this book is available from
the British Library. The paper in this book meets the
guidelines for permanence and durability of
the Committee on Production Guidelines for Book
Longevity of the Council on Library Resources.

10 9 8 7 6 5 4 3 2 1

for Clark Davis
too soon gone

Caminante, no hay camino.
Se hace camino al andar.

Traveler, there is no path.
Paths are made by walking.

—Antonio Machado

Contents

Introduction

The uprising began at the southern tip of Texas in the summer of 1915, as a series of raids by ethnic Mexicans on ranches, irrigation works, and railroads, and quickly developed into a full-blown rebellion. Groups of armed men—some from across the Rio Grande, others seemingly from out of nowhere—stole livestock, burned railroad bridges, tore up tracks, killed farmers, attacked post offices, robbed stores, and repeatedly battled local posses, Texas Rangers, and the thousands of federal soldiers dispatched to quell the violence. The groups ranged from two or three assailants who quickly vanished into the brush to scores of well-organized and disciplined mounted men.

The raids appeared to be the fulfillment of a manifesto titled the "Plan de San Diego," which was drafted in south Texas in early 1915. The Plan called for a "liberating army of all races" (composed of Mexicans, blacks, and Indians) to kill all white males over age sixteen and overthrow United States rule in Texas, Colorado, New Mexico, Arizona, and California. The freed territory would form an independent republic, perhaps to rejoin Mexico at a future date.

Although obviously a failure in its wider ambitions, the rebellion did make significant headway in south Texas. Aided for a time by a revolutionary faction in northeast Mexico, ethnic Mexican rebels—who came to be called *Sediciosos* (Seditionists)—killed dozens of Anglo farmers and drove countless more from their homes. Nellie Austin recalled what happened when an armed band held up her family's farm: "I then proceeded to the place where my husband and son had been shot; I first went to my husband and found two bullet holes in his back one on each side near his spinal column. . . . [M]y husband was not quite dead but died in a few minutes thereafter. I then proceeded to my son Charles who was lying a few feet from his father; I found his face in a large pool of blood and saw that he was shot in the mouth, neck and in the back of the head and dead when I reached him."[1] Many Anglo residents fled the region in the belief that the Plan and the violence meant that more such bloodshed lay in the future. "As soon as the bandit raids started the more timid ones commenced to move out at once, and inside of three months," remembered one local dairy farmer, "all the tenant farmers had left and a good many people there left their own farms, and others went up north or came to town and stayed until the bandit troubles were over." Hundreds, perhaps several thousand, clustered in urban areas. "[T]here was not anybody stayed in the country during those bandit raids. . . . There were no farms under cultivation that year."[2]

In response, vigilantes and Texas Rangers led a far bloodier counterinsurgency that included the indiscriminate harassment of ethnic Mexicans,* forcible relocation of rural residents, and mass executions. The wave of terror left few south Texans untouched. Prominent citizens formed "Law and Order Leagues" and carried out many of the atrocities. The Rangers and vigilantes took a high toll on the population. On a single day, for example, "[n]ear Edinburg . . . the bodies of two more Mexicans were found. They had been slain during the night. During the morning the decapitated body of another Mexican roped to a large log floated down the Rio Grande." Extralegal executions be-

---

*There is no graceful ethno-racial nomenclature for describing either south Texas or the border region as a whole. For purposes of consistency I have chosen to use "Mexican" to refer to Mexican nationals with no deep roots in the United States, "Tejano" or "Texas-Mexican" to refer to Texas residents of Mexican descent, and "ethnic Mexicans" to subsume both groups. The label "Mexican American" is reserved for those of Mexican descent who considered themselves to be U.S. citizens. Accordingly, it appears most often in the later portions of the book. "Anglo," following the common practice in Texas, refers to Euro-Americans not of Mexican descent. It is a more useful term than "white" because many Tejanos were in fact very light in complexion and in some circumstances considered themselves "white."

Racial and ethnic categories present themselves as natural and commonsensical. In fact, they are the products of history rather than the inherent or immutable properties of groups of people—how else could it be that a "white" woman can give birth to a "black" child, but the reverse is impossible under American racial terminology? I have chosen to use the term "racial" to describe conflicts between Anglos and ethnic Mexicans not to impute a biological basis to early twentieth-century social distinctions, but rather to capture the deep social gulf that came to separate the two groups.

came so common that a San Antonio reporter observed that the "finding of dead bodies of Mexicans, suspected for various reasons of being connected with the troubles, has reached a point where it creates little or no interest. It is only when a raid is reported or an American is killed that the ire of the people is aroused." "[T]he recent happenings in Brownsville country indicate that there is a serious surplus population there that needs eliminating," argued the editor of the *Laredo Times*. Whatever their station in life or their political sympathies, virtually all those of Mexican descent found themselves in an untenable situation. "[O]ne or more of us may have incurred the displeasure of some one, and it seems only necessary for that some one to whisper our names to an officer, to have us imprisoned and killed without an opportunity to prove in a fair trial, the falsity of the charges against us," pleaded residents of Kingsville. "[S]ome of us who sign this petition, may be killed without even knowing the name of him who accuses. Our privileged denunciators may continue their infamous proceedings—answerable to no one."[3]

Just as some of their Anglo neighbors fled north or to urban areas, so too did many Texas-Mexicans choose to cross the river into Mexico, then wracked by famine, epidemics, and warfare. The reprisals cleared large sections of ethnic Mexican residents. "Frequently we would find dead bodies," José Tomás (J. T.) Canales recalled of such areas, "and the ranches burned. Relatives were intimidated to the extent that they would not even bury their own relatives." Perhaps those who fled chose wisely, for even observers hesitant to acknowledge Anglo brutality recognized that the death toll was at least three hundred. Some of those who found human remains with skulls marked by execution-style bullet holes in the years to come were sure that the toll had been much, much higher, perhaps five thousand.[4]

The gap between the seeming importance of the Plan de San Diego and my own ignorance of it first prompted my interest in this topic. The uprising was comparable in scale to the best-known urban racial conflicts of American history—the New York City draft riots during the Civil War, more recent upheavals in Watts, Detroit, and Los Angeles—all of which were also ended only with the massive deployment of military force. Like these riots, the Plan de San Diego both reflected racial tensions and helped to systematize them. The defeat of the Plan de San Diego ushered in a system of harsh racial segregation in south Texas, one explicitly modeled on the south's Jim Crow. Anglos seized the rebellion as an opportunity to curtail ethnic Mexican voting and political power and to create separate school systems and public accommodations.

The uprising was thus violent, large, and had important consequences. Then why had neither I nor my parents, all of us natives of Texas and products of its school system, even heard of it? It was not until my mid-twenties, huddled in a dank library fifteen hundred miles from Texas, that I came across a brief description of the Plan de San Diego. I tracked down as much information as possible about the uprising. Although there were some sources available —a scattering of articles and a good book about the relationship between Mexican political exiles and the rebellion—it became clear that the events had been largely ignored by historians and the general public alike. In fact, I learned later, some of this was due to the fact that the Texas legislature deliberately suppressed evidence of the Texas Rangers' brutality, refusing to publish copies of hearings into their conduct and allowing Rangers to threaten their chief opponent in the legislature with death.

Recreating the uprising and looking into its causes and consequences became the focus of this book. From the start, the topic seemed to speak to important developments in American intellectual and social life. The remarkable growth of the Latino population—poised to become the nation's largest minority group and soon to outnumber Anglos in most southwestern states —makes the history of Mexican Americans, the largest Latino group, all the more important to the nation as a whole. Black–white relations were at the center of the American experience for our first two centuries of nationhood. The relations between Latinos and other groups may be just as decisive for this century. Events such as the Plan de San Diego, which struck most later observers as colorful but peripheral to the mainstream of American history, may thus take on a new importance in a nation where millions speak Spanish as their first language and where José is now the most common first name for newborn children.

If the Plan de San Diego is important to the history of the United States, then at the same time it cannot be encompassed completely within its bounds. The uprising was a transnational event. It took place on the border with Mexico and drew inspiration and some direct support from the Mexican Revolution, and its manifesto proposed redrawing the map of North America. In this sense it resonates with our own time, when the movement of people, culture, and capital across borders suggests to many that nation-states are not the almighty institutions that they once seemed. Historians are trying to free their accounts of the past from the assumption that nations are inevitably the sources of sovereignty and popular identities—precisely the assumptions that made border events such as this uprising seem so peripheral.

Writing about the events in south Texas in the early twentieth century provides a great opportunity to craft just such a history. And thus the heart of this book is a narrative of the Plan de San Diego uprising—its initial successes, the violent response that ended it, and the continued military occupation of south Texas through the end of the First World War. I set the stage for this narrative by tracing the specific people, institutions, and ideas so critical to the rebellion and its suppression, and linking them to broader developments in Mexico and the United States. Readers are therefore likely to encounter unfamiliar topics—social patterns on Mexico's northern frontier, ranching practices in the Rio Grande Valley, the Mexican Revolution—alongside more familiar subjects such as American notions of ethnicity, debates over the meaning of citizenship, the mobilization for World War I, and segregation. My hope is that this juxtaposition will prompt the recognition of how deeply entwined are the histories of Mexico, Mexican Americans, and the United States.

The process of researching and writing this book confirmed many of my initial hunches, particularly that what happened at the southern tip of Texas in the 1910s was a critical chapter in American race relations and the shared histories of Mexico and the United States. There was, however, one big surprise: the response of Tejanos (Texans of Mexican descent) to the Plan and its defeat. I had expected them to find the vigilantism a good reason to further resent American rule over what had been Mexican territory just two generations before, to see in the harsher segregation that followed the uprising all the more reason to embrace Mexican nationalism. But one influential group, amazingly enough, found reason for more optimism. They abandoned the irredentist project of returning the border region to the sovereignty of Mexico, and instead struggled to claim their full rights as United States citizens. A decade after the violence subsided, this group founded the League of United Latin American Citizens (LULAC), a sort of Mexican American counterpart to the NAACP (National Association for the Advancement of Colored People). During the uprising, although brutalized by local Anglos and dominant Texan political factions, these individuals found sympathy and even protection from the very army units dispatched to crush the Plan de San Diego. The United States, they came to believe, offered racial minorities a chance for effective and equal citizenship rights, not merely the iron hand of segregation and lynching. The defeat of the uprising, the last major movement seeking reunification with Mexico, marked the end of the American conquest of the Southwest. Absorption into the United States, however, did not spell a final defeat or unchallenged subjugation for ethnic Mexicans, but rather a turn toward a different form of struggle.

That the Plan de San Diego helped to create Mexican American identity at first only confused me. Why would a prolonged episode of savage racial violence prompt people to claim the same nationality as their victimizers? What did being an American mean to those whose daily language, culture, and identity bore more marks of Tamaulipas, Nuevo León, and Coahuila than of east Texas, Louisiana, or Arkansas? At the same time, the more I found my attention drawn to the first people to call themselves Mexican Americans, the more I was forced to reconsider my enthusiasm for postnational history, to

leaven my suspicion of nationalism with an appreciation for the need of oppressed peoples to assert their rights as members of a national community.
This book is, to be sure, a transnational history, one that draws on the archives
and histories of both Mexico and the United States to tell a story that has for
too long fallen in the cracks between nations. But to my surprise, it also became
a story of becoming American, a journey of some triumph in the midst of a
great tragedy.

1

Conquest

> We do not want the people of Mexico, either as citizens or
> subjects. All we want is a portion of territory, which they
> nominally hold, either uninhabited or, where inhabited at
> all, sparsely so, and with a population which would soon
> recede.
>
> —*Michigan senator Lewis Cass, 1847*

The Mexican-American War began in the territory that today is south
Texas—the strip of land between the Rio Grande and Nueces rivers, the lower
portion of which is known as "the Valley." In 1846, United States president
James Polk sent troops across the Nueces, which Mexico claimed was the
border, and toward the Rio Grande, which he insisted was the proper international line. Polk used the inevitable clash with Mexican forces as the justification for the massive invasion that eventually cost the weaker nation more
than half of its territory.

Nearly thirty years later, looking out at the huge expanse of plains and
brush that stretched for miles around him, General William Tecumseh Sherman
wondered if it had been worth it. Why anybody would fight over the land that
lay before him was a mystery. "We should go to war again, to make them take
it back," he concluded.

Not all visitors found the region so inhospitable. From the 1740s on,
Spaniards, Coahuiltecan peoples, Mexicans, and eventually Anglo-Americans
struggled for possession of what became south Texas. The Mexican-American
War seemed to answer the question of the nation to which it would belong.

But drawing a line on a map was one thing, and daily life quite another. What would it mean for Tejanos to live under United States rule? The Treaty of Guadalupe-Hidalgo, which ended the war, granted American citizenship to Mexican nationals who remained in what had become the United States. What would that citizenship mean in a country with its own deeply rooted racial hierarchy, and especially in a slave state such as Texas? The treaty protected the property rights of former Mexican citizens, including the land grants made in the Nueces Strip. But what would actually happen to those lands?

In some ways the challenges faced by Tejanos mirrored those faced by immigrants to the United States. How would being American change the way people made a living, married, voted, thought of themselves, and related to other ethnic and racial groups? Would the group struggle to maintain its culture in a new environment, or would it enthusiastically adopt the language, food, and customs of the majority population? Would it welcome marriages

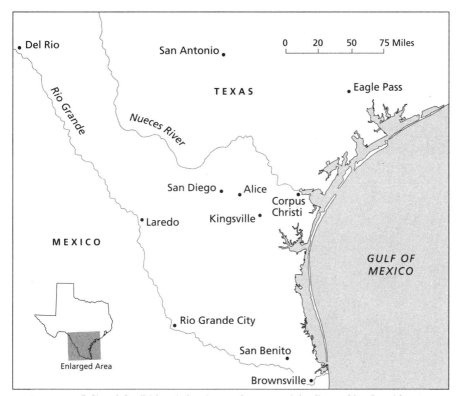

Texas map (left) and detail (above) showing south Texas and the disputed border with Mexico.

with outsiders or fear that they threatened the future of the community? What would the children and grandchildren of the first generation think of the choices that their ancestors made?

But in other ways the challenges faced by ethnic Mexicans in the Southwest were quite different. For they were not willing immigrants, but rather a conquered people subjected to the rule of their conquerors (as a Chicano slogan from more than a century later put it, "We didn't cross the border; the border crossed us"). They might choose to accommodate themselves to this conquest, making the best of a difficult situation. Or they could choose to resist it. Moreover, the ethnic Mexican community was quite diverse, encompassing wealthy elites who traced their ancestry to the original Spanish conquest of the region, modest ranchers, urban shopkeepers, laborers, deeply rooted residents, and more recent arrivals from Mexico. Would these groups' response to the challenges of American conquest bind them together all the more closely or widen the gaps between them?

The answers to these questions changed over time. The life of Tejanos in the 1910s was quite different from that in the 1850s or 1890s. From 1848 until the eve of the Plan de San Diego, Tejanos dealt with their absorption into the United States in different ways, at times rejecting American rule altogether, at other times reconciling themselves to it. Although they maintained much of their cultural autonomy and some of their power into the twentieth century, rapid economic changes brought by the railroad threatened all that they had struggled to defend, creating the grievances that would lead to the Plan de San Diego uprising.

Continuity and Change

The United States' conquest of the Mexican north was a traumatic event for the conquered, often bringing dramatic, wrenching changes. In some places hordes of Americans simply overran the previous Mexican and Indian residents. The several hundred thousand natives and less than seven thousand Mexican inhabitants of California, for example, watched with amazement as annexation and the Gold Rush drew immigrants from all of the states of the Union and from places as diverse as south China, Chile, Sonora, England, France, and Belgium. This demographic upheaval was particularly catastrophic for the state's native peoples, whose ranks dwindled from about one hundred fifty thousand in 1850 to thirty thousand just a decade later. California's Anglo and European population increased tenfold from 1848 to 1850, with San Francisco alone growing from a sleepy village of one thousand to a bustling city of thirty-five thousand. Across the entire Southwest, ethnic Mexicans found themselves outnumbered by Anglos by a margin of eight to one by 1860, scarcely more than a decade after the war.[1]

The Treaty of Guadalupe-Hidalgo guaranteed Mexican nationals who remained in the newly annexed territory "the enjoyment of all the rights of citizens of the United States" and promised that "[w]ith respect to political rights, their condition shall be on an equality with that of the inhabitants of the other territories of the United States." In practice, however, Anglo arrivals displayed little consideration for the rights of the established ethnic Mexican populations. Although many Americans had opposed the war with Mexico as a jingoistic endeavor that threatened to extend slavery from coast to coast, most doves and hawks alike agreed that Mexicans were racial degenerates. South Carolina senator John Calhoun warned of the dangers of annexing the heavily populated areas of Mexico, proclaiming that "Ours . . . is the Government of a white race. . . . [The] greatest misfortunes of Spanish America are to be traced to the fatal error of placing the colored races on an equality with the white race. . . . Are we to associate with ourselves as equals, companions, and fellow citizens, the Indians and mixed race of Mexico? I should consider such a thing as fatal to our institutions." The rapidity and completeness of conquest only confirmed such notions of racial triumphalism. One white woman living on the border observed "athletic Americans, and puny-looking Mexican laborers" pass before her, and could not help but conclude that the contrast "was that of an old race passing away—a new race pressing on its departing footsteps —a new scene in the history of the Country, a possession by conquest."[2]

These attitudes, not the treaty provisions, were born out in practice. In California, newly arrived Americans drove ethnic Mexicans out of the mine works, stole their land at gunpoint or by legal chicanery, and soon reduced even formerly wealthy families to subsistence farming or forced them to move into the incipient barrios of Santa Barbara and Los Angeles. This treatment particularly outraged the significant number of Californios (Mexican-descent settlers of California) who had actually supported American annexation. Near the end of his life, Mariano Vallejo, one of the most enthusiastic, could only curse the "government that promised to respect our rights and to treat us as its own sons."[3]

The status of Tejanos after Texas independence presaged Vallejo's lament. The Republic of Texas won its independence from Mexico in 1836, after rebel forces defeated the army led by Mexican president Antonio López de Santa Anna. Some Tejanos joined this rebellion, serving in the doomed band that defended the Alamo, participating in the triumph at the Battle of San Jacinto, and joining the new Republic's first constitutional convention and cabinet. But most Anglo Texans soon came to see their rebellion as the triumph of white people over "the mongrel and illicit descendents of . . . Indian, Mexican, and Spanish," as one writer put it.[4] They expelled Mexicans en masse from much of central and east Texas, from the very towns that they had founded.

The Texas Rangers played an important role in keeping Tejanos in their place throughout the nineteenth century, just as they would be at the center of vigilantism during the Plan de San Diego. In 1835, as the infant Republic of Texas sought its independence from Mexico, its Congress created the Ranger force. Organized along military lines, the Rangers were split into three companies, each led by a captain and two lieutenants. No mere law enforcers or state militia, Rangers were from the beginning the embodiment of the Texan version of the American frontier myth. Though employed by the state, early Rangers were recruited for their physical stamina, their skill with guns and horses, and their frontier-honed abilities to follow even the faintest trail for weeks upon end.

These were tough, fighting frontier heroes who courageously defended pioneers from marauding Indians, home-grown "bad men," and recalcitrant Mexicans. The men who wore the lone star badge were enshrined in legend even when still living. Many a Texan grew up on stories of such Rangers as "Big Foot" Wallace, Jack Hayes, Ben McCullough, and Frank Hamer. "There

is no question but that a definite potency exists in the name 'Texas Ranger,'"
crowed former Ranger commander William W. Sterling some forty years ago.
"Take two men of equal size and arm them with identical weapons. Call one
of them a deputy sheriff and the other a Ranger. Send each of these officers
out to stop a mob or quell a riot. The crowd will resist the deputy, but will
submit to the authority of the Ranger." The featuring of Rangers in dime-
store novels, the radio (and then television) show *The Lone Ranger,* the Texas
Rangers major league baseball team, and the more recent television series
Walker, Texas Ranger mean that even those Americans with no actual connection to Texas or to the Rangers can join in the celebration of their triumphs.[5]

Not everybody was so enamored with the Texas Rangers, however. Conquest has its victims, in Texas as everywhere, and in this case the conquered
often reserved particular spleen for the Rangers. Their brutality against civilian
populations during the Mexican-American War earned them the epithet *los
diablos Tejanos*—the Texan devils. During their occupation of the Nueces
Strip in the Mexican-American War, according to one American soldier, the
land was "strewed with the skeletons of Mexicans sacrificed by these despera-
does." Similar violence in occupied Mexico City prompted General Zachary
Taylor to threaten to imprison an entire Ranger unit. What was embarrassing
to national authorities abroad, however, was useful to state authorities back
home, especially along the border. One Texas Ranger stationed near the
boundary in the 1870s boasted of "a set policy of terrorizing the Mexicans at
every turn," adding that he "let no opportunity go unimproved to assert ourselves and override the 'Greasers.'" Border Tejanos had a special derogatory
term for the Texas Rangers—*rinche*—to reflect the Rangers' well-deserved
reputation for wanton violence.[6]

If conquest was a wrenching experience—a deadly one for those exposed
to the tender mercies of the Rangers—then nevertheless in some places in
the Southwest it did not immediately cause a wholesale dispossession of ethnic
Mexicans. Broadly speaking, where ethnic Mexicans remained a majority—
in parts of southern California, New Mexico, and the border regions of Texas
—they continued to hold significant amounts of land and to wield political
power. They therefore avoided becoming a despised and oppressed racial
caste. South Texas was one such place. The Nueces Strip saw no huge influx
of land-hungry white farmers or miners. Central and east Texas still had plenty
of land available for modest farms and slave plantations, and in any event the
region's aridity made it inhospitable to agriculturists. For more than fifty years,
Anglos were a small minority in south Texas, especially in the countryside.
And they knew it.

"Nine-tenths of the land is actually possessed by what is known as the
Mexican population," wrote an Anglo of the border area nearly three decades

after the Mexican-American War. "The great majority of these Mexicans (so-called) have been and are now recognized as citizens of the state of Texas, and are the principal industry of the country. . . . The Spanish language is spoken by them almost without exception. . . . They are jealous of their rights as they understand them." Even as late as 1910, just five years before the Plan de San Diego, Laredo newspaper editor Nicasio Idar could assert with confidence that "it would require many years to destroy the power of the Mexican masses of this town."[7]

The Anglos and the handful of Europeans who did come to the lower border region were an odd mix of soldiers, veterans, escaped criminals, merchants, and southern planters. Most settled in towns. Elites generally came in search of either mercantile opportunities, in which case they settled in Brownsville, Corpus Christi, or Laredo, or land for cattle raising, in which case they settled across south Texas wherever land could be purchased. The region changed the Anglo arrivals as much as they changed it. Nearly all newcomers learned Spanish, and many converted to Catholicism. Men constituted the overwhelming majority of the immigrants, and they often married into more elite Tejano families. Though their children bore surnames such as Leo, Lacaze, Decker, Marx, Champion, Krause, Margot, Volpe, and Ellert, they spoke Spanish and considered themselves Texas-Mexican culturally. Anglos became linked to other Tejano families through their incorporation into the *compadrazgo,* or godparent, system. "[S]o many of us of that generation had a Mexican mother and an American or European father," recalled one elite Tejano. "There were neither racial nor social distinctions between Americans and Mexicans, we were just one family." Anglos who bought ranch land raised their cattle and managed their workforce in much the same way as did the rancheros, adopting their generally paternalistic employment practices.[8]

The acculturation of Anglos, intermarriage, and alliances between elite Tejanos and Anglos created a distinct political system. A "machine" that would endure for more than a century in parts of the region dominated political affairs. The machine was generally understood by outsiders as the product of endemic corruption or the passivity of ethnic Mexicans. In fact, it looked much like political organizations in much of Mexico, and later in heavily immigrant cities in the United States, where private ties and kinship loyalties were strong enough to form enduring political regimes. In south Texas, while Anglos were generally the machine's candidates for upper-level offices, Tejanos were indispensable to its success. These Tejanos, usually ranchers or merchants, delivered the votes of their extended families and dependents—employees, cowboys, and laborers—in exchange for appointment to mid-level patronage positions such as deputy sheriffs and county school teachers. The machine also provided them with law enforcement and legal services. James Wells

A proud south Texas ranchero. Courtesy E. E. Mireles and Jovita González de Mireles Papers, Special Collections and Archives, Texas A&M University–Corpus Christi Bell Library.

inherited the leadership of the machine at the 1882 death of its founder, Stephen Powers, and was south Texas's preeminent political player for the next four decades. Wells and Powers essentially became the über-patrons for south Texas. Both men spoke Spanish (and Wells converted to Catholicism) and cultivated and retained close ties to numerous prominent rancheros. They had personal patronage networks among Tejanos of a more modest station, whom they provided with relief in droughts and with financial support for events such as weddings and funerals.[9]

What was a new place for Anglos was a familiar home for Tejanos. They lived in a complex class structure, one shaped above all by cattle ranching. At the top of this social hierarchy were the descendents of the leaders of Spain's 1746 colonization and large ranchers—often one and the same—joined by the wealthier merchants of Brownsville and Laredo. Independent ranching families and the skilled vaqueros who did the bulk of the ranching work for larger owners constituted the middle of the social strata. At the bottom were peones and remaining Coahuiltecan Indians. Tejano social life reflected these stratifications. Ranch cemeteries, for example, were segregated by class. Daughters of the wealthy families generally did not attend the dances that brought together middling and poor families from miles around. On a material level, peones depended upon their *patrones* for credit and for transportation beyond the property.[10]

If many Anglo-Americans boasted that the frontier had made their nation more democratic than the class-ridden societies of the Old World, then Tejanos could tell a similar story of their own culture. South Texas had its elites, to be sure, but at the same time a cultural and material egalitarianism strongly marked its society. Abundant land and a low population density allowed for many families—including many of those who would join the Plan de San Diego uprising—to own their own ranches. Any larger rancher who seriously abused his labor force risked losing his hands altogether. *"Peón,"* noted one native south Texan decades later, "had preserved much of its old meaning of 'man on foot.'" "Their servitude is not hereditary, and seldom even endures for life," wrote a Catholic missionary of the peones in the 1840s. "The peon engages his services for a certain number of years, during which he is to labor on the land, to tend the cattle and deliver the messages of his master . . . [his situation] is quite different from that of the niggers in the United States. In general, the peon eats with his master and is almost similarly clad; and it is hard at first sight to distinguish the one from the other." Furthermore, the lack of precious metals in the region precluded the development of the highly stratified societies based on coerced labor typical of mining districts in central Mexico. Unlike cotton and tobacco production in the South, cattle ranching required no such massive and tightly managed labor force.[11]

That the Plan de San Diego would speak of a "liberating army of all races," not merely an army of ethnic Mexicans, reflected something of the region's tradition of racial fluidity. If elite families like the Yturrias or the de la Garzas could claim the status of a Spanish blood lineage, the overwhelming majority of Tejanos were a mestizo, or mixed people. Some Coahuiltecans in the lower Rio Grande Valley married into nearby ranchero families, though surviving documents do not clearly outline the extent of this mixing. For those of African descent, the border could mean freedom. Slavery was outlawed in Mexico, and racial lines tended to be more fluid even on the U.S. side. Escaped and freed slaves found refuge in the Nueces Strip, sometimes blending in with the Tejano population. Nathaniel Jackson and Mathilda Hicks, for example, arrived in Hidalgo County in 1857, accompanied by their seven children and by eleven freed slaves. Jackson, described in some accounts as Cherokee, bought several thousand acres of land, which came to be known as Rancho Jackson. The settlement may have been a way station for runaway slaves. Blacks associated with the Jackson ranch married into the Mexican population, and to this day there are people in Hidalgo county with Hispanic first names and the last name of Jackson. The 1850 federal census found that about 10 percent of the inhabitants of south Texas "were of Negro or mixed background."[12]

On the other hand, Tejanos, including those in south Texas, could also embrace a more exclusive racial identity, differentiating themselves from Indians and blacks to cement ties with Anglos. A Tejano delegate to the 1845 state constitutional convention, for example, argued that Mexicans were "white" and therefore exempt from restrictions placed on free blacks. Similarly, in 1898 Laredo's Anglo and Tejano elite began to host an annual ceremony celebrating the birthday of George Washington, in which leading citizens dressed up as Indians surrounded and stormed the city hall. The ceremony united Tejano and Anglo colonists, portraying both groups as virtuous settlers attacked by savage Indians. Black soldiers stationed in Laredo, Rio Grande City, and Brownsville in the 1890s and 1900s became involved in numerous conflicts with local residents, including those who resented their sexual relations with Texas-Mexican women. The most notorious such instance, the 1906 Brownsville "Affair," in which black troops clashed with Anglos and Tejanos, resulted in the dishonorable discharge of three companies, outraging black leaders and civil rights advocates across the country. Even this conflict, however, did not stem from a clear line between blacks and Tejanos. At this time in Brownsville, Anglo-run bars served blacks in back rooms or not at all, while Tejano establishments served the soldiers with the other customers. Sixty years after American conquest, racial boundaries were still more easily crossed in south Texas than in the rest of the nation.[13]

Tejanos continued to live in much the same way as they had before American conquest. Nevertheless, the Anglos who came after 1848 did bring significant changes to the region. Most important, they became its economic leaders, more tightly linking its economy with the rest of the United States. Anglo merchants quickly dominated the real estate, shipping, and importing businesses of Brownsville and Laredo, the area's largest cities. At the same time, Anglo ranchers made the cattle business much more market-oriented. Where rancheros raised cattle first for local consumption and second for the export of their hides and tallow, Anglos made ranching a modern business, shipping livestock in mass quantities to railheads in Kansas and Colorado and turning a profit from by-products such as tallow and cured hides. The American cattle industry was born in south Texas out of this fusion of Anglo economic power and Tejano stock handling techniques. Thus, the familiar terminology of cattle and the open ranges are either Spanish phrases or English corruptions of them: bronco, buckaroo, burro, mesa, canyon, rodeo, corral, lariat, lasso, chaps, and even ten-gallon hat.[14]

The enormous King Ranch epitomized the new stock-raising model. Tejanos watched with amazement and resentment as the ranch grew and grew —by a strategic marriage, by purchases, and, many said, by fraud, outright murder, and theft. It totaled about five hundred thousand acres at the time of founder Richard King's death in 1885. His widow, Henrietta, and son-in-law Richard Kleberg continued to expand the operation, which reached nearly one and a quarter million acres by Kleberg's death in 1932. Like the Texas Ranger force that was so frequently called upon to defend it, the King Ranch was simultaneously a powerful institution and a legend. It pioneered the use of barbed wire, established its own rendering plants, and developed its own breeds of improved cattle, such as the Santa Gertrudis. The ranch and the Kings and Klebergs—or their thinly fictionalized versions—were featured in dime novels, numerous radio and television westerns, and classic movies such as *Giant*. The vast property is now a major tourist attraction.[15]

Tejanos viewed the King Ranch with a mixture of affection, admiration, fear, and resentment, and in some cases with unvarnished and profound hatred. Its labor practices resembled a plantation more than a corporation. By employing generations of the same families (some of whom were originally brought in from outside the region) and caring for those too old to work, it made itself the center of its employees' social and economic lives, securing a great deal of loyalty from most of them. Indeed, its employees often referred to themselves as *kineños* and took pride in the fact that it was their hard work and knowledge of livestock, passed down from generation to generation, that made the ranch successful. Other Tejanos, however, could—and can still—point to relatives' former ranchos that had been consumed by the voracious King Ranch. For them, the ranch and the Rangers that protected it were thieves and murderers who transparently cloaked themselves with the sanction of law and economic might. These Tejanos took pride in poaching game, running their cattle in the ranch's remote corners, and even in repossessing livestock that it wrongly claimed as its own.

One of the many advantages that the King Ranch boasted in its struggle with these Tejanos was the backing of the Texas Rangers. Because the Kings and Klebergs were major players in Texas's economic and political circles, they were always able to call upon the Rangers to protect their interests. Those Tejanos who thought that the Rangers were the private police force of the ranch were not entirely mistaken.

Even for those who did not lose their land to the King Ranch, Anglo economic dominance made for important changes in the fabric of Tejano life in the nineteenth century. The enclosure of the formerly open ranching lands was one of the most dramatic. When ranchers raised cattle mainly for local consumption, land ownership remained fluid and undefined. Boundaries between ranches were often unclear, and some land was even unclaimed or unused for long periods. "With the Mexican rancheros it is customary to let the cattle range upon each other's property, as oftentime the grasses are abundant in certain places not convenient to the homestead," noted an Anglo observer in the 1870s. "When one or more of these rancheros desire to brand their young stock, notice is generally given to their distant neighbors, and all interested are expected to participate in the 'drive.'" Indeed, in some parts of the Nueces Strip, it was almost as if money grew on trees: all that a person had to do to become a rancher was to corral some of the abundant feral stock and claim it with a brand as his own. Rancheros often used lakes or streams suitable for watering stock as common property, with access unrestricted by property lines or fences. The enormous cattle drives north that began in the 1860s, along with the introduction of barbed wire in the next decade, however, led to the enclosure of most of the range in south Texas by the mid-1880s.[16]

Enclosure made cattle raising more difficult for smaller rancheros by curtailing access to water and preventing the shipping of stock by overland trail drive. The expense of fencing and of drilling wells in turn strapped cash-poor operators, thereby pressuring them to devote more of their cattle production to the market. Tejano ranchers, whose land titles were often in litigation and in any event usually shared with numerous relatives, had much greater difficulty securing credit than did their Anglo competitors. The mix of a greater involvement in the cattle market and poor access to capital was a dangerous combination, for the cattle market was prone to violent fluctuations and vulnerable to periodic drought. Rancheros were forced to sell tens of thousands of acres to more highly capitalized operations such as the King

Ranch in the slow markets of the late 1880s and of 1902–1904. They had little credit to survive the drought-induced "die-ups" of the 1890s. As a local saying went, *con el alambre vino el hambre*—with the barbed wire came hunger.[17]

It would have been little solace for Tejanos to know that ethnic Mexicans in southern California and New Mexico experienced similar economic pressures in the decades after 1848. Before conquest, most ordinary Californios worked as vaqueros, shepherds, artisans, or common laborers on large ranches owned by a few elite families—in contrast with the Nueces Strip, where most of the population worked on their families' own lands. As legal disputes, squatters, property taxes, and increasing numbers of Anglos reduced their employers' lands, within a few decades Californios found themselves working as wage laborers for Anglo bosses, and consistently being paid less than Anglo workers. New Mexico's Hispanic villages proved more resilient, in part because ethnic Mexicans remained a majority of the state until the 1940s. Indeed, some ethnic Mexicans never lost their status as state economic and political leaders. During the three decades after conquest, more plebeian ethnic Mexicans also fared reasonably well, expanding their frontier settlements north into Colorado. Complemented by capital from seasonal labor and from selling stock, the subsistence farming and sheep raising that took place on village-owned land provided for the needs of this expanding people. In the 1880s, however, an influx of Anglos and the integration of the state with the national economy weakened the villagers' position, for the first time leading to significant land loss. Anglo settlers claimed millions of acres traditionally used by the villages as common pasture areas. Although these lands were in theory protected by the Treaty of Guadalupe-Hidalgo, courts confirmed the villagers' claims to less than 6 percent of this acreage—much of which had to be sold to lawyers to pay their fees. Weakened by Anglo control of credit and by competition from new stock raisers, ethnic Mexicans sold even more of their land and were forced, like their counterparts in California, into permanent wage labor at the bottom of the economy. But dispossession in New Mexico resembled south Texas more than California did. As in the Nueces Strip, thousands of ethnic Mexicans continued to own their own land. When pressed to the wall, they were a force to be reckoned with.[18]

Enclosure of the open range and competition from Anglo ranchers brought similar results in south Texas. Tejanos lost much of their land from these economic pressures. Although the number of Tejano land owners increased in tandem with overall population growth, Anglos claimed more and more of their land. The growth of the King Ranch, which Richard King significantly expanded by smuggling cotton for the Confederacy, made Tejano land loss in Cameron County particularly severe. In 1848 those of ethnic Mexican descent owned nearly all of the county. By 1892, a mere forty-six non-Spanish-surnamed owners controlled more than one million, two hundred thousand acres of land, almost four times the territory owned by ethnic Mexicans. The next county up the Rio Grande, Hidalgo, saw a similar if less severe pattern. In 1890 only a third of the land remained in the hands of Spanish-surnamed owners. Although Tejanos owned a greater proportion of the land farther upriver, in the counties of Starr, Zapata, and Webb, Anglo economic dominance was clearly changing south Texas.[19] The thousands of Tejano families who still ranched in the Nueces Strip in 1900 must have wondered how long they would be able to maintain their way of life.

Resistance

The shifting and uneasy accommodation that Anglos and Mexicans reached in the border regions after the Mexican-American War allowed the victors to maintain law and order without constantly resorting to the force of arms. Anglos inserted themselves into the previous social hierarchy, dominated business and politics, but often conformed to ethnic Mexican social norms. This system neither entirely degraded those of Mexican descent nor gave them the tools to resist growing Anglo economic might.[20]

Across the Southwest, however, smoldering resentment did erupt into open defiance — most often in the form of individual "outlaws" who gained the admiration of their communities, but also in concerted rebellions that seriously threatened the bargain struck by Anglos and their elite ethnic Mexican counterparts. In the decades following the American invasion of California, some ethnic Mexicans fought back against those who had taken their land and expelled them from the mines. In the early 1850s, Anglos came to attribute a rash of thefts, holdups, and attacks on their mining camps to a gang led by a Joaquín "Murieta" or "Murrieta." In response to these raids, California's legislature established its own ranger force, which soon began an indiscriminate manhunt for the mysterious "bandit." They claimed victory in July of 1853 after a battle in which they killed two Hispanic men, putting the head of the one they claimed was Joaquín in a jar to be displayed in the state capitol. Although it is not clear whether a Joaquín Murrieta ever existed, the legends told by Californios and Mexicans enshrined his name in folk memory. Where Anglo papers described him as a violent bandit, these legends recount that he was evicted from rich mining claims and turned to violence only after Anglos raped his wife and hung his brother. Joaquín Murrieta thus embodied the courageous struggle against dispossession and brutality.[21]

The Southwest abounds with legends of similar defiance, often of people whose individual histories are clearer than that of Murrieta. The story of Gregorio Cortéz, Texas's analogue of Murrieta, reflects the key role of the Rangers in suppressing ethnic Mexican dissent before the Plan de San Diego. A vaquero

Gregorio Cortéz (seated, center), Tejano outlaw and folk hero, surrounded by Texas Rangers. Courtesy Institute of Texan Cultures.

and ranch hand raised in south Texas, Cortéz lives on in legend nearly a century after his exploits. In 1901 a sheriff approached Cortéz at his farm in central Texas and attempted to arrest him for horse theft, wounding his brother in the process. Cortéz killed the sheriff and in the ensuing manhunt eluded the Texas Rangers and Anglo posses numbering up to three hundred men, taking them on an incredible journey of more than five hundred miles into deep south Texas and toward the border. Exhausted from his journey—he walked more than one hundred miles of it—Cortéz was captured just eight miles short of the Rio Grande. He was sentenced to life in prison for the murder of a second sheriff during his flight. Outraged Tejanos funded a legal defense effort and ultimately secured his pardon in 1913 from the Texas governor. Before his death three years later, Cortéz fought for a time in the Mexican revolution.[22]

A year after Cortéz's epic journey, a bloodier set of clashes showed south Texans how easily a spate of violence could make the contours of their distinct society seem very fragile. Ramón de la Cerda was one of many rancheros who disputed the King Ranch's land claims. He died at the hands of Rangers, and both his death and the disputed accounts of it would later strike many as a microcosm of the confusion and death during the Plan de San Diego uprising. In May of 1902, as a series of cattle depredations irritated the King Ranch's proprietors, Ranger A. Y. Baker came across several cattle tied to brush in the ranch's southern wilds. Ramón de la Cerda, burning his family's brand onto one of the calves, looked up and saw Baker and his men. Both the Ranger and the ranchero instantly fired. De la Cerda brained Baker's horse, dropping it dead in its tracks, but Baker simultaneously hit de la Cerda in the head, killing him.

To the Rangers and their beneficiaries at the ranch, this was a simple case of conflict between a family of rustlers and a brave officer sworn to uphold the law. To the de la Cerdas and to many other rancheros, it looked like assassination. The Rangers had long harassed them over running their cattle on territory disputed with the King Ranch but were too cowardly to confront the de la Cerdas directly, as this was a family whose menfolk were widely respected for their backcountry and marksmanship skills. Supporters alleged that de la Cerda's body had been bound and dragged along the ground before his death, and the surviving de la Cerdas said that a King Ranch worker told them that he had witnessed Baker and his fellow Rangers set the ambush, complete with the half-branded calf. The conflict continued. That September, unknown parties hidden in the chaparral fired on Baker and several other rangers, killing one and seriously injuring Baker. Shortly thereafter, the Rangers arrested Alfredo de la Cerda (Ramón's surviving brother) and a handful of supporters, including a justice of the peace who backed the de la Cerda account of the original ambush. Three weeks later, Baker encountered Alfredo, who had been released on bail, in a Brownsville store and shot him, claiming that he had reached for a weapon on his hip. Public outcry from Tejanos forced the withdrawal of the offending Ranger unit, but the conflicts that prompted the killings remained—as did A. Y. Baker, who would repeat his performance time after time in 1915 and 1916.[23]

Ramón de la Cerda and his killing were well known in south Texas, but it was Gregorio Cortéz—the man who fought the Rangers and lived to tell the tale—who became enshrined in folklore. Like Murrieta, his legend endures long after his own death. The "Ballad of Gregorio Cortéz," sung across Mexico and the Southwest, commemorates his masculine exploits in defying his hapless pursuers. "They let loose the bloodhound dogs," the song says, "[t]hey followed him from afar. But trying to catch Cortéz was like following a star." Tejano heroes were defeated, in this as in other legends. But it was only because they were so heavily outnumbered and outgunned. One on one, man to man, the proud rancheros were unbeatable. Most versions of the song end with the defiant Cortéz taunting the Rangers. "Ah, so many mounted Rangers / Just to take one Mexican!" Américo Paredes' lyrical description written in 1958 still holds true half a century later: "They sing of him still," he wrote, "in the cantinas and the country stores, in the ranches when men gather at night to talk in the cool dark, sitting in a circle, smoking and listening to the old songs and the tales of other days. . . . They sing with deadly-serious faces, throwing out the words of the song like a challenge, tearing savagely with their stiff, callused fingers at the strings of the guitar."[24]

Such legends used the deeds of individual men to embody defiance of the oppression brought by Anglos. A handful of larger uprisings in the Southwest during the nineteenth century reflected the potential of this defiance to spread to concerted action that might overthrow Anglo domination. In 1847, during the Mexican-American War, a brief rebellion in northern New Mexico captured Taos and managed to kill the American military governor before being crushed by the army. Forty-five years later, Las Vegas, New Mexico, saw large groups of masked men who called themselves *"las Gorras Blancas"* (White Caps) cut fences, destroy haystacks, wreck railroad infrastructure, and threaten those who encroached upon their land.[25]

The two largest rebellions took place in south Texas and may have helped inspire the architects of the Plan de San Diego to believe that their lofty goals were achievable. The first was known as the Cortina War. In July 1859, Juan Cortina, the son of a wealthy borderlands ranching family, witnessed an Anglo city marshal pistol-whipping a family employee. Outraged, Cortina shot the man, then fled the city to escape retaliation. Two months later he led an armed force into the city, released Tejanos whom he felt had been unfairly imprisoned, and executed four Anglos who had gone unpunished despite their murder of Tejanos. "Flocks of vampires came and scattered themselves in the settlements, without any capital except the corrupt heart and the most perverse intentions," he declared to his fellow Tejanos. "Many of you have been robbed of your property, incarcerated, chased, murdered, and hunted like wild beasts, because your labor was fruitful, and because your industry excited the vile avarice which led them." Cortina was not in a position to guarantee success, but he did vow that "[o]ur personal enemies shall not possess our lands until they have fattened them [with] their own gore." He also addressed Anglos, berating them for defying the principles of their own Declaration of Independence and Constitution.[26]

Cortina's appeal to Tejano resentment of loss of land and the arrogance of the new arrivals anticipated much of the rhetoric of the Plan de San Diego some six decades later. So did the response: the Texas Rangers struck back furiously, often arbitrarily, punishing any Tejano whom they suspected of being a Cortinista. At the same time, many ethnic Mexicans joined the effort to stamp out the rebellion. Prominent Tejanos from Laredo, and leading Brownsville merchants, wanted nothing to do with what they perceived as the ranchero's rash grab for power. Cortina did have a base of popular support, however, and so his rebellion was powerful enough to force the federal government to again send the army across the Nueces. "The whole country from Brownsville to Rio Grande City, 120 miles . . . has been laid waste, the citizens driven out," reported Major Samuel Heintzelman in early December 1859. "Business as far up as Laredo, two hundred and forty miles has been interrupted

Juan Cortina, an elite Tejano who led an 1859 rebellion that briefly captured Brownsville. He was ultimately defeated by the U.S. army. From the private collection of Jerry Thompson.

or suspended for five months." But soon enough the federal army, led by a colonel named Robert E. Lee, defeated Cortina's forces, forcing him into exile in Mexico. The Robin Hood of the Rio Grande, as Cortina was widely known, continued his military activities from Mexico. He aided Union partisans in Texas during the Civil War and fought with President Benito Juárez and other Mexican Liberals against a French invasion in the 1860s. In 1863 he was made a general in the Mexican army and soon became the acting governor of Tamaulipas. Anglo Texans attributed numerous cattle raids and border incursions to Cortina throughout the 1870s.[27]

The last major regional uprising before the Plan de San Diego, the 1891 revolt led by Catarino Garza, began as a plan to overthrow Mexico's government. It also became a protest against the oppression of ethnic Mexicans in the United States. Garza, born in Matamoros in 1859, moved to Brownsville at age eighteen. He became a newspaperman and an active organizer of mutual benefit associations throughout south Texas. Where Cortina was born into a position of wealth and privilege, and used his social position to rally Tejanos to his cause, Garza was more like his successors in the Plan de San Diego. It was his courage and ability to articulate the sufferings of a people abused by both Mexico and the United States that catapulted him to prominence. Garza lashed out at the marginalized status of ethnic Mexicans in Texas, which he attributed to Anglo racism and the corruption of machine politics. He criticized the rule of Mexico president Porfirio Díaz for its arbitrariness and denial of basic political rights to ordinary Mexicans. Like Cortina, Garza was steeped in the tradition of Mexican Liberalism. He thus appealed more to political freedoms such as individual liberty, personal security, and equality before the law—all described as in the best tradition of Mexican patriotism—than to economic grievances or class militancy per se. Like all Tejanos who set themselves against the region's ruling order, Garza made a number of enemies. And like so many dissident Tejanos before and since, he experienced the tender mercies of the Texas Rangers. When Garza asserted that a U.S. customs inspector had killed an ethnic Mexican in cold blood while escorting him to jail, Rangers swept through a passenger train and apprehended the brave journalist on a charge of libel. The next month, when the customs inspector shot and injured Garza himself, as many as four hundred Tejanos and Mexicans gathered in front of the U.S. army fort in Rio Grande City to demand the arrest and punishment of Garza's assailant.[28]

Three years later, Garza led a group of men across the Rio Grande, declared himself in rebellion against Díaz, and called on all patriotic Mexicans to join the uprising. Within months more than one thousand men followed his command. For the next year, Garza's forces clashed with the Mexican and U.S. armies. The numbers of his recruits and the difficulty that government forces had in capturing him suggest that he enjoyed widespread popular support in south Texas. "The fact that every inhabitant of the ranches and every Mexican the troops met was a secret sympathizer," wrote one journalist somewhat hyperbolically, was "a most important difficulty in the way of his pursuers." Army officers frequently expressed their frustration that locals lied and misled them when hired as guides or when they simply asked the whereabouts of Garzista forces. Once again, however, this popular support proved to be no match for the U.S. army. As his forces were scattered and the Rangers led a manhunt for him from Eagle Pass southward, Garza fled to Houston, Texas, and then to Colombia, where he died in 1895 while fighting for a Liberal army.[29]

Like Joaquín Murrieta and Gregorio Cortéz, Garza and Cortina live on in legend. To this day, in south Texas Tejanos still remember them as folk heroes courageously defying Anglos. Indeed, their memories are alive in much of Mexico as well; a recent fundraiser music recording for the Zapatista rebellion in Chiapas begins with "The Ballad of General Juan Cortina."

Ethnic Mexicans across the Southwest resented their mistreatment by Anglos. But there was something about south Texas that seemed to foster mass insurgencies. Ethnic Mexicans remained a majority, and although many cooperated with the structures that made Anglo economic dominance possible, others were willing to resort to arms to cast it off. Moreover, thousands of landowners still numbered among the ethnic Mexican population. Although the landless and truly dispossessed supported their rebellions, both Garza and Cortina were relatively well-off, born or married into fairly prominent families. Finally, rebels could sometimes find refuge on Mexican soil, just an easy river crossing away. All of these factors were still present in the start of the twentieth century, when dramatic changes gave Tejanos all the more reason to rebel.

The World Rushes In

Fifty years after their forcible incorporation in the United States, most Tejanos in south Texas found themselves poorer, more marginal, and with less land than their grandparents. And yet in many ways life in turn-of-the-century south Texas was not so different than it had been in 1848. Spanish, not English, was the dominant language, used in newspapers, business, political campaigns, and court trials alike. Mexican pesos circulated alongside American dollars. If virtually all manual laborers were ethnic Mexicans, then so too were many merchants, ranchers, politicians, and sheriffs. If Anglos now controlled most of the land, then thousands of Tejanos still owned their own ranches. Indeed, in 1900 ethnic Mexicans constituted 92 percent of the Valley's population, a significant increase from the 80 percent in 1850. At the dawn of the twentieth century, fewer than one thousand Anglos lived in the region's rural sectors. Unlike African Americans in the South, or ethnic Mexicans in most of the Southwest, Tejanos of the Nueces Strip were not a segregated racial minority shorn of all protection of the law. This was no golden age, even if those who lived through it and well into the twentieth century would often romanticize it. Material comforts were scarce, and work and daily life difficult. But neither did the world seem to insist on the humiliation of Tejanos. They did not yet have to stomach signs that read "No Mexicans Allowed" or answer their children's questions about why they couldn't use main entrances or sit in restaurants.[30]

Changes in the new century, however, would threaten all that they had managed to preserve. The region's isolation had allowed Tejanos and Anglos to create a distinctive racial order, different from the rest of the United States. But it soon collapsed under the weight of masses of Anglos and of the Plan de San Diego, giving way to a more thoroughly segregated and brutal society. In a sense this was all the fault of the railroad. In 1904 workers completed a line connecting Brownsville to the rest of Texas's burgeoning railroad network. The first passenger train of the St. Louis, Brownsville, and Mexico (S, B & M) Railroad arrived on July 4, as though to suggest that the lower border's distinctive society would finally have to face the fact that it was truly part of the United States.

The railroad's arrival represented the culmination of years of effort by many of the Valley's elite. Prominent merchants and landholders knew all too well that the region still remained a backwater, terribly marginal to national and even to state centers of power, culture, and wealth. (It was no accident that the army captain sent to crush the Garza rebellion referred to south Texas as "an American Congo.") But that might change, local elites hoped, if a railroad made it easy to get in and out of the Valley, to ship produce to markets, and—above all—to attract industrious American farmers to settle in large numbers. Developers made efforts to link Brownsville and Corpus Christi by rail as early as 1873 but were unable to attract sufficient local capital or outside support. A grandiose plan to run a railroad from Corpus Christi all the way to Panama collapsed in the midst of the economic crash of 1893, as did a more modest effort to connect Victoria, Texas, with the Rio Grande one year later.[31]

Just as it embodied so many of the changes brought to the region after 1848, the King Ranch played a key role in the construction of the railroad. In 1900, King Ranch proprietor Richard Kleberg planted an experimental crop of cabbage and onions irrigated with well water. The yield so impressed him that he contacted friends in the state's railroad business, and three years later he and other south Texas ranchers and businessmen formed a corporation to connect Brownsville to the national railway system.[32]

Although only one of the incorporators of the S, B & M Railroad was an ethnic Mexican, some Tejanos were important in bringing the railroad to the region. By 1903 the state of Texas was no longer as generous with railroad

The first passenger railroad car arrives in Brownsville, Texas, on July 4, 1904. Courtesy of the Hidalgo County Historical Museum.

grants as it had once been, and in any event the confirmation of Spanish and Mexican land grants left little public land in south Texas. Thus the railroad required private land donations if it were to be built. A varied group of merchants, bankers, and prominent ranchers stepped forward to provide cash and land for its construction. Anglo ranchers and merchants were joined by the likes of Francisco Yturria, the largest Hispanic rancher and an old foe of Juan Cortina; Brownsville banker and merchant J. H. Fernández; and members of established Tejano families such as the Garzas and the Velas. Fully a third of the railroad's fundraising committee boasted some Hispanic ancestry. Their contribution to the railroad would earn them the wrath of less fortunate Tejanos a decade later.[33]

Even before the final track was laid, real estate developers—including large operations such as the King Ranch—aggressively marketed the region to farmers, bringing them in by the score, hoping to entice them to stay. Their promotional material made south Texas out to be a near-paradise. Its eleven-month growing season, burgeoning irrigation network, and railroad connections added up to one thing: money. Farmers needed only to leave the cold Midwest and move to the border to make a killing. As the lyrics of one song, sung to the tune of "Casey Jones," indicated:

Come, all you people, who want to buy land,
And go with us to the Lower Rio Grande,
Where the corn and the cotton and the sugar cane grows,
Where the Sun always shines, and it never snows.

Come on, boys, to the Rio Grande Valley;
Come on, go to the Lower Rio Grande;
Come on, boys, to the Rio Grande Valley;
When we make the next trip to that promised land.
. . .
Here we have churches and schools to suit,
'Frisco railroad to market the fruit;
Social conditions as good as at home—
Now is the time to get ready to come.[34]

This was not only a matter of individual profit, but also of a triumphal story of national pioneering and progress. "Scenes in the Valley everywhere make one wonder at the change from the old and primitive to the beautiful and modern that has taken place in so short a time," marveled an Hidalgo County development company. "The golden glow of the brush fires against the night sky, where land is being cleared for cultivation, truly typifies the passing of the old civilization and the coming of the new."[35]

But who would clear the brush and do the other backbreaking labor to build this new "promised land"? On this count, the hopes of real estate developers must have made Tejanos quite nervous, for ethnic Mexicans were absent from these visions as anything other than manual laborers. Numerous yet out of sight, docile yet industrious, they were the ideal labor force. "The manual labor in the Lower Rio Grande Valley is performed by Mexicans. They have been found to be very satisfactory farm hands," described one railroad pamphlet. "Mexicans cannot be hurried or driven," it concluded, "but they are a quiet and industrious people and ask nothing better than to be employed, shown what to do, and let alone. They do not work rapidly, but they work continuously. On the whole, they are a kindly and courteous people, and in a slow and steady way, industrious and reliable." Though Mexican laborers were numerous and available, promoters seemed to promise that Anglo immigrants would not have to share their society with them. At times it seemed that Mexicans were not even residents. "Our lands being located just across the river from Mexico, where there is plenty of cheap Mexican labor to be had, there is no trouble in getting labor," one company claimed.[36]

The boom that followed the construction of the railroad confirmed the developers' optimism. The rail connection instantly made widespread market agriculture feasible, and south Texas soon became an agricultural empire to

Prospective farmers in south Texas. Courtesy Runyon Collection, Center for American
History, University of Texas at Austin.

Clearing brush in south Texas. Courtesy Runyon Collection, Center for American History,
University of Texas at Austin.

rival even the most productive acres of California or Florida. Although nature
had well suited the Valley for agriculture—its latitude made frosts rare, and
its soil, continually enriched by the deposition of silt from the Rio Grande's
frequent floods, was extremely fertile—the high capital costs of irrigation had
precluded much intensive agricultural development. After the railroad, though,
dozens of irrigation companies sprouted up, increasing the irrigated acreage
in Cameron and Hidalgo counties from fifty thousand in 1909 to more than

South Texas's agricultural bounty. Courtesy Runyon Collection, Center for American History, University of Texas at Austin.

two hundred and twenty thousand by 1919. The value of farm property in south Texas quintupled from 1900 to 1920. In 1924, Hidalgo County became the nation's highest-producing agricultural county.[37]

For the first time, thousands of Anglos moved to the lower border region, flooding Cameron and Hidalgo counties in particular, the future site of most of the warfare during the Plan de San Diego. From 1900 to 1910 Cameron County's population rose from just over sixteen thousand to more than twenty-seven thousand, and Hidalgo County's more than doubled, reaching almost fourteen thousand. Dozens of almost entirely Anglo towns sprung up alongside the railroad. "As if by magic," noted one Tejano newspaper, "the towns of Mercedes, San Benito, Chapin, Raymondsville, San Juan, Mission and other places have risen in the lower Rio Grande."[38]

The agricultural boom that so pleased its architects was a disaster for small Tejano landowners, threatening and even dispossessing many of those who would flock to the rebellion in 1915. The sharp rise in land prices was one of the first noticed and most discussed signs of the railroad's arrival. In the late nineteenth century, unimproved pasture land sold from fifty cents to two dollars per acre. Anticipation of the railroad's arrival soon pushed prices up to

Street scene in Mercedes, Texas, one of the towns born in the agricultural boom early in the twentieth century. Courtesy Runyon Collection, Center for American History, University of Texas at Austin.

between five and fifty dollars an acre at the end of the nineteenth century. By 1912 or so, undeveloped land cost between one hundred and three hundred dollars an acre, and property that was easily irrigated or had particularly rich soil went for five hundred dollars or more per acre. These rapid increases strained the ranching economy. Small ranches had always produced cattle and crops primarily for family consumption, selling whatever extra remained. Even rancheros blessed with abundant land were thus cash poor, and as a consequence found it extremely difficult to pay exponentially larger property tax bills. They were soon forced to sell portions of their land to pay the taxes. Some were still unable to foot those bills. Sheriffs sold three times as many parcels for tax delinquency in the decade from 1904 to 1914 as they had from 1893 to 1903, itself a period when intense drought caused economic dislocation. These sales almost always transferred land from Tejanos to Anglos. Only two of the purchasers in the latter decade had Hispanic surnames.[39]

The rise in the value of land intensified conflict over its ownership. Land titles at the turn of the century remained extremely complicated and poorly recorded. Multiple heirs often claimed ownership, ran stock, and lived on un-

Major towns and railroad routes in south Texas in the early twentieth century.

divided properties. With the agricultural boom, however, land became too valuable to remain unoccupied or infrequently used. "Clarification" of property ownership could be done by legal mechanisms, such as forcing the partition of an undivided tract by purchasing the interest of one of the heirs. In the Ojo de Agua tract of eastern Hidalgo County, for example, a white farmer named Fred Johnson began collecting rent in the 1910s on fenced land that surrounding Tejano landowners believed to be theirs. Even when such legal maneuvers were challenged in court, they often accomplished much of their purpose anyway, for the only way for cash-poor rancheros to pay their legal fees was often to sell part of their land. The growing value of real estate prompted some to resort to the simple expedient of occupying a desired tract and violently expelling previous occupants. Rancher and developer Lon C. Hill was fond of this tactic. As the railroad neared completion, he purchased an acreage in the Ojo de Agua grant. A small rancher with the last name of Barrera never-theless continued to use the portion he considered to be his own land. Hill bragged about his solution to this conflict to a jury in a subsequent lawsuit: "I told him to pack up his doll rags and piss on the fire, and he was gone." Real danger lurked behind Hill's bluster. A decade later, during the Plan de San Diego uprising, he would become one of the most savage vigilantes.[40]

The combination of economic pressure, title challenges, and outright theft led to significant Tejano land loss shortly after the railroad's construction. From 1900 to 1910 Hispanic-surnamed individuals lost a total of more than one hundred and eighty-seven thousand acres in Cameron and Hidalgo counties. In Hidalgo County alone, they ceded nearly half of their land to Anglos in this period. "The shepherd and cowboy are gradually disappearing, and agriculture has replaced the ranch," observed a Laredo newspaper in 1910. "The lands which mainly belonged to Mexicans pass to the hands of Americans . . . the old proprietors work as laborers on the same lands that used to belong to them." The new century had brought Tejanos a taste of the upheaval and dispossession that conquest had visited upon their counterparts across the Southwest some fifty years before.[41]

More and more Tejanos thus found themselves reduced to fieldwork, helping to enrich the very farmers whose arrival had so much to do with their own dispossession. To plant, tend, and harvest somebody else's crops was a very different matter than to work on one's own ranch. Ranch work had its seasonal variations but created no enormous peaks and troughs of workload. Family labor accounted for most work done on smaller ranches. Nonfamily members, who did most work on the larger ranches, relied on long-term relations with their employers, in many cases over several generations. Their work could certainly include brute physical force—building fences, pinning and branding cattle, pulverizing shells to make lime, digging wells, and the like— but nonetheless had its rewards as well. Vaqueros could find pleasure and pride in the horsemanship and stock-handling skills that their work required. Even the male peon on larger ranchos had varied tasks—in one description, "planting and harvesting, herding goats, digging wells, building dams and houses"—which he generally performed under his own supervision. Women's work was an essential part of the ranch economy. Women generally tended small family vegetable gardens located near their ranch homes or jacales. They laundered, cooked, and sewed in small groups, a pattern of labor that allowed for socialization even as it met basic material needs.[42]

To be an agricultural worker was very different. The physical labor itself was more repetitive, usually consisting of repeated hoeing or picking of a ground-level crop, and often done while stooped. People could not pace their own work: pay was based on piecework, that is, a flat rate for each unit of crop picked. Where ranch work served the needs of family and social life, farmwork

Onions in april, 1917

Fieldwork in south Texas. Courtesy of the Hidalgo County Historical Museum.

was a market transaction done in labor platoons closely watched and supervised by foremen. And because labor needs fluctuated so enormously with the season, farmworkers had no choice but to take to the highways to make enough money. They "begin cotton picking down near the Rio Grande about the first of June," described one Anglo farmer, "pick over the cotton down there, gradually work up our way, and up to where I live [two hundred miles north of the border] the cotton would be ready to pick up about the first of July, possibly, a month later than near the border."[43]

The folk song "El Bohimio" captures some of the sense of defeat that Tejanos associated with the forced transition to agricultural work. The song tells the story of a vaquero's failed efforts to break a horse.

> When Manuel mounted El Bohimio
> Who would have thought
> That in a few leaps
> Manuel was going to tumble
>
> When he found himself on the ground
> Manuel Rodríguez said,
> "It is better if I leave La Parra
> And quit trying to be a vaquero."

By the song's end, the vaquero is defeated and bids his ranch good-bye. The penultimate verse reads:

> Good-bye all my friends
> Good-bye all my loves
> And the road that he took,
> Went to Las Labores.

Labores is the south Texas Spanish word for fields. Farmwork was the product of defeat and humiliation, the sad lot of an oppressed people who had once lived better.[44]

The flood of changes brought by the railroad also threatened the political power that Tejanos had maintained over six decades of American rule. Most Anglos who moved to the region in the nineteenth century learned—rapidly —to accommodate themselves to the demographic, cultural, and economic weight of the region's ethnic Mexicans. In contrast, those drawn by the agricultural boom wanted ethnic Mexicans as laborers and nothing else. Financially lucrative agriculture had brought them to the region, and its high capital costs in expensive land and irrigation water required them to grow labor-intensive crops. What they most definitely did not want were Mexicans as neighbors, friends, or social equals.

The political machine's reliance on Tejano voting revolted the newcomers. Insurgent farmer politicians disparaged Tejano voting, offering lurid descriptions of drunken barbecues and painting them as "menaces" to American democracy. They saw the patron-client relations that were the basis of the machine's strength as evidence of innate Mexican passivity. As one Anglo put it in 1915, the year of the Plan de San Diego, Mexicans "retain vestiges of the primitive man's willingness to attach themselves as followers to any one who may have shown them a kindness."[45]

Ethnic Mexican voting was also the Achilles' heel of the machine, for the newcomers turned to disfranchisement as a logical tool to destroy its power. The Jim Crow regime of the South provided an arsenal of techniques for this effort. Texas implemented a poll tax in 1902, and a 1903 amendment required that it be paid between October and February, seven months before a general election. The following year, the state Democratic Party authorized "white primaries," a practice that soon spread to many county party organizations. Although these measures were aimed at black voting, they also threatened to undercut the machine's Tejano vote. State representative Alexander Terrell, the author of the poll tax legislation, accused machine boss James Wells of hatching a "conspiracy" to defeat the legislation. In south Texas, he charged, "Mexicans are induced on election day to swim across the Rio Grande and are voted before their hair is dry." Not content with mere social separation, Anglo farmers in south Texas ran against the machine, arguing that "the Mexican vote" had to be curtailed. Stripped of more and more of their lands, forced into demeaning migratory labor, Tejanos now faced the prospect of becoming a despised racial caste.[46]

Conclusion

"A day will come when the mesquite trees of the state will hang with the bodies of the white bandits ... who have denied the Mexican the right to life in this savage state of the south," predicted the Mexican exile newspaper *Regeneración* in 1914. "To be ready for this day," its writer said, "each and every Mexican worker needs to arm himself. When the shout of rebellion sounds, there is nothing to do but join the battle.... Bourgeois Texan bandits: each and every one of you will pay with as many tears, as much suffering, as you have caused to thousands of men, women and children who have worked year after year in your rich cotton fields!" Later that year a similar prediction circulated in south Texas. A manifesto titled "A los Hijos de Cuahtémoc, Hidalgo y Juárez en Texas" (To the Sons of Cuahtémoc, Hidalgo and Juárez in Texas), dated November 26, 1914, called for the expulsion of the "forces of Washington in Texas" and the proclamation of an independent republic, to join with Mexico when the latter reformed its own political system.[47]

Less than a year would pass before parts of these visions would be realized in south Texas, as a small army of dispossessed rancheros took up arms in a doomed effort to regain the power and independence that they once boasted. The rebellion not only prompted a backlash from Anglo segregationists, but it also pitted Tejanos against one another. This civil war eventually helped prompt some to begin to think of themselves as Mexican Americans. To understand why not all Tejanos would choose to side with the "sons of Cuahtémoc, Hidalgo and Juárez," we must first take a deeper look into how they responded to the new world that confronted them early in the twentieth century.

2
Trouble in Mind

> "Look at the mess we've got ourselves into," Colonel
> Aureliano Buendía said at that time, "just because we
> invited a gringo to eat some bananas."
> —*Gabriel García Márquez*, One Hundred Years of Solitude

Don Antonio Yznaga knew that trouble was brewing in south Texas.
"Things did not look right," he remembered of late 1914, little more than six
months before the Plan de San Diego uprising was to begin. "Something
queerly fantastic, unnatural, seemed to be hovering over the Valley and along
the river front. Riding along the road . . . I met people who looked at me with
sidelong glances, people whom I had known for years, and in every face there
was that something I could not exactly fathom, but I knew that behind those
masks danger of some kind was kindling, and found expression in the eyes
that glinted ominously whenever they looked at me." Others, of all ethnicities
and walks of life, shared Yznaga's sense of alarm. Scores of requests for additional law officers, signed by newly arrived Anglos and long-standing Tejano
ranchers alike, poured into the statehouse in Austin. The anxiety was obvious
even to outsiders. "The Rio Grande Valley is fast becoming an armed camp,"
wrote an army scout the day after Christmas. "[N]early every man is carrying
a six shooter rifle or shot gun. It is uncommon to see a farmer plowing and if
you will notice there is a rifle hanging in a scbbard [*sic*] from the hames of
one of the mules."[1]

If few south Texans anticipated a rebellion on the scale of the Plan de San Diego, then many had good reason nevertheless to suspect the eruption of some sort of trouble. Relations between whites and ethnic Mexicans had been unsteady and occasionally violent since the region's subjugation to United States rule at the conclusion of the Mexican-American War in 1848. Indeed, nearly every long-standing resident knew of—or had witnessed and perhaps had even participated in—the uprisings led by Juan Cortina in 1859 and Catarino Garza in 1891, both of which showcased Tejano resentment of Anglo power and arrogance. The arrival, for the first time, of thousands of Anglos unfamiliar with the region's delicate racial balance could only further unsettle matters.

But another reason that so many were so nervous by 1915 had nothing to do with what the residents of south Texas had or had not done to one another. Mexico was in the throes of a revolution, in which peasant armies took to the battlefield to destroy the corrupt old order that had robbed them of their land and independence. Some hoped—and others feared—that the revolution would inspire a similar effort, just across the river, where ethnic Mexicans also watched more and more of their land slip away.

New arrivals to south Texas were generally blind to differences among the ethnic Mexican population. But in actuality the Texas-Mexicans of the lower border responded in different ways to the influx of Anglos and the Mexican Revolution. Some attempted to preserve the region's structure of racial accommodation, shoring up the political machine against Anglo disfranchisement and ethnic Mexican militancy alike. Their hope was that south Texas could continue much as it had since American conquest, with elite Tejanos using their power to broker a peace with sympathetic white leaders. The Mexican Revolution inspired others with the hope that a resurgent Mexico could be a refuge for Texas-Mexicans—or that a violent redistribution of land was just as feasible north of the Rio Grande. Still others, the "Tejano Progressives," looked to ethnic groups beyond south Texas for the answers to local problems, hoping to fuse Mexican and American traditions to restore political and economic power to a revitalized Tejano community.

In the years immediately following the railroad's arrival, these three groups had not crystallized into hard factions. Some individuals who played roles in the machine also joined the Progressives' efforts to develop independent and robust mass political power. The Mexican Revolution deeply moved both the Progressives and those rancheros willing to resort to arms to regain their lands. But soon enough the modernization of south Texas and the tumult of revolutionary Mexico created deep divisions within the Tejano community. It was with good reason that Antonio Yznaga saw danger in the eyes even of those he knew best.

The Machine

By decisively linking the southern tip of Texas to the rest of the United States, the railroad confronted Tejanos with the reality of being a racial minority in a nation with stark racial hierarchies, and in a region whose white leaders had turned to Jim Crow segregation to reassert those hierarchies. The influx of Anglo farmers and the rise of segregationist politics thus directly threatened old rights and privileges maintained when south Texas was a border enclave cut off from the rest of the nation. "The rapid industrial and agricultural development of the lower Rio Grande daily brings to our land . . . numerous elements unfamiliar with our prior rights as old inhabitants of the border," warned a Tejano newspaper in 1910. Given "our lack of political foresight," its author concluded, "[t]he newcomers," with their "new ideas, resources and lofty ambitions, will not hesitate to fleece us . . . of the representation that we have collectively exercised for many years in banking, commerce, society, and politics."[2]

The old order, embodied in the machine, did not simply melt away in the face of these tensions. The Anglos and Tejanos who ran the machine struggled to use the Tejano vote to defeat segregationists at the polls. That they were successful for a time was largely due to the persistence of a landed Tejano elite. Despite the pressures to which the agricultural boom subjected rancheros, some of the large Hispanic ranching families so instrumental in the creation of the machine in the nineteenth century managed not only to survive, but even to prosper in the new world created by the railroad. If they played their cards carefully, large ranchers with access to capital and the requisite language and business skills could benefit from the land boom. They could continue their cattle-raising businesses, made more profitable by the reduced shipping costs, and speculate in farm or even urban real estate on the side. The entrepreneurship of Brownsville's Francisco Yturria, a descendent of Spanish immigrants, exemplified this strategy. Yturria, an old foe of Juan Cortina's, helped to finance the railroad. It was a shrewd move, as "Don Pancho" added thirteen thousand acres to his ranching empire in Cameron and Hidalgo counties during the first decade of the twentieth century. At his death in 1912, Yturria left his heirs an integrated commercial empire. Not only was the family one of the region's major landholders, but his descendants also inherited the Yturria Cattle Company, Yturria Town and Improvement Company, and the Yturria Mercantile Company.[3]

Well-connected individuals without Yturria's preexisting land base and commercial interests also used the agricultural boom to their advantage. McAllen merchant and rancher Deodoro Guerra was a good example. Guerra's cousin Manuel was the head of the Starr County Democratic machine, and an important lieutenant for James Wells. Deodoro Guerra used his economic power and political connections to become one of the main labor contractors for the Valley. The process of clearing brush was arduous and labor-intensive, but necessary for planting crops. Guerra provided this service. He "employed large labor gangs that were transported daily by wagons to sprawling worksites. In some instances, if the *campos de desenraiz* [grubbing camps] were distant from town, the laborers encamped at the worksite in tents until the project was completed. Contratistas made good profits not only in land clearing, but also in other businesses, such as wholesale stores and taverns which they set up to serve laborers and the growing population. For instance, Guerra made a fortune in land clearing and the wholesale business, investing much of his money in ranching and farming in the San Manuel area."[4]

Another Hidalgo County resident used a similar strategy to profit from the Valley's boom. Florencio Saenz was a direct descendent of Captain Juan José Hinojosa, a beneficiary of one of the earliest Spanish land grants north of the Rio Grande. Saenz served as Hidalgo County commissioner from 1852 to 1905, delivering the numerous votes of his tenants, retainers, and kin to the Hidalgo County machine. As early as the 1880s he grew cotton, sugarcane, melons, and numerous truck crops. In the 1890s he began an integrated ranching, farming, and mercantile operation on his Toluca Ranch. Saenz continued ranching and expanded his sugarcane plantation, adding numerous farming tenants, a church, and a schoolhouse to his compound. He also operated a store that he claimed did more than fifty thousand dollars in business each year.[5]

Even if they did not have the capital or land to create multifaceted operations like Saenz did, more than a few Tejanos become successful large-scale farmers. Northwest of Edinburg in Hidalgo County, Tejanos were among the leaders in cotton farming. Rancher Ramón Vela added over three thousand acres to his holdings from 1900 to 1910. Members of his family and the Alamía family engaged in agriculture as well as ranching. By the 1920s they had as many as three thousand acres in cotton cultivation and frequently won the national prize for the first bale of cotton produced each season. These growers had tenants, generally sharecroppers, of their own, often former vaqueros.[6]

Relying on the votes delivered by Tejanos such as Vela, Saenz, and Guerra, the machine resisted insurgent Anglo politicians, who won most of the votes of newcomer farmers by promising to "clean up" elections by curtailing ethnic Mexican voting. In the context of open calls for segregation, this resistance often took on a quasi-populist tone. After Independents won control of Brownsville city government in 1910, for example, W. T. Vann, the machine's candidate for Cameron County sheriff in the next election, presented himself as the champion of the downtrodden. He accused his opponent, Fred Stark, a former customs inspector, of political corruption and of ignoring important crimes while punishing "some poor humble Mexican" for smuggling "two

bits' worth of mescal across the river." Vann defeated Stark by a margin of
more than two to one. His rhetoric, the size of his victory, and the fraud that
the machine employed to ensure it—James Wells sent the county judge into
hiding for several weeks to avoid the appointment of Independent election
judges—made Vann a hated figure for insurgent Anglo political factions. Despite this opposition to segregationists, however, the machine also continued
its tradition of dampening Tejano militancy. Deodoro Guerra would make
the arrest that first uncovered the Plan de San Diego, and Florencio Saenz
would find himself one of the uprising's principal targets.[7]

The Tejano Progressives

If the machine embodied sixty years of accommodation between Anglos
and ethnic Mexicans, then the Tejano Progressives sought to create a new
sort of accommodation, one based on equal economic opportunity, ethnic
pluralism, and respect for Mexican cultural heritage. They sought to fuse
what they thought of as the best of both Mexico and the United States. The
Progressives aimed inward, addressing their fellow Texas-Mexicans in the
hopes of remolding them as an educated, enlightened, prosperous people.
At the same time, they sought to represent the Tejano community to the outside world, insisting that Anglos respect Mexican culture and the political
rights of all peoples of the United States. The Progressives were enormously
ambitious, hoping to transform both race relations and what it meant to be
Tejano.[8]

Tejano Progressives steered a difficult course through the minefield of
south Texas. They admired the region's growing agricultural bounty but
feared the dispossession of Tejanos; they looked to the United States as a
model of a liberal democracy yet venerated aspects of Mexico's political tradition; they fiercely defended Tejanos against white arrogance even as they
condemned many of their own people as backward. The Mexican Liberalism
in which so much of their own ideology was steeped accounts for many of
these ambiguities. The ideal Liberal society was one dominated by autonomous
individuals equal before the law, unfettered by economic dependency or such
corporate entities as an established church or Indian communities. A central
government with powers authorized by a written constitution and private
property rights were the foundational institutions of such a society. Mexico's
Liberal elites and intellectuals sought to curtail the political and social power
of Catholicism and to transform—by force, if necessary—common lands into
private property. They admired the United States as a nation where political
liberty and a virtuous middle class reigned supreme. As the industrial revolution lifted western Europe and the United States to new heights of economic
wealth and global power, Mexican Liberals struggled to modernize their own

country by preparing and even forcing its citizens to compete in a market economy. A sort of folk Liberalism, however, also enjoyed wide support among the Mexican populace for much of the nineteenth century. This tradition emphasized local self-rule and constitutional checks on central government more than it did the need to transform ordinary Mexicans into acquisitive and rational citizens of a modern state.[9]

Most Tejano Progressives were small businessmen, skilled workers, or merchants. Though deeply rooted in south Texas, many had experiences and knowledge beyond the region that allowed them to envision a fusion of Mexican and American traditions. Laredo's Idar family was a good example. The family produced *La Crónica,* the newspaper that did more than any other venue to articulate the Progressive viewpoint to south Texas's Tejano community. Nicasio Idar was publisher and editor. He was born in Port Isabel, Texas (on the Gulf Coast near Brownsville), in 1855 but lived in northern Mexico for much of his early adulthood, working for the railroad into the 1880s. Idar helped to found a union on the San Luis Potosi–Nuevo Laredo railroad line. In the late 1880s or early 1890s he settled with his wife, Jovita Vivero Idar, in Laredo and soon become a civic leader and editor of *La Crónica.* Three of the Idars' children—Jovita, Clemente, and Eduardo (who worked for newspapers in San Benito and Brownsville)—were the principal writers and workers for the newspaper in the early 1900s. After the ordeal of the Plan de San Diego, Clemente and Eduardo would help to pioneer Mexican-American politics.[10]

Brownsville lawyer and politician J. T. Canales was the most important Progressive figure in the Valley itself. Born in 1877 in Nueces County, Texas, into one of the borderland's most distinguished and important families, Canales was much more aristocratic than most of the Progressives. His ancestors included the Tamaulipan secessionist and regional leader General Antonio Canales, the founders of Brownsville, and numerous ranchers on both sides of the border. By the first decade of the twentieth century, J. T. Canales's own life had taken him far from the borderlands. He received his elementary education with his grandparents in Nuevo León, Matamoros, and Tampico, returning to his father's ranch at age ten in 1887. After a few years in south Texas public schools, he briefly attended a business college in Austin. In 1892, at fifteen, he accompanied a shipment of his father's cattle sent to Indian Territory to escape a terrible drought. He did not return to south Texas until 1896, by which time he had completed high school in Kansas and had converted to Presbyterianism. From high school he went to the University of Michigan law school, graduating in 1899. The opportunity to do legal work for railroad companies brought J. T. Canales back to south Texas. In 1900 he began practicing law in Laredo with T. W. Dodd, the general counsel for the Texas-Mexican and Mexican Railway Company. Three years later he moved

Jovita Idar, ca. 1905. The University of Texas Institute of Texan Cultures, San Antonio, Texas. Courtesy of A. Ike Idar.

Nicasio Idar (center) with his sons Clemente (left) and Eduardo (right) in 1906.
The University of Texas Institute of Texan Cultures, San Antonio, Texas. No. 84–589.

to Brownsville and set up his own practice, because, as he put it, "by that time it was certain that a railroad was going to be constructed to Brownsville."[11]

The combination of Canales's bilingualism, local roots, family ties, and education suited him well for south Texas politics. Canales began his on-again, off-again involvement with the machine almost as soon as he arrived in Brownsville, supervising the Cameron County tax survey in 1904. In 1906 he won election to the State House of Representatives, serving as its only Tejano member. Canales steered his own course in the House, often voting against the wishes of the machine. He opposed greater scrutiny of railroad companies' political power and voted against an inheritance tax but supported corporate taxes, greater transparency in corporate finances, the regulation of the insurance industry, the creation of mine safety standards, anti-nepotism measures, and the establishment of the Texas Department of Agriculture. Sometimes using his family ties and economic power to buttress the machine, other times joining insurgent factions, Canales was one of the most pivotal figures in south Texas electoral politics.[12]

The agricultural boom stimulated Progressives such as Canales with the hope that economic development would make their people more industrious and give them a much-needed base of economic security. Canales saw the railroad's arrival as "the beginning of a new era in the Valley: the Era of Progress." *La Crónica* waxed more rhapsodic, declaring in 1910 that "where merely five years ago only the howl of the coyote could be heard, now one can hear the melody of the locomotive and the pump." The Idars were so impressed with the Valley's transformation that they called for ethnic Mexican landholders farther upstream to construct their own rail system. "The stream of immigrants that would invade this region upon the line's construction," they argued, "would be immense and the land would rise in price to 10 or 15 times its current value," and a large number of crops could be grown profitably. Without the railroad, on the other hand, the land's "immense riches will remain unexploited as they have up to now, and its proprietors will continue to be wealthy, but only in the sense that they produce enough to continue vegetating, without bringing any benefit to the region or its inhabitants."[13]

At the same time, though, the Progressives knew full well that the agricultural boom was literally taking the land right out from under Tejanos. In public speeches, harried conversations, and newspaper editorials, in fact, Progressive authors repeatedly called attention to this, at one point offering the stark prophecy that "Mexicans are condemned to be the Jews of the American continent, to an eternal wandering, first from North to South, and now from South to North."[14]

The loss of land was not only an economic hardship, but also reduced Tejanos' ability to resist segregationists. The Progressives who traveled outside of south Texas often feared that they saw their own future in the whites-only train cars, restaurants, and waiting rooms in the rest of Texas. Octavio García's memories are a good example. His first experience with segregation occurred early in the century, when he moved from a modest ranch in south Texas to attend a Catholic college in San Antonio. More than seventy years later, he still recalled how surprised he was to see a sign for a "Negro" waiting room once he had left the ranching zone of south Texas. Although fairly isolated from the white and black parts of San Antonio while at the school, García was so stunned by Jim Crow that he immediately wondered if Mexicans in south Texas were not headed for the same fate. Indeed, the Progressives watched as segregation spread over the rest of Texas, subjecting Tejanos outside of border enclaves to separate and poorly funded schools, denial of service at restaurants and hotels, and exclusion from public accommodations. "In San Antonio, Corpus Christi, Seguín, Goliad, and other currently important cities, founded by Mexicans," lamented *La Crónica,* "there is no public place for Mexicans except for the inferior and poorly-paid jobs allowed them."[15]

Individual education, ethnic unity, and economic success would allow Tejanos to avoid such a fate. Although the Progressive position obviously demanded changes from Anglos—an end to lynchings, an undoing of segregation, respect for Mexican culture and traditions—it also insisted that Tejanos transform themselves, collectively and individually. "The time has come," *La Crónica* editorialized in 1910, "for the Mexican element to adopt a strategy to achieve the dignity and position that it deserves, leaving the shadow of ignorance that humiliates it, and this strategy is education . . . we will thereby advance ourselves as many Brownsvillians and youth of Hidalgo and Starr have." The paper lauded those who followed such a strategy. "All lines of work are open for the educated Mexican, as we have seen with the Yturrias, Celedonio Garza, José T. Canales and many other educated Mexicans who now figure prominently in business and the different paths of human activity."[16]

Just as men and women in immigrant communities often adopted very different gender roles in their new home, so too did Tejanos begin to rethink old family patterns. Weakening patriarchal family patterns became an important part of the Progressive project of racial uplift. On the one hand, Progressive rhetoric consistently associated the accomplishments of Canales and other leaders with masculine virtue. On the other hand, it called for the "moral and physical education" of women and girls and sharply criticized the "false love" that discouraged women from learning gainful trades. Indeed, the Idars pointed to the increasing number of American women working outside the home as excellent proof of the advanced nature of the United States. They also endorsed women's suffrage, achieved in six states by 1911.[17]

Typically the proponents of modernizing visions such as that offered by Canales and the Idars were highly nationalist, linking their revitalization efforts to the redemption of a nation from backwardness or to its liberation from colonial rule. For the Progressives, however, matters were more complicated. It was unclear whether Mexico or the United States offered the greatest chance for the fulfillment of this political vision—or if such a choice even had to be made. Were Tejanos Mexicans or Americans? Both? Neither? The Progressives never fully grappled with these questions—they did not have to, until the Plan de San Diego forced them to make excruciating choices—but chose instead to emulate different aspects of each nation's politics and culture.

In some ways the Progressives maintained themselves within the trajectory of Mexican Liberalism, frequently condemning Catholicism and other "superstitious" beliefs, while lauding such national heroes as Benito Juárez. The outbreak of the Mexican Revolution in 1910 only strengthened this tendency. The fall of the ancien régime prompted the Idars to speculate that Tejanos could find refuge in "the sacred native ground of our ancestors." At the same time, however, their rhetoric frequently invoked American political traditions, and they often encouraged Tejanos to press their claims on the national community. The Idars sometimes referred to ethnic Mexicans in the United States as "Mexican-Americans"—some two decades before this term became common usage. On a practical level, they thought, American democracy offered an opening for Tejano power. "[V]ote always and loyally for men of your own race who aspire to public positions and have the aptitude to fill them agreeably for their own voters," *La Crónica* urged its readers. Indeed, the Idars went so far as to call for the replacement of ethnic Mexican support for the machine with a "party of Mexican-Americans." Such a party, they hoped, "would be . . . indivisible, without a place for the other elements who, with Machiavellian intent, introduce divisions among the Mexicans and take advantage of our different factions in order for their candidates to triumph, with detriment to the interests of the very same Mexicans."[18]

Ideologically, the Progressives had high praise for American political traditions. In opposing the poll tax, for example, *La Crónica* referred to the "glorious and sublime principles of individual liberty and civil rights embodied by the Declaration of Independence and the Federal Constitution of the American Republic." Such freedoms might protect ethnic Mexicans from discrimination and violence. The Idars printed the First Amendment in the hope that knowledge of it would "avoid the commission of abuses against some Mexicans in Texas who aren't aware of the constitutional rights that they enjoy when they live under the auspices of the American government, which they may invoke with the absolute security that justice will be done them." They demanded protection for Texas-Mexicans from lynchings and believed that such protection was more likely to come from federal power than from either Texas or the Mexican government.[19]

Although south Texas remained an isolated region well into the twentieth century, larger developments in North America and, indeed, around the globe, deeply influenced the Progressives, accounting for some of their ambivalence on the question of national identity. If the spectacular growth of European empires in the nineteenth century drew a color line across the globe, then growing anticolonial movements in the early twentieth century threatened to erase it. The rise of Japan particularly impressed the Idars. It opened itself up to Europe and the United States, they believed, sending its brightest children to Western universities. While Mexico and other nations were mired in cultural and economic backwardness, Japan epitomized a "modernized nation."[20]

Progressives found the ethnic transformation of the United States even more relevant to the changing fortunes of Tejanos. More than thirty million immigrants entered the United States from the 1880s to World War I, more than ten million from 1905 to 1914 alone. By the end of this wave of immigration, nearly one of every nine Americans was foreign born. The scope of this ethnic transformation raised fundamental questions about ethnic pluralism and cultural diversity. What would hold such a cosmopolitan country together? Would newcomers view their time in the United States as an exile to be endured, preferably temporarily, or was this their new home? Did they need to shed their old ways, adopting dominant WASP cultural patterns, or could they maintain themselves as ethnic enclaves with their own folkways? Would immigrants secure enough political power to serve their own interests, or could they hope for only a second-class citizenship at best?[21]

The national response to immigration offered no clear answer to these questions. On the one hand, the new arrivals prompted a ferocious backlash. While most native-born white Americans were Protestants of northern European descent, most immigrants in this period were Catholics and Jews from southern and eastern Europe. Established Americans often condemned them as racial degenerates unfit for social equality or citizenship. In 1891, for example, when a New Orleans mob lynched eleven Italian immigrants accused of plotting against the city's chief of police, the *New York Times* praised the lynchers as the city's "best element" and damned "[t]hese sneaking and cowardly Sicilians" as "to us a pest without mitigation. Our own rattlesnakes are as good citizens as they." Such sentiments conflated American nationality—and, by extension, the nation's avowed democratic principles—with an Anglo-Saxon heritage. Madison Grant systematized these views in his enormously influential 1916 book *The Passing of the Great Race*. "Democratic theories of government," he noted, "are based on dogmas of equality formulated some hundred and fifty years ago, and rest on the assumption that environment and not heredity is the controlling factor in human development." Grant insisted that racial differences were powerful and immutable, and thus that American support for continued immigration reflected "a pathetic and fatuous belief in the efficacy of American institutions to reverse or obliterate immemorial hereditary tendencies." To see the consequences of mixing the separate "races" of the earth, Americans needed to look no further than across the Rio Grande, "where the absorption of the blood of the original Spanish conquerors by the native Indian population has produced the racial mixture which we call Mexican, and which is now engaged in demonstrating its incapacity for self-government." In the early 1920s, Congress essentially codified Grant's philosophy into legislation. The Immigration Act of 1924, based on the report of a committee headed by the eugenicist, used a national origins quota to bring immigration to its lowest level in eighty years, drawn mostly from western Europe.[22]

Not all shared Grant's assumptions. Some established Americans hoped to "Americanize" the immigrants, making them culturally indistinguishable from those whose families had lived in the United States for generations. Others, including many immigrant leaders, offered their own visions of Americanization, in which cultural homogeneity was not the inevitable or even desirable outcome of successful integration into the larger society. Social scientist Horace Kallen, who coined the term *cultural pluralism,* argued that the United States was becoming a "great republic consisting of a federation or commonwealth of nationalities." Kallen lauded the "chorus of many voices each singing a rather different tune" and urged his readers to make the chorus "a symphony of civilization" rather than hewing to the "righteous and pathetic" rejection of immigrant diversity.[23]

These running conflicts made it easier for the Tejano Progressives to see how they, or at least their children, might become respected members of the national community. They knew that the segregation and disfranchisement sought by so many Anglo Texans were not all that the United States had to offer. Progressives lauded the United Sates as a polyglot nation, one that welcomed people from scores of nations and provided them with freedom and economic opportunities of which their ancestors could only have dreamt. In his examination of Minnesota's Swedish community, for example, Clemente Idar argued that Tejanos had much to learn from American ethnic groups. Gaining full acceptance and social standing did not require abandoning a distinct cultural heritage and group identity. "In this country, from its founding," he wrote, "even when all lived loyally under the national flag and as American citizens, its inhabitants have always divided themselves into peaceful factions along lines of racial origin." The Progressive emphasis on modernizing the Tejano community, moreover, resembled the strategies of some immigrant leaders, who sought dramatic cultural change to equip their communities for success in their new home. Like these immigrants, the Progressives knew that they could not hope to change the Tejano community for the sake of Tejanos until they had changed Tejanos to ensure the survival of their community.[24]

The poverty and severe marginalization faced by African Americans in

both the South and the northern cities that received the most immigrants allowed newcomers to claim the mantle of whiteness. They could press established Americans to recognize them as racial equals, as fellow white people
with greater capacities and more rights than those of black people. The very
concept of an "ethnicity"—a distinct yet mutable culture of a self-conscious
group, as compared with a "race," a supposedly biological and therefore un-
changeable category—reflected the importance that so many attached to dis-
tinguishing themselves from blacks. Mass culture, intermarriage, and the
shared experiences of Depression and war erased many of the lines separating
distinct ethnic groups, making "Polish" or "Italian" subcategories of "white,"
rather than separate racial categories.

In Texas, those who could claim whiteness could gain considerable
benefits. If Tejanos could force Anglos to recognize them as white, they would
avoid judgment under segregation statutes, they might preserve their voting
rights, and they could send their children to the best public schools. There
was thus a clear logic behind *La Crónica*'s condemnation of Anglo labeling
of ethnic Mexicans as non-white. But the Progressives displayed little interest
in the whiteness strategy. They did not seem to think of themselves as white,
or even to aspire to such a status. Noting that in the United States "the problem of race is a question of color," *La Crónica* matter-of-factly referred to
Mexicans as a "latin multicolor race." Moreover, the paper frequently put its
discussion of anti-Mexican discrimination and violence in the context of wider
Anglo racism. In an attack on Texas's poll tax, for example, one editorial argued
that the tax was not only a blatant violation of the United States' democratic
principles, but was also the "creation of purely political interests in retaining
power with the authorities of the Democratic party in Texas." The tax hurt
not only Mexicans, but others as well: "[T]here are many poor and illiterate
Germans, Bohemians, Jews and Negroes, just like many Mexicans, who cannot
pay their poll tax, and by an extraordinary coincidence among these class of
residents of Texas one will find the great majority of citizens who are not
Democrats and who profess other political creeds that are in open conflict
with the perpetuation in office of the Democratic party of Texas." Racism,
not ethnoracial diversity, was the scourge of Texas and of Tejano aspirations.[25]

The question of language clearly revealed the Progressive ambivalence
about national identity. As superintendent of Cameron County's school system,
J. T. Canales emphasized the need for students to learn English, instructing
teachers that "the English language should be spoken both in the school-
room as well as during recess; and, also, that school children should be taught
to sing, in English, either sacred or patriotic songs." The Idars similarly urged
Texas-Mexicans to learn "the language of the country in which they live." On
the other hand, living in the United States put Tejanos at risk of losing

something of their "Mexicanness." Houston resident J.J. Mercado, for example, argued that Anglicisms corrupted the Spanish spoken by Texas-Mexicans. For Mercado the use of terms like *bordeando* for the English *boarding* showed that the isolated social life of Mexicans in Texas stunted their culture and even their mental faculties. These attitudes reflected how Progressives considered themselves Mexicans in some sense but were also aware of an increasing social distance between Tejanos and Mexicans. "They have their own ways of living in their own country," Emeterio Flores said of Mexican nationals, "and it is absolutely different from ours. We people who were born in this country feel for them because they are our own race, although we were born and educated here in this country; we feel for those poor unfortunates, and we would not like to see them come here any more unless conditions changed a great deal."[26]

The Primer Congreso

The Progressives made some headway in their project of ethnic revitalization. In September 1911 they hosted delegates—as many as four hundred, by one count—at the Primer Congreso Mexicanista (First Mexicanist Congress, literally) in Laredo. Nicasio Idar used the pages of *La Crónica* to advertise the meeting and sent broadsides to ethnic Mexican newspapers, mutual benefit associations, and Masonic lodges across Texas and northeast Mexico. He hoped that the meeting would help Texas-Mexicans to be "treated with more respect . . . and given justice when we demand it," to improve the quality of their children's education, and to establish some sort of organization that would work continually for such goals.

The Primer Congreso was the largest ethnic Mexican civil rights gathering held to date. Delegates—mostly men, but some women—came from dozens of Texas towns and from as far away as Houston and Mexico City. South Texans dominated the conference, just as the region dominated the population and culture of the Tejano community. The meeting elected board members from Brownsville, Laredo, Kingsville, and Rio Grande City. Most presenters stressed the themes of Tejano Progressivism: loss of economic power, exclusion from schools and public accommodations, and growing racial violence. The solutions were similar as well. Delegates advocated the political unity of ethnic Mexicans, economic advancement through education and mutual-benefit associations, instruction in both English and Spanish, the education of women, and the modernization of family life.[27]

The question of national identity, however, played itself out differently at the conference than it had with most Progressives over the previous decade. Whereas the Idars were conflicted in their sense of national identity, most of the delegates at the Congreso emphasized that Texas-Mexicans' future lay within the institutions and culture of Mexico. Most of the speakers invoked the symbols and figures of Mexican nationalism to make this point. Faustino Rendón, the Grand Chancellor of the fraternal association Caballeros de Honor, began his comments on the status of Mexicans in Texas by lauding the fact that the Congreso was being held on September 16, the anniversary of Mexico's independence. He closed his speech by urging delegates to struggle for the well-being of Mexicans so that "our beautiful [Mexican] tricolor flag may always fly proudly at the crest of our efforts." Delegate Gregorio González of Nuevo Laredo, Tamaulipas, made perhaps the strongest statement that agitation on behalf of Mexicans in Texas was based on the embrace of Mexican national identity. Mexico's "absent children," he argued, "who have been obliged to seek their living outside the patria, have regathered today . . . to seek ways to make their exile less sad."[28] Conspicuously absent from the convention was any mention of how American institutions or politics might offer assistance, or at least be used as tools in the struggle to protect Texas-Mexicans. Instead of advocating for rights granted by the U.S. Constitution, or drawing useful lessons from the experiences of other ethnic groups, speaker after speaker urged the delegates to join the long line of Mexican patriots and political movements.

The meeting's final act was to establish a Gran Liga Mexicanista, an organization to struggle for the advancement and protection of Mexicans across the state. The Liga was to hold an annual convention on September 16, Mexican Independence Day. Shortly thereafter, led by Jovita Idar, the women delegates created a group, called the Liga Femenil, to work with the Gran Liga.[29]

If these groups had lasted and fulfilled the ambitious program of the convention, the Gran Liga might today be a familiar organization to most Americans. Just two years earlier, a similar meeting in New York City resulted in the formation of the National Association for the Advancement of Colored People. But whereas the NAACP quickly became a nationwide organization in the forefront of black struggle, the chaos of the Mexican Revolution soon wrecked the prospects of what might have become the first ethnic Mexican civil rights organization. Almost two decades would pass before Tejanos would again form such a statewide body, this time as self-declared American citizens. Although several of the Tejano Progressives in attendance at the Congreso would in fact spearhead this effort, in 1911 they were still very much caught in the borderlands between American and Mexican nationalism.

Conclusion

Those who lived through the first decade of the twentieth century were aware of just how much south Texas had changed. The Nueces Strip was still an isolated enclave at the beginning of the decade, with a political system and race relations that differed dramatically from those of the rest of Texas and the United States. The long whistle and smokestack of the railroad signified that this had changed, however. Thousands of Anglos came, intent upon making the Valley much more like the rest of the country. Finding their homeland thus tied more closely, some Tejanos realized that the nation itself was changing, trying to reckon with its growing ethnic diversity and burgeoning industrial economy. They hoped that south Texas could adopt the best of the United States and avoid Jim Crow, one of the nation's most contemptible practices.

Perhaps the Tejano Progressives asked themselves how much of an impact they had been able to have on the mind of average Tejanos. If so, they had abundant reason to be pessimistic. Few could afford to keep their children in school, to receive the kind of education that J. T. Canales so lionized. Many continued to dutifully vote for the machine's candidates, even when these politicians showed no interest in protecting Tejanos against the forces of the new agricultural economy.

Even many of those who shared the Progressives' insistence on standing up for themselves resorted to very different means. Since 1848, the Tejanos most discontent with Anglo rule had turned to violence to combat it. Courageous individuals such as Gregorio Cortéz and the de la Cerdas eluded and fought the Rangers, succumbing only when tricked or vastly outnumbered. Others, among them Juan Cortina and Catarino Garza, had rallied hundreds, forcing outmatched regional leaders to call in the federal troops.

Whatever the new century had changed, and whatever the Progressives' great ambitions were, violence remained an appealing option for the most discontented of Tejanos. The new south Texas of the railroad and the Anglo farmer gave rise to yet another Tejano hero. Jacinto Treviño lived and ran a modest herd of cattle just upriver from Brownsville near Los Indios, a small settlement that would be deeply involved in the Plan de San Diego raids. Like so many Tejano families by 1911, the Treviños could no longer entirely rely on their own land to support themselves, so Jacinto's brother went to work for a nearby Anglo farmer. A dispute with his boss left him so badly beaten that he soon died from his wounds. This was too much for his grieving brother Jacinto, who took swift revenge, killing the farmer and fleeing to Mexico. Anglo farmers raised money for a reward, and together with the Texas Rangers decided to use a distant relative to lure him back across the border to a remote meeting place where they would arrest or kill him. But the ranchero was a step ahead of his pursuers; he lay in waiting in the chaparral as they rode to meet him. Firing upon the hated *rinches,* he killed one Ranger, a deputy, and his traitorous relative. Using his intimate knowledge of the terrain, Treviño eluded his numerous pursuers and slipped back across the river—just as so many of his fellow rancheros would do four years later.[30]

3
The Promise of the Revolution

> History says, Don't hope
> On this side of the grave.
> But then, once in a lifetime
> The longed-for tidal wave
> Of justice can rise up,
> And hope and history rhyme.
> —*Seamus Heaney,* The Cure at Troy

Delegates at the Primer Congreso had good reason to place so much confidence in Mexican nationalism. Their meeting took place during a seismic political shift in Mexico, one that would eventually transform the United States as well. In 1908, Coahuila hacendado Francisco Madero began a daring presidential campaign against Porfirio Díaz, who was planning to reelect himself for the eighth time two years later. Madero, the scion of one of Mexico's wealthiest families, damned the "corruption of the spirit, the disinterest in public life, a disdain for the law" rampant in Porfirian Mexico, linking Díaz's rule—the longest in the western hemisphere—to growing foreign power. "In the society that renounces the responsibility of governing itself," he proclaimed, "there is a mutilation, a degradation, a debasement that can easily translate into submission before the foreigner."[1] Free elections, an independent judiciary, and an uncensored press, he argued, could free Mexico from its shackles and prepare it to join the modern world.

Madero won enormous publicity for himself, but at first his campaign seemed to fail completely. The regime used wholesale fraud to prevent his forces from winning a single congressional seat in the June elections. Madero

Mexico at the time of the Mexican Revolution.

himself spent election day in prison, charged with sedition. In October he
jumped bail and fled from San Luis Potosí to San Antonio, Texas. There the
exiled hacendado issued a manifesto declaring himself provisional president
and calling on Mexicans to revolt against Díaz in November.

For years after the Plan de San Diego, federal and Texas officials would
wonder how Tejanos came to believe that they could force one of the world's
most powerful nations to cede a large portion of its territory to the descendents
of those it had conquered. Their incredulity failed to take into account the
breathtaking events in Mexico that followed Madero's call for revolt. Although
the uprisings that he had planned mostly failed to materialize, often easily
crushed by the federal army, the courage of ordinary Mexicans filled the
breach. In the southern state of Morelos, a peasant army led by Emiliano Zapata continued to tie down critical portions of Díaz's army, just barely to the
south of the capital. Other revolts that Madero had not planned soon erupted,
first in Chihuahua under the leadership of Pascual Orozco and Pancho Villa,
and then in many other parts of the country by March 1911. By April a majority
of the countryside was in rebel hands. Late that month, Ciudad Juárez, just
across the river from El Paso, became the first major city to fall to Madero's
supporters. On May 21, 1911, a humbled Díaz agreed to resign and to yield to
a provisional government that would hold new presidential elections in October. The Primer Congreso met just three weeks before these elections.[2]

Madero handily won the election and ascended to the presidency. But overthrowing the Díaz dictatorship was a simple matter compared with building a new order that could rule the country and meet the enormous and conflicting expectations of the Mexican people. Porfirian Mexico, much like the Gilded Age in the United States, witnessed explosive economic growth coupled with deepening inequalities. The railroad network grew from less than four hundred miles in 1876 to fifteen thousand by 1910, sparking booms in textile manufacturing and export crops such as sugar and cotton. Metal mining, which previously was dominated by foreign nationals, more than quintupled. In 1906 Mexican industrialists built Latin America's first steel mill in Monterrey. But hunger and dispossession walked hand in hand with this unprecedented growth. Wages remained flat as prices of staple foods (corn, beans, and chile) spiraled upward. Violence, fraud, and economic forces stripped millions of their lands. By 1910, landless peasant families constituted nearly two-thirds of the national population. In the densely populated central plateau, more than 90 percent of the villages had been stripped of their communal lands. The Porfirian regime provided no form of redress for those harmed by the nation's transformation. It banned opposition political parties and used the federal army and the *rurales,* a paramilitary police force much like the Texas Rangers, to crush strikes and other protests.[3]

Madero's campaign became the outlet for this stifled dissent. Many agreed that Díaz had to go, even if they could agree on little else. Some elites and much of the middle class, especially in Mexico's north, resented their exclusion from political power and the concessions made to attract foreign investment. They saw Madero as an apostle of democracy, the leader who could finally make Mexico a modern nation with a free citizenry. Other political factions simply saw his campaign as an opportunity to gain power previously denied them. Many peasants—a large majority of Mexico's population—hoped that his rule would allow them to recover their land.

Once in office, Madero proved himself true to his liberal principles, devoting his energies to formal legal and political reform while rejecting burgeoning calls for land redistribution. He was neither a dictator nor a democrat, willing neither to rule with an iron fist like Díaz, nor to let what he called "the ignorant public" run the nation. This middling course proved impossible to maintain. The key constituents of the old regime—regional political bosses, wealthy hacendados and industrialists, and the federal army—never accepted his rule, believing him perilously weak, unable and unwilling to prevent the lower orders from tearing society apart. On the other hand, those who hoped for a sweeping reform of landholding were angered by Madero's unwillingness to heed their calls. Zapata, refusing the new president's order to surrender his weapons and disband his soldiers, again found himself fighting the federal army.

These diverse groups initially struggled for control of Madero's regime, but were soon to clash directly on the battlefield. In early 1913 General Victoriano Huerta, commander of the federal army, had Madero assassinated and dismissed the congress elected alongside him. Led by Huerta, the ancien régime desperately fought back against the revolution. Coahuila hacendado Venustiano Carranza established the "Constitutionalist" opposition to Huerta, seeking to restore Madero's liberal and moderate rule. Some radicals, including Pancho Villa, soon joined him, while others, like Zapata, fought on alone. A plethora of local rebellions and alliances, often unconnected to larger factions or ideologies, also emerged by the end of the year. Civil war—at first between Huerta and the revolutionaries, and then among the different revolutionary factions—would wrack Mexico for the rest of the decade, killing a tenth or more of its population, driving perhaps another tenth of its population to flee to the United States, prompting two American military occupations and at times threatening the nation's very existence.

The land question hung over the entire revolution, transforming what had been a conflict between some of Mexico's wealthiest citizens into a struggle for the soul of the nation. Three-quarters of Mexicans lived in the countryside. Agrarian discontent drew tens of thousands to the armies of Zapata, Villa, and lesser-known leaders, and even impelled moderates like Carranza to recognize the importance of land reform. While Zapata spoke for a close-knit village society that saw its collective lands taken by sugar plantations, Villa came from a northern frontier culture more familiar to Tejanos. Chihuahua's military colonies, founded in the eighteenth century at roughly the same time as the Spanish settlement of the Nueces Strip, formed a bulwark against the Apache and other militarily formidable Indian nations. Military service provided ordinary Chihuahuan men with greater access to land and political power than their counterparts had in the rest of Mexico. After the subjugation of the Apache in the 1880s, however, a clique headed by a powerful family came to dominate the state's economy and politics, taking what many Chihuahuans thought of as their birthright.[4]

The followers of Villa, Zapata, and others fought for land not only because it was the most important form of wealth in an overwhelmingly rural and agrarian society, but also because they considered it essential to be truly free. A free man—rural Mexicans, particularly in Chihuahua, linked agrarianism to manliness—was above all one who worked for himself, his family, and his community, not as somebody's peon or employee. It was no accident that "Tierra y Libertad" (Land and Liberty) was one of the most common revolutionary slogans. And if control over land made people free, then a free country was one that secured such control for its citizenry. These revolutionaries thus linked their struggle to the redemption of the entire nation from those who

had betrayed its promise. As Zapata put it, "[T]he land will be our own possession, it will belong to all the people—the land our ancestors held and that the
fingers on paws that crushed us snatched away from us."[5]

The Mexican Revolution had an enormous impact on the United States.
The arrival of hundreds of thousands of refugees dramatically expanded ethnic
Mexican settlements, restoring their ties to Mexico and ultimately redrawing
the ethnic geography of the Southwest. Where Americans had once flooded
into Mexico's territory, now Mexicans flooded into the United States. In 1900,
for example, Los Angeles County's ethnic Mexican community was a tiny
and isolated enclave of around five thousand people—a smaller settlement
than the Tejanos of Cameron County alone, and a minor presence in a metro-
politan area of one hundred and seventy thousand. By 1930, when this huge
migration ceased, the two hundred thousand ethnic Mexicans living in the
county formed nearly a tenth of its population. As many as one million Mexicans
may have found refuge in the United States over the course of the revolution,
and while many soon returned to Mexico, the aggregate number of ethnic
Mexicans in the United States nonetheless tripled between 1910 and 1920.
This wave of immigration also began to tip the balance of the Mexican-descent
population away from Texas and toward California, though it would not be
until the 1950s that more ethnic Mexicans lived in California than in Texas.
Indeed, for more than eighty years after the Mexican-American War, the Lone
Star State contained more than half of all those of Mexican descent living in
the United States.[6]

Political ferment accompanied demographic explosion. From the turn
of the twentieth century well into the 1920s, a plethora of Mexican politicians,
military leaders, and intellectuals found refuge in the United States, most often
in Texas. The overthrow of Díaz had created a window of opportunity to pursue the wide spectrum of political philosophies and aspirations they had
brought with them. Although they had relocated north of the border, these
exiles mostly continued to focus their energies on politics back in Mexico,
encouraging their fellow refugees—who now outnumbered American-born
ethnic Mexicans—to do the same. As the discussions at the Primer Congreso
suggest, the Mexican Revolution even turned many of the Tejano Progressives,
deeply rooted in south Texas, away from their experimentation with the American political system and toward the prospect of finding sanctuary in a redeemed
Mexico. Four years after the meeting, Emeterio Flores reflected on the effects
of the revolution on Texas-Mexicans. Flores was a supporter of the Congreso,
a close associate of the Idars, and the head of a mutual benefit organization
called the Mexican Protective Association. "[T]he activities of the association
in 1911 and 1912 were greater than in 1913 and 1914," he recalled, "due, probably, to the failure of the association in several cases in 1913 and the influx of

refugees from Mexico who, it seems, are almost generally revolutionarily inclined at all times and have great influence with their countrymen already here prior to them."[7]

Flores needed look no further than the Idar family to illustrate his point. Many influential merchants from Nuevo Laredo, Monterrey, and Saltillo found refuge in Laredo, strengthening commercial and political connections with Mexico's north. After Huerta's forces took Nuevo Laredo during his 1913 overthrow of Madero, the city soon became a center of support and organizing for the Constitutionalists. Though no record remains of activities by the Liga Femenil, Jovita Idar joined with a Mexican émigré in founding a nurses' corps for the Constitutionalist army. She helped to quarter wounded soldiers in Laredo and traveled for a time with Constitutionalist forces in northern Mexico. In 1916 she wrote to Venustiano Carranza to ask for his financial support for pro-Carrancista newspapers along the border, which she hoped would help "elevate the mother country."[8]

Regeneración and Radical Exiles

In the end, however, the politics of the Mexican Revolution also led Tejanos to address their plight in the United States, not merely to hope for the redemption of Mexico. Indeed, Ricardo and Enrique Flores Magón, two of the earliest and most influential exiles, would become the intellectual inspiration for the Plan de San Diego.

Born in Porfirio Díaz's hometown of Oaxaca in the 1870s, the brothers were active in liberal anti-Díaz political circles by the early 1900s. Their fondness for publishing anti-Porfirian newspapers and their flirtation with advocating the armed overthrow of the government earned them several prison sentences. In January 1904 the two men fled to Laredo, where they worked for a time as manual laborers to support themselves. They soon saved enough money to move to San Antonio, where, with other anti-Díaz émigrés and with funding from Liberals still in Mexico, they resumed publishing their newspaper *Regeneración*. Harassed by Díaz's agents, and quarreling with other exiles, in 1905 the brothers moved to St. Louis, Missouri, where they became part of U.S. anarchist circles and published the paper whenever possible. Ultimately relocating to Los Angeles, the Flores Magóns achieved remarkable success in spreading *Regeneración* across the Mexican community in the United States and into Mexico itself. By 1906, nearly twenty thousand people in both nations paid for subscriptions. In July 1906, the brothers founded the Partido Liberal Mexicano (PLM). Their new party called for formal political reforms such as a four-year presidential term with no reelection, classical liberal proposals such as taxing church property, and social reforms such as an eight-hour workday and an end to child labor. Their manifesto circulated across Mexico, prompting the formation of local Liberal groups. It inspired several major industrial strikes and numerous small and unsuccessful uprisings in Mexico's north—all decisively crushed by the federal army and the rurales.[9]

By the time that Francisco Madero became president in October 1911, Enrique and Ricardo had become both more explicitly radical and less influential. Whereas liberals such as Madero viewed private property as a sacrosanct institution, the Flores Magón brothers believed that a massive redistribution of property was necessary to create an egalitarian and just society. They denounced Madero as a "traitor to the cause of liberty" and called for an armed struggle to redistribute land and wealth and destroy the power of the church, foreigners, and the rich.[10]

Like most exile publications, *Regeneración* devoted most of its attention to Mexico and to the course of the revolution. In sharp contrast with the Tejano Progressives, the Flores Magóns saw the United States as an unremittingly hostile land whose people and institutions, with the possible exception of a handful of radicals, had nothing to offer Mexicans. The paper's column "In the Defense of Mexicans" regularly documented the violence and discrimination they faced. The column's authors complained bitterly of segregation, discrimination, economic exploitation, and racial violence, particularly in "the savage state of Texas." For the Flores Magóns, the mistreatment of Mexicans in the United States reflected the debasement of Mexicans in Mexico. "The Mexican is a pariah here, just as he is a pariah in Mexico," wrote Ricardo.[11]

In the teens, the Flores Magóns had trouble enough paying their bills and staying out of U.S. prison, let alone leading a successful revolution. Nevertheless, *Regeneración* continued to be an influential publication for Mexicans. Indeed, it may have influenced Mexicans residing in the United States—and especially in Texas—more than those in Mexico. By 1915, the year of the Plan de San Diego, almost half of its papers circulated in the Lone Star State, twice as many as in Mexico and California combined. Mexicans and Tejanos formed scores of local PLM *grupos* in small towns and cities across the state. The organizations wrote to *Regeneración* to announce their formation and to report their recent activities. Correspondence from these grupos, often named "Tierra y Libertad" or some variant thereof, came to *Regeneración* from places like Brownsville, Laredo, San Antonio, and El Paso in the traditional Mexican areas of Texas, from coastal towns such as Port Lavaca, from Amarillo and other towns on the panhandle plains, from the mixed Anglo-Black-German-Czech area in central Texas around Schulenburg, from the Dallas-Fort Worth area in northeast Texas, and even from Oklahoma. Mexicans from Texas to California wrote to *Regeneración* in search of relatives whom they had lost contact with during their migrations.[12] The grupos met to apprise themselves of developments in the course of the Mexican Revolution, to discuss PLM writings and other anarchist tracts, to commemorate holidays such as the Dieciseis de Septiembre and May Day, and to raise money and write letters in defense of jailed Mexican exiles—the Flores Magón brothers themselves, as often as not.

The PLM's platform spoke to many Tejanos in the Nueces Strip, offering them an explanation for their plight and the hope that the resolution of the land question in Mexico might address their own needs. South Texas Magonistas were typically small or middling ranchers, ranch hands, or urban shopkeepers and skilled laborers who generally owned their own homes. Both men and women joined the PLM. For the Flores Magón brothers, much as for the Tejano Progressives, patriarchy was part of the ossified old society of which Mexicans needed to rid themselves. They therefore denounced authoritarian families and advocated greater sexual equality. In both Mexico and the United States, women played active roles in the PLM, helping to circulate the party's literature and to found local grupos. When the brothers first arrived in the United States in 1904, they were welcomed by Laredo resident Sara Estela Ramírez, whose home soon became the party's headquarters. She remained a close confidant of Ricardo's until her death in 1910. A frequent contributor of poems, essays, and literary articles to Spanish-language newspapers across south Texas, Ramírez supported mutual aid societies, labor unions, and the liberation of women from strict patriarchal norms. "Rise Up! To Woman," she proclaimed in 1910. "Rise up! Rise up to life, to activity, to / the beauty of truly living; but rise up radiant / and powerful, beautiful with qualities, splendid / with virtues, strong with energies."[13]

Aniceto Pizaña, a rancher who lived near Brownsville, appears to have been the single most active PLM partisan in the region. The ranchero became a devoted follower of the Flores Magón brothers, in one account shortly after meeting them in Laredo in 1904. Pizaña not only faithfully donated to the legal defense of jailed PLM partisans, but he also raised money and sold party literature in the Brownsville area, proudly distributing what he called "the propaganda of Land and Liberty for all." He even named his son, Praxedis, after PLM leader Praxedis Guerrero. He founded a grupo named "Perpetual Solidarity," reading *Regeneración* out loud to some of the men who would soon join him in south Texas's own version of the Mexican Revolution. The anarchist condemnation of wage labor as a form of servitude had enormous resonance with rancheros like Pizaña, who found such labor exploitive and humiliating. Pizaña himself had gone on a long cotton-picking excursion into central Texas in the 1890s while in his mid-teens. Decades later, he still remembered the backbreaking work and still boasted of how he worked slowly enough to gain the most pay for the least amount of toil.[14]

Pizaña supported PLM efforts in Tamaulipas, where small ranchers and rural workers were demanding land reform to break up large haciendas. In 1910 PLM partisan Higinio Tanguma led about forty men under the banner "Viva Tierra Libre y Libertad!" in occupying an hacienda headquarters near Aldama, Tamaulipas, and burning its records and account books. Shortly before this raid Tanguma visited Pizaña's ranch and gave speeches about the PLM that deeply impressed his host. Pizaña later wrote that had it not been for his aged mother and an injury to his leg, he would in fact have joined Tanguma's uprising. Soon enough he would find himself at the head of a much larger force.[15]

Agrarian Radicalism in Texas

Although the Flores Magón brothers had little but contempt for the United States—and especially Texas—some ethnic Mexicans found kindred spirits among the dispossessed of the American south. The migratory stream that Aniceto Pizaña and so many others joined took Tejanos out of their distinctive regional community and exposed them to agrarian discontent in both Texas and Tamaulipas. If Tejano Progressives were influenced by the diversity of the American populace, so too, in their own way, were the architects of the Plan de San Diego uprising.

The lives of its adherents made the PLM a transnational organization. The members of many central Texas grupos migrated back and forth from Texas's cotton fields to those of the Laguna region of southwestern Coahuila. Indeed, Laguna planters complained of the belligerence of workers returning from Texas. As early as 1906, a PLM faction from central Texas led an unsuccessful armed revolt against an army post in Laguna. At the same time, some PLMers may have begun to consider their time in the United States as something more than a temporary exile. In July 1912 in Lehigh, Oklahoma, for example, members from around the region gathered to discuss the history of the PLM and the "social conditions of the Mexican proletariat on both sides of the Rio Grande." A suggestion of a union of "our movement with the American, Italian, Polish, and Negro compañeros" became one of the objects of the meeting. A "diversity of races and nationalities attended" a similar meeting in August, at which "American and Negro compañeros spoke in favor of the Mexican Revolution."[16] This was the radical tradition out of which the interracial appeal of the Plan de San Diego grew.

As the apparent sympathy of non-Mexicans at the Lehigh meetings suggests, the PLM was not the only voice in favor of land redistribution that ethnic Mexicans encountered in the United States. The roads that south Texans took to central Texas and to as far as Oklahoma and Arkansas brought them to a region with its own legacy of agrarian radicalism. Much as the villagers of Morelos and the settlers of Chihuahua found themselves dispossessed by their country's economic modernization, so too did many of the South's small farmers. Incredibly scarce capital—at one point, Arkansas had barely thirteen cents in circulation per capita—forced middling farmers to become indebted to merchants, signing away their future crops and most of their possessions in the process. As more and more lost their land and slipped into tenancy or wage labor, these farmers founded the Populist, or People's, Party, the largest challenge to the American two-party system to this date. The Populists sought to use the powers of government—to regulate monopolies, tax the wealthy, and expand the currency—to serve the Jeffersonian vision of a democratic nation of independent proprietors. Political democracy required the direct control of productive resources—land, above all. The independent middle or "plain people" was the nation's salvation. The Populists expressed their solidarity with laborers, condemned the violent suppression of strikes, and warned of the dangers of creating "two great classes—tramps and millionaires." Though led by white farmers, in many cases the People's Party made an appeal for interracial solidarity in the face of a common threat. "You are made to hate each other because upon that hatred is rested the keystone of the arch of financial despotism which enslaves you both," Georgia Populist Tom Watson told black and white farmers in the 1890s, promising that the People's Party would "wipe out the color line and put every man on his citizenship irrespective of color." [17]

Populism crested a decade before the railroad forced so many south Texans to head north. The imposition of segregation and the disfranchisement of blacks and poor whites across the South killed the People's Party. But it nonetheless left a strong mark on the region's political culture. In the teens in Oklahoma and Texas, the United States' Socialist Party garnered its highest level of support, which came from small landowners, tenant farmers, and migrant farmworkers. This brand of Socialism owed as much to Thomas Jefferson and Jesus Christ as it did to Karl Marx. Oklahoma and Texas Socialists called for more family farms rather than for the traditional Marxist collectivization of land, and they often used the language of evangelical Protestantism to damn the harshness of the capitalist marketplace. Although more committed to electoral politics than to the Flores Magóns' anarchist vision of armed revolution, these Socialists nonetheless condemned the monopolization of land and other productive resources by the rich. As one Texas farmer put it, "the land must come into the possession of those who labor." [18]

The defense of besieged communities could easily translate into a wholesale rejection of "outsiders," and so white agrarians could be just as racist as the farmers that were turning south Texas upside down. Some Populists, including Tom Watson later in his career, numbered among the nation's most vehement white supremacists. Similarly, many white Socialists viewed black sharecroppers and farmhands as prisoners of their own stupidity and docility, and they often extended such sentiments to Mexicans as well. For example, one white supporter wrote to the *Rebel* (based in Hallettsville, Texas)—at the time, the third-largest Socialist newspaper in the United States—that Mexican immigration was going to ruin Texas. Mexicans were worse than the Chinese and Japanese had been on the West Coast, he argued. They were ignorant, cost taxpayers money, and crowded white people out of the labor market. "In five years," he predicted, "there will be one million Mexicans . . . in Texas; then we will have a constant gangrene upon our social body and our moral atmosphere will be so rotten that it will require oceans of carbolic acid to disinfect it."[19]

On the other hand, agrarians often felt deep sympathy with the plight of landless Mexicans and therefore supported their revolutionary struggle. They saw something of themselves in the followers of Pancho Villa and Emiliano Zapata. The coming of the revolution struck the *Rebel*'s editors as a hopeful sign that Mexicans were casting off the shackles of the oppressive past. They frequently printed Villa's and Zapata's manifestos. "Why should not the Mexican masses own the soil, where they were born, and which they till, and where their ancestors were born, slaved, and died?" asked the paper's editors. "All the leaders of the present social revolt realize the urgent necessity of destroying the unjust and feudal agrarian system which is the real cause of most of the ills under which the people labor." The parallels between rural Mexico and the rural United States were inescapable: "[T]hings are rapidly shaping themselves for a similar revolution in Texas where four-fifths of the tillable land is held out of cultivation by . . . landlords who raise fake issues to distract the minds of our people." Perhaps a similar revolution would erupt in the United States. The *Rebel*'s introduction to one of Zapata's manifestos, for example, argued that if the Socialist proposal "[t]hat use and occupancy be the title to land" were not accepted, "then look out for another Zapata to arise on this side of the Rio Grande who will precede to hang as high as Haman those who have by subterfuge, trick and fraud secured possession of the land upon which the people must live and have their being."[20]

Socialists also showed some interest in addressing the problems of Mexicans in Texas. Although by the teens the Flores Magón brothers' anarchism had estranged them from most American socialists, nonetheless the *Rebel* continued to publish English translations of PLM documents and occasional excerpts from *Regeneración.* Editor Tom Hickey raised money and editorialized on behalf of the brothers' legal defense. Socialists such as Hickey took steps to incorporate Mexicans into their organization. In 1910, the party organized predominantly Mexican locals in Bridgeport and Matagorda Bay, and hired an organizer named Antonio Valdez to work in areas with high levels of Mexican population. A late April 1912 meeting in Uhland, Texas, co-organized by the Land League and the PLM, brought over a thousand delegates from central Texas. By 1914, Hickey's Land League organizer, F. H. Hernández, corresponded with twenty ethnic Mexican locals in central Texas. By the middle of 1915, when the Plan de San Diego uprising began, the socialist Land League boasted around a thousand Mexican renter-members in southern Texas and formally hired PLM member J. A. Hernández to organize locals "among the Mexican farmers and renters" of the state. Although state repression would soon crush such efforts, by 1915 an alliance of dispossessed Anglos and Mexicans seemed to be getting on its feet.[21]

Across the River

South Texans such as Aniceto Pizaña were surely aware of this ideological ferment—by reading *Regeneración* or by virtue of their own migrations —but events directly across the Rio Grande provided more dramatic confirmation that land reform was not only necessary but possible. By the teens, the concentration of land ownership in Tamaulipas spawned numerous calls for an armed uprising to redistribute land. Higinio Tanguma made several such efforts, including the 1910 raid that Aniceto Pizaña had been so tempted to join. After his arrest in the United States in early 1911 for violating neutrality laws, Tanguma returned again to Tamaulipas to resume his leadership of armed uprisings. In October of that year he issued a proclamation titled "The Red Flag in Tamaulipas," announcing his willingness to shed blood in the struggle for "Bread, Land, and Liberty." Tanguma told Mexicans that "you are poor because a handful of the rich have everything in their hands. They own the earth, they own the mines, they own the forests, they own the houses, they own the water, they own the railroads, they own machinery and all the tools of work are in their power." By March 1912, Tamaulipan hacendados were complaining to Francisco Madero that Tanguma was robbing people in the southern part of the state under a banner labeled "Tierra y Libertad"—one of the very slogans that Pizaña and his cohorts would soon use in south Texas.[22]

The small proprietors of Tamaulipas faced similar threats, as did their counterparts north of the border. By the time of the revolution, only 8 percent of Tamaulipans owned their own land. The massive hacienda known as La Sauteña bore a particularly striking resemblance to the larger ranching and farming operations north of the Rio Grande. Located along the Texas-Tamaulipas border, La Sauteña was Tamaulipas's version of the King Ranch. At about two million acres, it constituted nearly one-tenth of the land surface of the entire state (and more than one-half of the district of North Tamaulipas) by the beginning of the revolution. The property had its origin in an enormous royal land grant awarded to a Spanish colonist in Nuevo Santander in 1781. As early as 1825, nearby small landowners complained that the huge enterprise was restricting their access to grazing lands, comparing its proprietors to "an orchard owner's dog, which neither eats nor allows others to eat the food he guards."[23]

Later in the nineteenth century, the heirs of the original grantee sold the property to a group of Mexico City investors and politicians with strong ties to the Díaz regime. The property remained a traditional if enormous hacienda until the 1905 construction of the Matamoros-to-Monterrey railroad. Iñigo Noriega, a businessman with strong political connections to Díaz's regime, then decided that it had enormous promise as a site for modern agriculture. Noriega began raising capital for a massive development project modeled after the economic transformation of south Texas. He and other investors intended to put dams on several tributaries of the Rio Grande, and then to use the water to create an irrigated landscape of small farms, towns, and food processing factories such as sugar mills and cotton gins—all to be linked by railroad. Noriega envisioned that European and U.S. settlers would buy most of the land in small, family-sized tracts. The development project secured the support of both the Mexican federal government and Texas investors, who hoped that North Tamaulipas would witness its own version of south Texas's agricultural transformation.[24]

Just like the situation north of the Rio Grande, these heady ambitions caused the forcible dislocation of numerous small ranchers and farmers. By 1910 small proprietors were in dispute with the hacienda over more than half of its territory. The conflict grew most heated in La Sauteña's northern portion and on the banks of the Rio Grande and other waterways. Naturally enough, then, the property was a lightning rod for Tamaulipas revolutionaries. In April 1911, a group based just outside of Matamoros issued a manifesto vowing to raise an armed struggle until an agrarian reform was carried out in Tamaulipas along the lines proposed by the PLM. Their proclamation condemned La Sauteña and called for dividing its lands among the people whom it had dispossessed. Alberto Carrera Torres, Tamaulipas's most powerful agrarian radical during the revolution, echoed this call. He singled out the hacienda as an egregious example of political corruption and concentrated land ownership, and called for its complete dispersal and redistribution as part of the "imperative need to violently solve the agrarian problem." Even some Tejano Progressives, generally averse to calls for land redistribution, condemned the political connections that made the property's size possible. In October 1911 *La Crónica* urged Tamaulipans to vote for the pro-Madero gubernatorial candidate, condemning his principal opponent as a tool of reactionary Porfirians—described

Lucio Blanco (seated at table) at the Los Borregos land distribution ceremony.
Courtesy Runyon Collection, Center for American History, University of Texas at Austin.

as "an aristocracy of great speculators"—who hoped for the protection of their investments in La Sauteña. In a classic liberal stance, *La Crónica* insisted that whoever was elected governor should both protect the legitimate property holders of Tamaulipas and return the lands stolen by corrupt politicians from small proprietors.[25]

The Mexican Revolution allowed Tamaulipans to do what Tejanos could only dream of doing. Although La Sauteña survived the early years of the revolution even without the federal political and financial support its developers once boasted, in 1913 it became the target of the first revolutionary redistribution of land in Mexico's north. General Lucio Blanco, who had joined Carranza's opposition to Victoriano Huerta, led the assault on the federal army in Matamoros, taking the city in June 1913. Two months later, he decided to redistribute part of Los Borregos, an hacienda previously part of La Sauteña and recently sold to Porfirio Díaz's nephew Felíx. Blanco organized an enormous ceremony to commemorate the event, sending formal invitations to land recipients, journalists, photographers, and numerous residents of Brownsville and Matamoros. A playing of the "Marseillaise" began the ceremony. The general spoke briefly but forcefully to the assembly, portraying the land redistribution as the revolution's return to "to our people, the humble,

The beneficiaries of the land distribution. Courtesy Runyon Collection, Center for
American History, University of Texas at Austin.

the disinherited" of the land taken from them under the "tyrannical government" of Díaz. He praised the revolution's soldiers for "sacrificing all: home,
family, interests for this liberating cause" and promised that they would all
receive land upon "the triumph of our ideals." Then the first thirteen beneficiaries, former laborers on the hacienda, marched past Blanco's soldiers and the
audience to a table where they were handed certificates confirming the land
donations. The drama of the ceremony, its connection to the wider conflict
in Mexico, and Blanco's search for publicity spread word of the redistribution
far and wide. "Now I know why they are fighting in Mexico," commented
one French Socialist leader.[26]

Conclusion

The Los Borregos redistribution was the most dramatic sign that Tejanos
living in south Texas had good reason to believe that the tide of history had
turned to favor the dispossessed. To be sure, they faced severe challenges, watching more and more of their land pass to others' hands and hearing calls for
their outright disfranchisement. But ordinary Mexicans fought longer odds.
And now they seemed to be winning. Just across the Rio Grande from Brownsville, a revolutionary general doled out land unjustly seized by wealthy outsiders.

Little wonder, then, that some Tejanos would soon bring the Mexican Revolution to Texas. The revolution, however, was not just the graceful dethroning of a corrupt old order by a united citizenry, but rather a bloody and protracted conflict among Mexicans with very different visions of the nation's future. And the signs of Tejano division were clear even before the Plan de San Diego uprising began. The course of the Mexican Revolution split many Tejano Progressives from their more radical counterparts. Although Nicasio Idar, for example, had briefly been an associate of the Flores Magóns after their arrival in Laredo, by 1911 they had clearly split. The Idars supported Madero and his successors, the Constitutionalists. *La Crónica* condemned the Flores Magón brothers for their break with Madero, ridiculing their utopian plans and referring to them as "traitor[s]" who were "enriching some American tramps." Progressive Emeterio Flores told a federal commission that "how the United States has ever consented to [*Regeneración*] to go through our mails is something we can not understand. . . . Several copies of this filthy paper have reached our offices and we think it very disgraceful to let such a thing be transmitted."[27]

The machine Tejanos and Progressives were similarly divided. Although some leaders, such as J. T. Canales, at times had allied themselves with the machine, the Progressives became convinced that the south Texas political machine was an obstacle to their plans for unification and uplift. Indeed, they could be as anti-machine as the most rabid of newcomer Anglo racists, believing that the personal ties that the machine relied on to deliver its votes reflected a weak-willed and dependent attitude. In 1910, for example, Canales publicly broke with the machine, declaring that "from now on, let us give our support not to those candidates recommended by corrupt politics, but rather to those persons who share our ideas . . . who are just, honorable and virtuous, and who protect the rights of the people."[28]

These divisions would only widen in the years ahead. Tejanos would find themselves walking down very different paths. Radicals would try to bring the Mexican Revolution to United States soil by starting the Plan de San Diego uprising. Machine loyalists, whose ranks included the wealthiest of Tejanos, would find their power stripped by Anglo segregationists and their political dominance reduced to rural enclaves. Some Tejano Progressives would eventually find refuge in the embrace of American citizenship. These divisions ensured that the Plan de San Diego would be a Tejano civil war as well as a racial conflict.

4
Rebellion

Sometime in January 1915, Basilio Ramos crossed the Rio Grande, heading north from Matamoros into Texas. On the surface, there was nothing extraordinary about his journey: tens of thousands of his fellow Mexicans had made such trips in the last few years, and millions more would do the same in the decades to come. In Ramos's time, the crossing itself was most often an anticlimactic middle episode in a generally grueling trip—by foot, animal, or train—from war-torn central Mexico to a much more prosperous United States. People crossing from one border town to another could freely walk or ride across the bridge, declare themselves to be Mexican citizens on the rare occasions they were challenged, and then be on their way. The many others who either simply swam across the Rio Grande, took one of hundreds of simple ferries, or ambled across the desert did not yet concern the populace or government of their new home. Existing laws could have been used to restrict this immigration: those seriously diseased, morally questionable, previously contracted for labor, or "likely to become a public nuisance" were nominally barred entry. But in practice immigration officials did not go to the trouble to determine who fit these criteria. The aggressive labor-recruitment agents standing outside of immigration buildings at major entrepôts were a vivid sign that these new arrivals would have no difficulty finding employment in rail yards, fields, and mines of the Southwest. In the more densely settled portions of the border, such as the south Texas–Tamaulipas frontier, frequent crossings by local residents in both directions were an accepted part of daily life in a community that straddled the river. The border patrol, whose distinctive green trucks and uniforms are the scourge of migrants today, would not exist for more than a decade.[1]

Ramos's crossing was uniquely momentous because he carried with him a manifesto that envisioned redrawing the international boundary, pushing it far north of the Rio Grande, beyond even the territory wrested from Mexico by the Texas Revolution some seventy-nine years earlier. If Ramos's hopes came to fruition, the Rio Grande—or the Rio Bravo, as Mexicans know it—would again be another river well in the interior of Mexico.

The Plan de San Diego, a signed copy of which Ramos bore, called for an armed uprising against the United States to commence in little more than a month, on February 20, 1915, at two o'clock in the morning. The first goals named, according to a translation later made by U.S. authorities, were the "proclaiming [of] the liberty of the individuals of the black race" and "the independence and segregation of the states . . . Texas, New Mexico, Arizona, Colorado, and California, of which states the Republic of Mexico was robbed in a most perfidious manner by North American Imperialism." These states, once liberated, would in the best case rejoin Mexico when the mother country was itself redeemed, but might be made for a time into an independent nation. In any event, blacks would be aided in "obtaining six [other] states of the American Union . . . and they may form from these States a republic and they may be therefore independent." The "Liberating Army for Races and Peoples," to operate with formal military discipline under the command of a "Supreme Revolutionary Congress" based in San Diego, Texas, would be the vehicle for these ambitious goals. All prisoners taken in the process would be executed, as would Anglo males of sixteen years or more. Ancestral lands would be returned to the Apache and to other Indian groups of the region in exchange for their support.[2]

Ramos was commissioned to form juntas in Texas, New Mexico, Arizona, Colorado, and California to implement these plans. He believed himself well equipped to gather the "Liberating Army." Ramos was born in Nuevo Laredo but graduated from high school in Norman, Oklahoma, and lived for several months in San Diego in 1914. Letters of introduction to residents of Brownsville, San Pedro (a small town west of Corpus Christi), Eagle Pass, and San Diego itself, as well as a safe conduct pass from General Emiliano Nafarrate, commander of the forces in control of the Texas–Tamaulipas boundary, were to help him start his work. It required incredible nerve even to contemplate the provisions of the document he bore with him, but Ramos must have thought that the combination of support from revolutionary forces in Mexico and his knowledge of the bitter fruit of white supremacy in the United States made him a fit messenger.

And perhaps others had already laid the groundwork for his mission. Several months before Ramos again entered the United States, a small party of men visited the merchant Alberto Guzmán in his store in the small town of San Benito. Identifying themselves as representatives of the "San Diego Junta," the men "bought nothing, but asked me many questions about my business, how I was getting on, if I were making money, how many members of my family and how long I had lived in the United States," according to Guzmán. They soon returned and "made inquiries about other Mexican merchants in San Benito, how many of them were born in Mexico, how many were natives of Texas and were they all making money." The letter that the two men left with Guzmán deepened his concern. It requested a one hundred dollar loan and informed the merchant that "[i]f you do not help us you will be injured in everything possible. We would also have you know that if at the time you receive this you make it known to the authorities, as soon as our forces take the town you will be shot immediately as a traitor to the fatherland." "[I]f these men ever find out that I have talked to any of the authorities," Guzmán told a friend, "it will mean the death of me and of my family and the burning of my store and home." [3]

San Benito would indeed become the scene of some of the most intense fighting and greatest bloodshed in south Texas over the next few years. But Basilio Ramos did not participate in these events, despite the high hopes that he carried with him across the Rio Grande. Shortly after his return to Texas, Ramos approached Andrés Villareal in Hidalgo County in the hopes of gaining his support for the proposed insurrection. No record remains of why Ramos thought Villareal would be sympathetic, but in any case it was a grave miscalculation. Villareal immediately went to his friend Deodoro Guerra, who was a major landowner, businessman, labor contractor—and an Hidalgo County deputy sheriff. Guerra and Villareal feigned sympathy, soon tricking Ramos into explicitly asking their help in "carrying out a revolution against the United States." Ramos soon found himself not in the arms of fellow revolutionists, but rather in the hands of federal authorities. [4]

The arrest of Ramos and the unveiling of the Plan exacerbated the growing fears of south Texans. Domestic racial tensions and the Mexican Revolution, which by 1915 had entered a period of intense mass warfare, had already convinced many Anglos and Tejanos that a day of reckoning might not be far away. The Plan de San Diego, whose provisions were reported in national papers, linked these domestic and foreign events in the specter of a violent revolution by ethnic Mexicans on American soil. As February 20, the scheduled date for the start of the rebellion, drew near, these fears reached something of a crescendo. "Since the newspaper articles and comments on the 'Plan of San Diego,'" wrote an army commander in Harlingen, "many white people in this district have been alarmed lest there may be some truth in the report." An elected authority in McAllen, where Ramos had been arrested a month before, approached the closest army unit "for advice and assistance in case of an uprising . . . in the next few days."[5]

As the months stretched on, and nothing resembling Ramos's far-flung plans materialized, fears of an uprising abated. To be sure, south Texans continued to complain of robberies and livestock theft, and they still lived with the bottled-up racial tensions. But fewer believed that the turmoil of the Mexican Revolution would be brought to the United States. The army was particularly dismissive of any such belief. Its officers found themselves exasperated by what they saw as the paranoia of Anglo south Texans. "Every time a Mexican gets 'tanked up' with mescal and informs the bystanders in forcible but rude and impolite language what he proposes to do to the Gringos when the proper time comes," commented General Tasker Bliss, "everybody in the community thinks that Huerta is just around the corner." Bliss, the commander of the federal army divisions stationed on the border, could scarcely hide his contempt for such alarmists: "a one-eyed, one-legged, rheumatic, octogenarian Mexican with a wooden gun would make them throw up their hands. Every old woman in south Texas who has lost a hair pin claims that a detachment of Mexican troops came over and robbed her. The situation thus far is one that calls for horse whips, cold douches or whatever remedies are resorted to in lunatic asylums."[6]

Basilio Ramos ended up as a beneficiary of such sentiments. In May, some four months after his arrest, he came to trial in the Brownsville federal court on charges of sedition. The judge, dismissive of the prospects of an armed revolt to free the Southwest of American rule, did not look kindly on the severity of the charges. Ramos "ought to be tried for lunacy, not [for] conspiring against the United States." The judge set a modest bail for the would-be revolutionary. Ramos posted it and again crossed the Rio Grande, this time heading south.[7]

The Rebellion Gathers

In July, the Valley, warm even in the winter, becomes almost unbearably hot. Native vegetation turns brown or shrivels, waiting for the return of cooler temperatures to grow and flower. Crops, if they get enough water, do grow quickly, but tending them is grueling work. The temperatures, which on average break one hundred degrees for weeks on end, make the rural tradition of the mid-afternoon break a virtual medical necessity. This inferno must have seemed extremely foreign to the Valley's Anglo farmers, so many of whom could not have helped but compare the parched land and shimmering waves of heat with their recent, much more moderate summers in Iowa, Minnesota, and Wisconsin. If the sun meant wealth in the form of their crops, the suffering that it inflicted seemed to suggest that there was a price to pay for this worldly ambition.

The Fourth of July, like other holidays, provided something of a respite from work and summer's heat. On Independence Day in 1915—the 139th birthday of the nation and the 11th anniversary of passenger service on the Brownsville railroad—some Anglo farm families hitched their wagons or drove their cars to attend picnics or more formal celebrations to mark the occasion. Some chose to stay home, commemorating the Fourth with their families and perhaps a few friends.

But not everybody was celebrating. Ten miles outside of Harlingen, in western Cameron County, frightened residents reported the presence of a band of mounted and armed "Mexicans," whom they variously numbered from twenty to fifty. After the group took four horses and mounts from the Los Indios Ranch, locals and army units slowly followed the men toward Lyford. The next day, July 5, another army unit received notice that a small ranch eleven miles northeast of the town had been raided, apparently by the same men.[8]

Anglos were unsure who those raiders were. Some, believing that the "bandits" did not know their way around the ranchos and chaparral in the area, felt certain that they were intruders from Mexico. Others thought that the culprits were homegrown, possibly even their neighbors. "Eusebio Porras, Rudolpho Muñiz and brother, natives of the Sebastian region, were missing from the neighborhood and believed to be members of one gang or another running about in this section," stated one informant. Tejanos were of little help. They "appeared to know more about the whereabouts of the band than they would admit," in the words of one officer. "All these natives," he wrote to his commander, "seemed to be much frightened and disinclined to talk."[9]

An unknown number of other raids occurred over the next several days. "Marauder bands have crossed from Mexico into Cameron County, penetrating as far as fifteen or twenty miles from the Rio Grande. They have stolen horses and other equipment and terrorized American citizens," wrote Cameron County judge H. L Yates to General Frederick Funston on July 8. The judge's warning reflected the extent to which the week's events had resurrected the fears of south Texas Anglos: "The people of Brownsville and other towns of the Rio Grande Valley are practically helpless against an attack by a strong armed force," he declared. "[W]e have less than three hundred American soldiers in Brownsville and no other town has half as many. . . . We regard the danger as very real and unless we can interpose the moral effect of a large American force the danger will certainly materialize." The next day, an army patrol in western Cameron County "found much alarm among people [and] generally also evidences of marauding parties, but saw none." Although the patrol's commander received eyewitness accounts of armed parties, they continued to elude his pursuit.[10]

Still the raids continued, growing more brazen by the day. On July 12, eleven armed ethnic Mexicans captured farmer Nils Peterson about four miles south of Lyford, forcing him to open his small store and give them food and ammunition. Five days later, in northern Cameron County a group of armed men killed another farmer, Bernard Boley. There were growing reports of "larcenies of private property from farmers" that same week. On July 22, slightly more than two weeks after the raid on Los Indios, a Texas Ranger reported that "many ranchman [*sic*] are moving their families into town," because "the bandits are still in the country . . . conditions are so bad."[11]

The growing ambitiousness of the raids deepened such concerns. On July 25, somebody burned a seventy-five-foot railroad trestle and cut telegraph lines outside of Harlingen, forcing an early evening passenger train to return to its station. The manager of the mighty King Ranch requested that another company of Texas Rangers be sent to the vicinity of the property.[12]

The following week, an army unit finally encountered one of the bands approximately six miles north of Brownsville. The largest one yet reported —variously estimated from twenty to fifty men—briefly took hostage a milkman and several residents. After releasing their captives, the raiders fired on some land surveyors. The next day, a pursuing squadron of twenty U.S. soldiers happened upon the band. In the resulting battle, the raiders killed one soldier and injured two more, while the army unit managed to capture three of its foes. Events elsewhere the same day destroyed any hope that the army had ended the violence. Another group of raiders burned a railroad bridge and cut telegraph wires near San Sebastian, later firing on the work train sent to repair the damage. This incident took place eight miles north of Harlingen, almost thirty miles away from the clash with the army and at virtually the same time. These were particularly well-organized "bandits."[13]

On August 6, as Alfred Austin, his adult son Charles, and several other farmers were feeding the summer's corn harvest into the small mouth of the Austin's shelling machine, about fifteen armed ethnic Mexicans roamed through the nearby town of Sebastian, robbing several stores, taking prime horses, and burning the outbuildings of several nearby farms. Their work in town done, the raiders headed for the Austin farm in search of Alfred and Charlie.

Since their arrival in the Valley six years before, the Austins had done

Railroad trestle burned by Sediciosos. Courtesy of the Hidalgo County Historical Museum.

more than enough to attract the attention—and enmity—of neighboring Tejanos. The Austins were not simply reflections or embodiments of the new
Anglo farming ascendancy, though clearly their farm prospered, perhaps well
enough to entice other Anglos eager to emulate their success. They were also
important local segregationists whose personal behavior had angered many
Tejanos. The senior Austin was the head of the local Law and Order League
and had quite a reputation for brutality against local Texas-Mexicans; Charlie
was the group's secretary. "The father was said to have been a very hard
taskmaster and unused to the ways of the Mexicans. He was of a fiery temper
and on occasion used the toe of his boot a little too freely on those whom he
considered laggardly in their field work, and every time he kicked a Mexican
he made an unrelenting enemy," remembered Deputy Sheriff Virgil Lott.
"Some six men are said to have been thus treated," according to Lott, "and
these six men were among the bandits who made up the attacking party."[14]

Nellie Austin was working in her kitchen when suddenly the raiders
burst into the house, dragging her husband and son in with them. They demanded all of the family's weapons and then marched the two Austin men
outside. Minutes later Nellie heard shots from the adjacent field. Running
out, she saw Alfred and Charles sprawled on the ground. "I then proceeded

to the place where my husband and son had been shot," she later reported in an affidavit. "I first went to my husband and found two bullet holes in his back one on each side near his spinal column. . . . My husband was not quite dead but died in a few minutes thereafter. I then proceeded to my son Charles who was lying a few feet from his father; I found his face in a large pool of blood and saw that he was shot in the mouth, neck and in the back of the head and dead when I reached him."[15]

If the events since the Fourth of July seemed a random frenzy of robbery, theft, destruction, and murder, then the killing of the Austins suggested that there was a method to this madness. That very day, Samuel Spears, a Valley resident who was a regular informant for the federal Department of Justice, wrote of a growing local suspicion that the past month's violence was a concerted and premeditated effort. He told his superiors that "representative men here, American and Mexican . . . [have] three theories with respect to those who are making the disorder here." Locals whom he interviewed first thought that "for years, perhaps always . . . there has been [a] lawless and irresponsible element in the back country" and that these "operators" were responsible for the raids. Second, Spears's contacts blamed "bandits [who] have crossed from the other side, who are operating more or less independently of the local element with the general purpose of plunder." But now, Spears concluded, there was growing suspicion that the raids, killings, and attacks on railroads were related to an even larger purpose: "There are others . . . who believe that the purposes above mentioned are merely incidental, and that the real object and purpose look to a more important movement. The Mexicans on this side visited by the so-called bandits are told that this section of the country was taken away from Mexico, and does not really belong to the United States, and as the United States will probably busy itself in the pacification of Mexico, then will be a good time for Mexico to recover this lost territory."[16] The Plan de San Diego, dismissed as a bad joke just months before, now seemed an ominous reality.

As Samuel Spears's letter reveals, south Texans intensely speculated about the motives and meanings of the events of the first half of 1915. Who was behind the issuance of the Plan de San Diego? Was it a vision foisted upon Texas by Mexican revolutionaries or a homegrown conspiracy? As the violence grew in July, these questions took on an added urgency and were joined by others. Were the raids and murders a sustained effort to fulfill the Plan's provisions or a less-orchestrated breakdown in law and order? Would the raiders continue their apparent successes, or would state and federal authorities soon crush their efforts?

Tejanos must have asked themselves such questions, and added others to them: should these raids be supported or condemned? Did they offer a chance for liberation from growing Anglo economic and political might, perhaps the opportunity for regaining a beloved ranch? Or would the unrest just make life all the harder, providing Anglo farmers with the perfect excuse for their own violence?

Anglos could openly deliberate these questions, speaking freely to one another, to the press, to police and military authorities, and to their elected leaders. But few Tejanos could do the same; the wrong response or statement could bring down upon them the wrath of their neighbors or the authorities. So most conducted their debates privately, as far as possible from outside scrutiny. Little wonder that army officers time and again reported their frustration with the reluctance of Tejanos to give them any information or to volunteer any opinion on the origins or intentions of those responsible for the raids.

The actions of Tejanos in mid-1915 suggested something of the outcomes of their hidden deliberations. The attack on the Austins made it all too clear that some Tejanos embraced the raids, turning toward violence to even the score for the wrongs done to them by newcomer farmers. Even when the motive for a particular raid was not as clear as it was in the Austins' case, the grace with which the parties wound their way across fields, around and over fences, and through the chaparral, easily shaking most of their pursuers, pointed to local participation, support, and leadership. On the other hand, some Tejanos opposed the uprising from its beginning. It was Deodoro Guerra, after all, who arrested Basilio Ramos to uncover the plan in the first place. Guerra's clear motives for doing so—he owned large tracts of land and had profited handsomely from the agricultural boom—were shared by other Tejanos of his social class.

The Plan de San Diego

But what of the Plan de San Diego itself? Did it inspire Tejanos to launch the raids? Or were they simply evening up scores against neighbors with no ambitions of a wider conquest or reunion with Mexico? Only the raiders could answer these questions, and they never did, at least not in public. None of the men who killed the Austins, nor those who burnt the railroad bridges, nor those who shot at American soldiers, proclaimed their devotion to the Plan. Perhaps they knew Basilio Ramos or his compatriots. Perhaps they did not.

Nevertheless, there were strong signs that the issuance of the manifesto was more than coincidental to the raids of July. Those who looked closely could see that the Plan reflected the local tensions of south Texas and the Mexican Revolution. It invoked a generic Mexican nationalism that would have been attractive, or at least inoffensive, to adherents of most of the factions then vying for control of Mexico. It singled out the United States, and not any particular Mexican social group or practices, as its target. The army's slogan, "Equality and Independence," was a staple of revolutionary rhetoric. It offered no clear ideological basis for action such as Emiliano Zapata's call for the return of land to the pueblos or the Flores Magóns' anarchism. In fact, there was no provision for land redistribution at all. Ten of the fifteen articles dealt with the specifics of the military organization, stressing above all the need to establish a clear chain of command and to obey superior officers. Indeed, the Plan stipulated that "[e]very stranger who shall be found armed and who cannot prove his right to carry arms, shall be summarily executed, regardless of his race or nationality." As much as it invoked any ideology, the Plan celebrated armed struggle and the rights and power of those who led it.

The Plan was adapted most to the borderlands in its interracial appeal. The document began with the call for "the liberty of the black race" and focused on African Americans as much as on the plight of Mexicans in the United States. Other aspects of the Plan indicated familiarity with the borderlands. The offer of lands to Indian peoples mirrored calls made by the Partido Liberal Mexicano (PLM), which had made such appeals to the Yaqui of Sonora, though the specific naming of the Apache could simply have reflected knowledge of their historical military importance in the borderlands. Finally, the Plan's name offered some clue as to the regional consciousness of its framers. Although Ramos claimed to have lived in San Diego for several months in late 1914 while working for a beer distributor, there was no indication that any of the signatories had deep ties to the town. Ramos stated that they were from Nuevo Laredo and Monterrey. So why name the manifesto after San Diego? The decision may have reflected the homegrown revolutionary tradition of south Texas. Those steeped in the region's history knew that San Diego had been the seat of support for Catarino Garza's rebellion some twenty-four years before.[17]

The grievances of besieged Tejanos dominated the second version of the Plan. Titled "Manifiesto ¡A los Pueblos Oprimidos de América!" (Manifesto to the Oppressed Peoples of America), the second broadside had nine signatories, none of whose names was on the Plan in Ramos's possession, and it was dated February 20, 1915, from San Diego, the day that the original plan called for the uprising to begin. The signatories identified themselves as members of "The Revolutionary Congress" created by the Plan de San Diego. The United States, it charged, "not being merely content with daily lynchings of men . . . now dedicates itself to the lynching of an entire people, an entire race, an entire continent." As proof, it cited the oppression of all "proletarians" in the United States and particularly in Texas. The authors were most impassioned in their discussion of segregation, the "hatred of races which closes the doors to schools, hotels, theaters and all public establishments to the Mexican, black and yellow, and divides the railroads and all public meeting places into areas where the savage 'white skins' meet and constitute a superior cast." Whereas the document in Ramos's possession avoided mention of the land question or economic radicalism, the Manifiesto openly proclaimed the movement's goal as "Social Revolution" and called for the return of all arable land to the hands of "proletarians" and combatants for the revolution, who could either keep the land in individual hands or proclaim "complete communization" as they saw fit. All railroads and means of public transportation were to be collectivized, and the new nation would create "Modern Schools" where "Universal Love" would be taught to students without regard to their race or nationality. The document subsumed the provisions of the original plan, adding Utah and Nevada to the list of states to be liberated. This second version of the Plan ended with the hope that the struggle would spread beyond the new republic to "all oppressed people of all despised races" who would one day overthrow their oppressors and join "the concert of universal fraternity."[18]

To Anglo, Tejano, and Mexican onlookers alike, the connections between the two manifestos were as hard to decipher as was the relationship between the Plan and the raids of July. The signers claimed to be implementing the provisions of the Plan de San Diego, but who could be sure? The additions that they made to the first Plan suggested that they were a more radical group than the original drafters, more tied to Texas and thus to the concerns of Texas-Mexicans—or at least that they knew enough about Tejano anger to expect that a more militant declaration might attract greater support. Those familiar with *Regeneración* clearly recognized the PLM's influence in the calls for land redistribution and collectivization of the railroads and other infrastructure, and in the utopian vision of universal education and brotherhood. On the other hand, the strict military structure preserved from the original Plan conflicted with the PLM program and more closely resembled the militaristic radicalism espoused by such leaders as Lucio Blanco, author of the Los Borregos land redistribution.[19]

Perhaps these hybridities and continuities reflected the compromises struck by a small group coordinating the uprising. Or perhaps there was no such centralized operation. Accounts of Ramos's arrest and the discovery of the Plan could have inspired unconnected parties to issue the second manifesto and, perhaps, to start the July attacks. Indeed, the origins of the manifestos and the influence of their authors were so unclear as to allow some to speculate that the Plan itself was a forgery, altered, or even wholly fabricated by Texas Rangers or south Texas Anglos to justify their aggression against Tejanos. The Spanish original of the first version of the Plan did not survive, affording

Ramos's captors the opportunity to doctor it. The clause calling for killing all Anglo males over age sixteen seemed particularly well suited to create mass hysteria, and beginning the document with a call for black rebellion would have had much the same effect.[20]

The testimony of Basilio Ramos, who had long since fled to Mexico, offered little help in resolving this dilemma. His claim that he and other followers of Victoriano Huerta drafted the document while imprisoned in Monterrey convinced nobody. Huerta was a reactionary, leading the old federal army in a desperate effort to crush the wide array of revolutionary forces. All of the incriminating documents in Ramos's possession had been generated in territory controlled by the Constitutionalists. The subsequent issuance of the more radical manifesto and July's sustained raids made an immigration official's description of Ramos's arrest as "a rather peculiar case" ring all the more true six months later.[21]

The Hidden Tejano Civil War

The visage of a race war, embodied in the Plan's call for the execution of all Anglos over sixteen, preoccupied both Anglos and Tejanos. At the same time, the Plan's instruction to execute all armed strangers "regardless of . . . race or nationality" suggested that its authors knew that Anglos would not be its only opponents.

On July 11, scarcely a week after the marauding bands first seemed to present a larger threat, the Magnolia dance ground in Brownsville filled with people eager to forget the week's work with beer, music, and companionship, as it did on many nights. Pablo Falcón, a deputy constable working for the city government, and Encarnacion Cuellar, a county deputy marshal, leaned on the fence surrounding the dance area, watching the crowd and chatting. The two men were among the many Tejano law officers in the county, and the Magnolia was part of their regular beat. Just the week before, they had arrested a man named Ignacio Cantú. As Falcón and Cuellar watched the dancers this night, somebody suddenly called out sharply behind them. As the two men turned, shots rang out and struck both officers in the back. Falcón immediately crumpled to the ground, unconscious. Cuellar managed to fire several shots at his assailants, whom he recognized as Ignacio Cantú and his brother Adelair. The Cantús fled the scene and soon crossed into Matamoros. Both Pablo Falcón and Ignacio Cantú died shortly from their injuries.

To most Anglos, this fight was unremarkable, the predictable outcome of the mixture of drink, dance, and a weekend crowd ready to blow off some steam. "The Magnolia baile [dance] ground is a notorious resort," opined the *Brownsville Herald*, "and has been the scene of many shootings and several killings in late years." Others, however, were sure that the incident was part of the unfolding insurrection, less obvious but no less direct than the clashes between Anglos and the rebels. Falcón was "the raiders' first victim," Brownsville lawyer Harbert Davenport later wrote. A sometimes law partner of J. T. Canales, Davenport prided himself on his close connections with Tejanos in Brownsville and rural Cameron County. Had Falcón not been murdered, Davenport maintained, he "would have undoubtedly warned me of the trouble brought about by the 'Plan of San Diego.'"[22]

Pablo Falcón was not the only Tejano killed under highly suspicious circumstances in the early stages of the uprising. Two weeks before, deputy sheriff Carlos Esparza of Cameron County was killed near his home on a small ranch outside of Brownsville. Although his assassins were never identified, those familiar with the deputy had reasons to see his killing as part of the uprising. The Esparza family had a long-standing feud with the nearby Escamillas, several of whom joined the raiding bands. Perhaps a similar motive was behind the killing of José María Benavides during a raid on the Los Indios Ranch two weeks after Pablo Falcón's murder.[23]

Even the most powerful and well-connected Tejanos had reason to fear attack. Indeed, they had the most reason. Their complicity with the agricultural boom, their power in the Anglo-run political machine, their wealth, and even their willingness to kill their own Tejano enemies had allowed them to navigate the tumult brought by the railroad. It also made them irresistible targets for the uprising.

Florencio Saenz learned this lesson repeatedly. Over the previous twenty years, Saenz constructed a small agricultural and commercial empire in eastern Hidalgo County, even as many of his Tejano neighbors lost their land to back taxes and outright violence. By 1915 he owned more than forty thousand acres split into farm fields and cattle pastures and served by a private irrigation system, a post office, and a store for the use of his many sharecroppers, vaqueros, and laborers. At the same time, "Don Florencio," as he was known, wielded considerable political power. As one neighbor put it, "[H]e practically controlled the votes of the eastern part of Hidalgo County for years and years."[24]

More than any other target, rebels attacked the heart of Saenz's holdings, on the river in eastern Hidalgo County. Progreso was, "for some unknown reason, down in the raiders' books for punishment. They seemed to have an especial grudge against the little town and centered their activities in that vicinity."[25] Four clashes occurred there in August and September. Soldiers and raiders exchanged gunfire on August 17 and 25, a four-day battle raged in the area September 2–5, and another sustained and bloody fight took place on September 24. Saenz's store had also been robbed in May 1914, before the wider-scale uprising began.[26]

Saenz's disgruntled Tejano neighbors spearheaded the largest attacks on Progreso. On September 2 a small band crossed the Rio Grande and again robbed his store and several other buildings. The raiders helped themselves to general supplies and ammunition, picking up several mounts from nearby residences in the process. As they penetrated farther into U.S. territory, two cavalry troops based in Mission, and a party of deputies under the command of Sheriff A. Y. Baker of Hidalgo County, gave chase. Their quarry doubled back and crossed the river the next day. When the pursuers approached the river the band of raiders opened fire from the heavily wooded Mexican side. The two forces exchanged intermittent fire for the next three days, with injuries to at least one of the soldiers and to an unknown number of their antagonists.[27]

On September 5, as the desultory gun battle continued, Sheriff Baker heard familiar guitar chords wafting across the river during a lull in the shooting. Baker was convinced that the musician was a Tejano he knew well and sought to use the knowledge to his advantage. He left the safe cover of the brush, walked a few paces onto an unprotected sandbar, and, feigning injury from the barrage of bullets that greeted him, threw himself on the ground. As Baker anticipated, the gunmen on the other side of the river were overjoyed—Baker was hated by most of the Tejanos whom he was sworn to protect as Hidalgo County sheriff, and his brutality would gain him additional enemies in the months ahead—and so they began celebrating his apparent death. Their carelessness, as Baker had hoped, exposed their positions and made them easier targets for his deputies, who injured and perhaps killed several with their carefully timed volley. Baker then scrambled back to cover, pleased with the success of his ruse.[28]

If Baker hoped that he had put an end to the attacks on Florencio Saenz, he was sorely mistaken. Three weeks later, on September 24, a large band of perhaps eighty men crossed the river in the early morning hours. They again fell upon Saenz's store, this time setting it afire and attempting to destroy it with dynamite. They killed one soldier who was present at the scene, injured another, and pinned some ten more under a barrage of fire until cavalry reinforcements arrived. A pitched fight with the fresh troops lasted from about eight to ten o'clock in the morning, at which time the attackers withdrew. During the retreat they took Private Richard Johnson captive, killing him after reaching the south side of the river. What they did next left a lasting impression on many a south Texan. "They cut off his head and put it on a pole and stuck it right in the sand just right south of Toluca Ranch, right where the Progreso bridge is," recalled an unnerved Andrew Champion, a nearby resident of mixed Anglo and Mexican ancestry.[29]

If the ferocity unleashed against the powerful and wealthy Saenz was unique, then more middling Tejanos, even those not working for law officers, also fell prey to the raiders in September. On September 9, for example, a

Tejano resident was killed by a party of four or five raiders near Lyford. Nearby soldiers gave pursuit but quickly lost the band in the chaparral. The next day, in the same area, Tejanos joined Anglos to repel a band of about twelve mounted raiders from a ranch. On September 11, the Lyford area saw its third consecu-tive day of killings: "[T]wo Mexican-Texans, one known and the other thought to be pro-American, have been killed by bandits, our troops near hunting the bandits and making them scatter or take to the dense brush and disappear," reported nearby army officers. A Tejano mail carrier was fired on by four or five men as he made his normal Edinburg–Del Fino run in Hidalgo County.[30] Tejanos who clashed with the raiders, with the exception of elites such as Saenz, were less likely than Anglos to attract or to seek the attention of the army and law enforcement officials. So the recorded incidents in July, August, and early September—the assassination of at least three Tejano deputies, the attacks on Saenz, the killing of Tejanos in isolated raids—may have been only a small portion of what was beginning to look like a serious dispute among Tejanos.

Whatever their feelings about the United States, armed revolution, or their Anglo neighbors, Tejanos knew by late summer that they were as vulner-able to attack as farmers like the Austins. Particularly astute Anglos recognized the Tejano predicament. "There are a number of well-known Mexicans who are law abiding and good citizens, whose condition is worse at present than that of the Americans," wrote Samuel Spears. "They or many of them are in the country, at the mercy of the lawless element, and yet are afraid to talk freely to the Americans." Despite their fear, these Tejanos were willing to cooperate with the army and local law enforcement officers to put an end to the raids. "Most all Mexican ranchmen in this section [near Brownsville] are ready to cooperate and do all they can to aid militia with aid of scouts and Mexican-Texas ranchmen who know the country," wrote one resident to the commander of the Texas Rangers. The risk of any such cooperation was considerable. "The better class of Mexicans are willing to co-operate with the better class of Americans, if this cooperation will afford relief," wrote Spears, "but if it should not their condition would be worse than it is now . . . [for] if they should tell what they know, their lives will also be endangered."[31]

The Vigilante Response

By early fall, the position of ordinary Tejanos was even more tenuous than Spears had imagined. The threat of summary justice at the hands of vigi-lantes soon joined with the fear of the raids themselves. The vigilante response closely followed the start of the rebellion. On July 24, less than three weeks after the initial flurry of raids, sheriff's deputies shot the brothers Lorenzo and Gorgonio Manríquez. Lorenzo fell near the headgate of the Mercedes

Canal, part of the region's irrigation system, while Gorgonio apparently died in the town of Mercedes itself. The deputies claimed that the men had been shot while trying to resist arrest. If Tejanos accepted this explanation at the time, they would have ample reason to dismiss it in the years to come, for vigilantes would make similar claims in the deaths of scores of suspects. And in any event the explanation seemed transparent, for Florencio Saenz had denounced the two brothers, convinced that they had been involved in the May raid on his store that cost him valuable merchandise and five hundred dollars in currency. Disturbed by what seemed to him an illegal execution, lawyer and local historian Frank Cushman Pierce began making a list of such victims.[32]

Only four days passed before Pierce had occasion to add another name to his list. Vigilantes executed Adolfo Muñoz near San Benito. Local Anglo farmers accused Muñoz of planning to rob the San Benito bank and of being connected with the murder of an Anglo in Raymondville the previous year. Some informants named him as a member of one of the armed bands sighted in the area in early July. At about ten o'clock in the evening, two Texas Rangers arrested Muñoz in San Benito and drove off with him toward Brownsville, where he was to be held in jail while charges were filed. According to the Rangers' accounts, seven armed men in masks stopped their car several miles outside of San Benito and insisted that they turn over the prisoner. The next day, the sight of Muñoz's body hanging from a tree greeted travelers on the San Benito–Brownsville road.[33]

South Texans who disagreed about the causes and importance of the raiding would all agree that this lynching unleashed a flood of violence. For Tejanos, the mute body spoke a simple warning: to be arrested was to risk summary death. The killing, according to J. T. Canales, "immediately had this effect: that every person who was charged with crime refused to be arrested, because they did not believe that the officers of the law would give them the protection guaranteed to them by the Constitution and the laws of this State." At the same time, the murderers' impunity—no one was charged for the crime, nor were the Rangers involved disciplined or even investigated—bolstered the courage of would-be vigilantes. San Benito developer Alba Heywood remembered that the incident "opened the ball, breaking the ice for mob law and violence."[34]

Indeed, some Anglos openly voiced support for the perpetrators. "The news of the hanging was received with relief by the public for the reason that he [Muñoz] was believed to be a menace to the security of the community," reported the *Lyford Courant.* The paper openly advocated vigilantism. Since the legal authorities in south Texas could not control the growing raids and violence, the people would have to: "Judging from past experience it is doubtful if the courts could have done anything with him and he probably would have secured his release promptly. Lynch law is never a pleasant thing to contemplate, but it is not to be denied that it is sometimes the only means of administering justice. This instance seems to indicate the temper of the people. There is evidently a determination to put an end to the reign of crime that has been growing worse rather than better." For the article's authors, the incident was in fact a model for how to restore peace and order to south Texas: "The time has evidently come to rid the community of thieves and murderers and we hope that officers and courts will awake to the gravity of the situation and meet their responsibilities fairly and squarely. . . . It is now time for vigorous action and it should not stop until the community is cleared of the criminal element."[35]

The designation "criminal element" came to encompass an enormous range of ethnic Mexicans. Shortly after the killing of Muñoz, farmers near Sebastian, angered by the killing of the Austins, took the law into their own hands. "Several Mexicans who were 'undesirable' citizens, were made to leave Sebastian and it is thought that the killing of these two men [Alfred and Charlie Austin], when no one else was molested, was through revenge, as several of the bandits were recognized and proved to be erstwhile citizens of Sebastian and vicinity," reported the *Lyford Courant*.[36]

A few days later, several Texas Rangers and local deputies approached the Flores family's ranch outside of Harlingen. An anxious eighteen-year-old Josefina Flores watched as the men searched her family's outbuildings. Vigilantism had prompted others to leave their ranches. But her father, Desiderio, vowed to stay, telling his family that "El que nada debe nada teme" (He who is guilty of nothing fears nothing). Finished poking around the buildings, the Rangers called Desiderio to the porch. Angry words were exchanged, and Josefina watched in horror as a ranger shot the unarmed ranchero. She then witnessed her brother fall under a hail of bullets when he came to his father's defense. The Rangers returned the following day, and a frantic Josefina and her mother hid her oldest surviving brother under a bed. But to no avail: the lawmen searched the house and found him. Knowing his fate was sealed, he fatally shot one of his assailants before they took his life. Traumatized, Josefina went insane for a time. She huddled in the house with her mother and remaining siblings for two days, at which time a passing army detachment helped them to bury their deceased. The surviving Flores family members then moved to Brownsville, never to return to their ranch.[37]

The killings of the Manríquez brothers, Adolfo Muñoz, and the three Flores men, along with the expulsions near Sebastian, suggested the mounting likelihood of widespread vigilantism. Two days after the Flores's killings, Samuel Spears ended a long letter to his supervisor in the Department of Justice with the warning that "the greatest danger immediately, is in controlling ourselves. The cooler heads are doing their best to keep things in due bounds, but conditions have been growing worse, with no relief in sight, till the usual and ordinary methods of a civilized community are considered inadequate." The scale of the raids prompted the vigilantism. "It is no use to say to these people that the law should prevail, they answer what is the law doing for us, and what guaranty have we that it will be any better? I hope something may be done at once that will relieve the situation, and believe Government troops will go a long way towards preventing trouble, which once it gets going, will be a long time before it stops," he concluded.[38]

Aniceto Pizaña

Aniceto Pizaña had continued his interest in the Flores Magón brothers and their PLM after founding a local grupo in 1908. The officers who later searched his house would find abundant evidence of this commitment: buttons with the PLM slogan "Tierra y Libertad," numerous issues of *Regeneración*, correspondence with PLM leaders, copies of the party's broadsides, and a poem by Pizaña protesting the recent arrests of radical Mexican exiles.[39]

Nevertheless, Pizaña had nothing to do with the Plan de San Diego. Joining or fomenting an uprising would have put his land and extended family at risk. "He was a man that was unusually well-fixed," remembered developer Lon Hill, who called the ranchero as "honorable, and high-class and as straight a Mexican citizen as there was in that country." Believing that he had too much to lose, Pizaña declined to join the 1910 PLM expedition into Tamaulipas and avoided any entanglement with the raids in July 1915.[40]

Pizaña's security, embodied in his land and cattle, bred envy as well as respect. In early August, nearby rancher Jeff Scrivener informed military and law enforcement authorities that his neighbor was harboring the band suspected of burning a nearby railroad trestle. A captain in the cavalry repeated this allegation, implicating other area rancheros in the arson. Scrivener bore quite a grudge against Pizaña, labeling him and his associates "notorious cattle and horse thieves." J. T. Canales would later charge that a long history of personal enmity existed between the two.[41] In the early morning hours of August 3, Sheriff W. T. Vann of Cameron County, several of his deputies, Scrivener, a handful of Anglo citizens, and a detachment of about ten U.S. army troops approached Los Tulitos, Pizaña's ranch.

Their arrival interrupted the normal ranch routine, to which Pizaña was so devoted. The ranchero "and his mother were in the kitchen, the latter pouring him a cup of coffee," wrote a judge several years later. "The other men were out working about the corral; the girl was preparing breakfast, and the boy was feeding the hogs, and another girl had gone for water." Jeff Scrivener and the rest of the posse "rode around the end of the corral and saw several men run to a building fifty or sixty yards distant from the corral, and one of the civilians halloaed: 'There they are.'"[42]

Widely disparate and contradictory accounts of the ensuing clash would circulate around south Texas in the years to come. Pizaña later wrote simply that "I was attacked in my own home." Harbert Davenport similarly argued that the encounter did not even deserve the term "fight," as it involved "a squad of cavalry with a half dozen Deputy Sheriffs, and several emergency officers, on one side, and a frightened Mexican small boy—trying desperately to defend his mother's domicile—on the other." Sheriffs and army officers at the scene, in contrast, painted a picture of a military battle between two large and well-organized forces. One went so far as to claim that he "was fired upon by a large number of Mexicans. . . . [I]t was evident that there was at least 50 or 60 well armed and mounted Mexicans in this party," though later investigators dismissed this account altogether.[43]

Whatever the truth about the brief gunfight, Aniceto Pizaña fled his ranch, leaving behind his aged mother, his brother Ramón, and his twelve-year-old son, Gabriel, who suffered a serious bullet injury to his right leg. One soldier was killed—Ramón was charged as an accomplice to his murder—and two deputies (one a Tejano) injured. The commander of another cavalry detachment that arrived at Pizaña's ranch several hours after the fight may have prevented more bloodshed. Sheriffs found two men hiding in the ranch house. The cavalry commander wrote to his superiors that "two or three civilians came to me urgently requesting that I take charge of Mexican prisoners in order that they could be protected from being killed 'while attempting to escape'. . . . As I had positive knowledge that it would at least suit the purpose of the armed civilians there [in nearby San Benito], if they could obtain possession of these prisoners, I informed them, that I would personally take the prisoners to San Benito, and would use every power at my disposal to protect them as long as they were in my charge."[44]

The attack on his ranch confronted Aniceto Pizaña with difficult choices. No longer could he afford the luxury of supporting the PLM in principle, yearning for its success in Mexico while remaining above the fray in south Texas. A peaceful life as a respected ranchero and family man was now impossible. But should he flee to Mexico, severing his ties with Texas and abandoning decades of hard labor on Los Tulitos with the hope of re-creating an ordinary life in Mexico? Or should he cast his lot with the uprising in the hopes of an eventual return, or at least the prospect of some sort of vengeance?

Pizaña mulled over this question during his flight. Much as Gregorio Cortéz had done fourteen years before, he headed for safety on the other side of the river, using his horsemanship, physical stamina, and knowledge of the chaparral to elude the numerous army patrols and posses intent on capturing him. Unlike Cortéz, however, Pizaña was on his home ground. Sympathetic rancheros and kinsmen provided him with food, shelter, and information about his pursuers. They also brought him word of the killing of the Flores men, the expulsions near Raymondville, and the amputation of his son's leg. And Pizaña needed only his own eyes to see the "ranches [that] remain un-inhabited for fear of the injustices that are being done."

During his flight Pizaña decided to cast his lot with the uprising. Perhaps being joined by other displaced and angry Tejanos—several other men from Los Tulitos and, shortly thereafter, by other members of his PLM grupo—raised his estimation of the rebellion's prospects. Or perhaps being driven from his own home and hounded like a common criminal was simply too great an affront to his sense of dignity. Whatever the motive, he decided to fight, as he put it decades later, "in defense of my sacred rights as the citizen of the world that I am."

Joining the rebellion was a relatively straightforward matter. Luis de la Rosa, a butcher or grocer who lived in Hondo near Pizaña's ranch and who was acquainted with the fugitive, received word of Pizaña's plight and sent a messenger with a request to unite with his armed forces, already responsible for numerous raids in the past month. (Although de la Rosa had not yet been named as a participant in any of the raids, a description of "a large light com-plected Mexican, freckled face, red hair and mustache" as one of those respon-sible for the early July attack on Los Indios closely matched his distinctive physical appearance.)[45]

Pizaña may have had misgivings about fighting alongside de la Rosa—he later referred to his comrade-in-arms as "el viejo culón" (the old asshole) and blamed him for "all that has happened to me"—but evidently he was will-ing. Pizaña agreed to fight in "Cameron, Hidalgo and Starr counties where we can defend against the gringo sons of bitches," taking personal responsi-bility for the southern portions of these counties, leaving the north for de la Rosa. Avoiding more soldiers, he and his compatriots slipped across the border east of Brownsville and prepared to exact their revenge.[46]

The High Tide of the Plan de San Diego

Bolstered by such recruits, the Sediciosos—as some came to call the rebels—engaged in more than two dozen battles and raids in the seven weeks following the attack on Pizaña's ranch. These engagements ranged from burn-ing railroad infrastructure to attacks on prominent Anglo and Tejano land-holders, and to clashes with pursuing federal troops or law enforcement officials. Pizaña soon divided his own sixty-odd followers into five bands, three with ten people each, one with six, and his own command with about twenty. The leaders of these groups—the brothers Antonio and Lionso Esca-milla, Antonio Rocha, Evaristo Ramos, Jose Benavides, Adrian Mejía, Eusebio

Luis de la Rosa (date unknown). Courtesy of the Huntington Library.

Torres, and Juan Martínez—seem to have been drawn from his old ranchero acquaintances. A few were also Mexican devotees of the PLM, including "Teodoro el Japonés" and four other Japanese men from Monterrey. Luis de la Rosa commanded another body of an undetermined number of men.[47]

The Sediciosos mounted one of their most daring raids just before Pizaña committed himself to their cause. In the early evening of August 8, just five days after Pizaña's flight began, Luis de la Rosa led about sixty men in an assault at the King Ranch on the headquarters of one of its sections called the Norias division. Caesar Kleberg, the manager of the ranch, had feared for some time that the operation might become the target of such a raid. Although the Norias headquarters was much farther from the river than were the targets of previous raids—it was along the rail line some seventy miles north of Brownsville—Kleberg was well aware of the deep resentment against his operation. In late July he urged the adjutant general to assign Rangers to protect the ranch. Four days before the attack on Norias, Kleberg and James Wells telegraphed the adjutant general that the "situation seems serious and ask you by all means to meet us here at Kingsville by tomorrow morning's train."[48]

De la Rosa's band, which included Constitutionalist Major Miguel Guevara, several members of Aniceto Pizaña's PLM grupo, and (in Samuel Spears's words) "Mexicans of bad reputation residing this side [of the] Rio Grande," struck the ranch house at a fortuitous time—a total of just eight U.S. soldiers, six Tejano employees of the ranch, and several civilians were there to defend it. A larger group of some two dozen cavalrymen, Rangers, and sheriffs had left that same morning to investigate reports of a nearby band, probably de la Rosa's very party. As they approached the house, one of the columns of Sediciosos came upon a Tejano ranch employee and demanded to know "how many gringos are over there?" "You cowardly jackass, why don't you go and see," she retorted. These were the last words she ever spoke: one of the raiders put his gun in her mouth and pulled the trigger, blowing her brains out.[49]

The occupants of the ranch house were surprised and badly outnumbered. For the next two and a half hours they managed to stave off the much larger raiding party, killing five Sediciosos and badly wounding several more. Running short on ammunition, the defenders breathed a sigh of relief when their assailants withdrew. "If the bandits had stayed a little longer, they would have won," recalled one of the men in the Norias house. Unbeknownst to him, the raiders were also running short of ammunition. Pizaña later described the battle as "[t]he defeat of de la Rosa," sharply criticizing him for launching the attack with poor arms and insufficient ammunition, and for leaving his soldiers' bodies on the field of battle.[50]

A series of clashes followed on the heels of the Norias battle. In some cases, the Sediciosos clearly planned to attack army units or guard posts manned by soldiers, such as the firefights near Progreso (August 17 and 25) and Los Indios (September 13). But more often the sheer number of soldiers in the Valley made it difficult for the rebels to avoid them. Pizaña noted that, after the Norias attack, "units and more units of soldiers were deployed in the counties of Cameron, Starr, and Hidalgo."[51]

The Sediciosos continued attacking railroads and other infrastructure. Units burned four railroad bridges within a twenty-mile radius of Brownsville and cut telegraph lines connecting Harlingen, San Benito, and Brownsville. Some of these attacks resulted in pitched battles, as did one that occurred September 2. In this skirmish, an army unit fourteen miles north of Brownsville surprised a band of raiders in the process of setting fire to a railroad trestle. The subsequent chase and running fight lasted for the rest of the day, resulting in the death of two civilians and at least one Sedicioso. The pursuing cavalry and law enforcement officers captured about one hundred pounds of dynamite as well, indicating that the raiders intended to commit further acts of sabotage.[52]

Hints of the Sediciosos' ambitions and hopes trickled into public view alongside news of their many raids. A mortally wounded member of the party that attacked Norias confessed that the daring raid was part of a plan for a regional uprising. "One of the bandits who was wounded and captured at the battle of the Norias, realizing the approach of death, confessed to us and told us the plan and purposes of the raiders and bandits," recalled Sheriff W. T. Vann. "He stated to us that the bandits or raiders were a well organized force of Mexican citizens who had their headquarters and rendezvous in the State of Tamaulipas, Mexico, and the purpose of the raids into Texas was to get ammunition, supplies, and equipment and ultimately it was their purpose to kill and drive out all Americans from the territory comprising Texas, New Mexico, Arizona, and California."[53]

Whether the Sediciosos were either directly inspired by the Plan de San Diego or responsible for drafting it remained unclear. No news of any public affiliation to the Plan by Pizaña or de la Rosa reached south Texans. In his later recollection, however, Pizaña did refer to an effort to regain the territory lost by Santa Anna, the Mexican ruler who presided over the loss of Texas and the Southwest. De la Rosa may have been more taken with the Plan. Early in their collaboration, he apparently shared some military plan in relation to San Antonio with Pizaña, who angrily dismissed it. Extending the raids beyond south Texas, of course, would have been consistent with the provisions of the Plan.[54]

Whatever the role of the Plan de San Diego in shaping their ambitions, the Sediciosos clearly thought of their rebellion as part of a larger struggle and hoped that pan-Mexican solidarity would boost their efforts. As they raised their military ventures to new heights, they cast their struggle in Texas as a fight for the rights of all Mexicans aggrieved by the chauvinism and brutality of the United States. "Mexicans, we have to fulfill a sacred duty," began a circular published in August in the Monterrey pro-Constitutionalist newspaper *El Demócrata*. "The revolution in Texas in a few days will have acquired a gigantic proportion. We should unite with our brothers there and take the same chances that they are taking, for this is the solemn moment for the vindication of right and justice lost to us for so long a time. Help us in this combat ... in order that our efforts may be crowned with success."[55]

Three weeks later, de la Rosa and Pizaña, identifying themselves as "First Chief of Operations ... and Second Chief of the General Staff," respectively, issued a manifesto that forcefully condemned anti-Mexican violence, lauded the uprising, and called for all Mexicans to support it:

The Mexicans in arms in the southern part of the United States issue a statement to our compatriots the Mexicans of Texas; a cry of real indignation and wrath has arisen from the depths of our souls at sight of the crimes and outrages which are daily being committed on defenceless old women and children of our race by the bandits and miserable rangers who guard the banks of the Rio Grande. Just and righteous indignation which causes our blood to boil and impels us, orders us to punish with all the energy of which we are capable, that crowd of savages that would put to shame a hungry tiger or a loathsome hyena. How can we remain indifferent and calm in the face of such crimes. How can we permit such offenses inflicted on our race. Is it possible that our feelings of humanity and of patriotism have ceased to exist.... Enough of tolerance, enough of suffering insults and contempt. We are men conscious of our acts, who know how to think as well as the "Gringo," who can and will be free, who are intelligent enough and strong enough to choose our authorities, and who will do it.

They invoked the Plan de San Diego—though not by name—as the antidote to such virulent racism. "The moment has arrived. It is necessary for all good Mexicans ... to repair to arms, and at the cry of 'Viva the independence of the states of Texas, New Mexico, California, Arizona, part of Mississippi and Oklahoma' which from today shall be called the Republic of Texas, to unite with our companions in arms who have already begun the conflict, giving proof of courage and patriotism viva independence, land and liberty."[56]

The Social Geography of Rebellion

The Plan de San Diego purportedly provided for the killing of all Anglo males above age sixteen. In practice, however, the Sediciosos' violence was much more targeted. Not only did their wrath fall upon some Tejanos, but their purposes in attacking—and sparing—Anglos were much more specific and personal than allowed for by the Plan's stark racial categories.

On September 24, for example, a dozen or more men fell upon the ranch house of James McAllen in western Hidalgo County. McAllen, described by the officer who investigated the raid as "the largest land owner and rancher in this part of the country," presided over more than fifty thousand acres at the time and had helped to found the city of McAllen a decade earlier. The three occupants of the home—McAllen, a teenage girl, and an unnamed Mexican cook—managed to hold off the raiders, killing two of the men and several of their mounts, and injuring several more over the course of the hour-long fight.[57]

Perhaps the Sediciosos attacked McAllen simply because he was a prominent Anglo landowner, one whose real estate business helped to draw

Banner captured from rebels by U.S. soldiers. Courtesy of the Hidalgo County Historical Museum.

so many more Anglos. Or the raiders might have held specific grievances against the rancher. Some of McAllen's employees may have taken part in the attack. The rancher told a Department of Justice investigator that some of his employees had been "pressed into the service of the bandits," but the men could just as easily have joined of their own will. Indeed, many ranchers subjected to such raids made the same claim as McAllen, refusing to acknowledge —or even to believe—that their closest Tejano associates could turn on them so brutally.[58]

Another account of the raid suggested that family members of McAllen's Mexican companion likely orchestrated the attack. "McAllen's family lived in Brownsville where they had a nice home," recalled neighboring ranch hand Roland Warnock. "He stayed out at the ranch during the summertime and had a Mexican woman cook and a girl there. The girl had come across the river looking for a place to hide from the revolution. He gave this girl a job to take care of the house during his absence and keep it clean when he was there." Warnock noted that "[t]he girl's parents back in Mexico did not care a lot for these living arrangements," as though to suggest that the two were lovers as well. "These fourteen Mexicans had been sent in there by that girl's family to kill old man McAllen," he concluded. Warnock's explanation for the attack may not have convinced those who knew McAllen, for there was long-standing animosity between the two families. But it did suggest the potential for any past dispute or entanglement to become a motive for armed attack during the chaos of 1915.[59]

While the motives for particular incidents could be disputed, few doubted that the raids were homegrown. "[I]t is undoubtedly true that majority of bandits operating in Cameron, Hidalgo, Starr, and Willacy counties are residents of the United States," concluded General Frederick Funston in August. If this was indeed the case, then the Sediciosos not only could count on local residents for security, they could also count on still more Tejanos to offer them shelter, food, and water as they misled their pursuers. "The population of the county is more than 95% Mexican birth and a very large proportion of this element is in sympathy with the raiders or bandits, now apparently trying to get together," wrote a frustrated army commander in Rio Grande City at the height of the raids. "This makes it most difficult to get information. I am endeavoring to work in harmony with civil authorities but these are active only in protection of towns."[60]

That the Sediciosos often knew the people they were attacking could lead to mercy as well as to vengeance. Such was the case on September 2, when a group of about thirty armed men, allegedly under the command of Aniceto Pizaña himself, held up S. S. Dodds and his crew at the construction site of the Los Fresnos pumping station. Pizaña and other members of the band were residents of nearby ranchos, and at least one had done manual labor on irrigation works in the area as well. Dodds moved to south Texas in 1911 to help construct a sugar mill and subsequently worked as a contractor on similar projects.[61]

As the holdup began, Dodds quickly pulled one of his Mexican employees in front of him, an act which he later stated prevented his immediate shooting. The band took as hostages Dodds and his foreman, Smith, and apparently also held several of the Mexican workers at the scene. They destroyed the partially built pump, engineering equipment, Dodds's car, and nearby construction materials. Their captors forced Dodds and Smith to exchange clothing with their own worn-out garments before leading the two men on a forced march of several miles. Along the way the band captured another Anglo, identified only as "Mr. Donaldson."

As they were marched toward a particularly dense patch of brush, Dodds feared that he and his companions were about to be executed. A heated argument broke out among his captors, however, with several insisting that his life be spared. He recognized some of these men, recalling that several years before he had given a ride to one after finding him injured along a road. Another benefactor was Jesús Esparza, a nearby ranchero who seemed to think highly

The ruins of Stanley Dodds's automobile. Courtesy of the Hidalgo County Historical Museum.

of him. Donaldson and Smith had no such defenders, and were taken into the chaparral and summarily shot just before Dodds was set free. Dodds's seemingly cordial relations with Tejanos were not enough to protect his property—two weeks later, a larger group again occupied his construction site, abandoning it after exchanging fire with a patrolling cavalry unit—but they had saved his life.[62]

The Taste of Victory

The Sediciosos must have been proud of their accomplishments in August and September. The number of raids—more than thirty in eight weeks —was impressive enough. As many as eighty men participated in the largest attacks. During these raids, such as the August 8 attack on Norias or the September 24 battle at Ojo de Agua, they adhered to a military-style command structure, differentiating between officers and soldiers. And they struck multiple targets at the same time: on September 2, for example, one band burned two railroad bridges, another held up Dodds's construction site, another clashed with cavalry near Harlingen, and yet another attacked the post office and other buildings at Ojo de Agua. Despite being heavily outnumbered by U.S. soldiers, the Sediciosos fought no major pitched battle that could have eliminated their force. The rebels' knowledge of the area and support from the local population made it very difficult for pursuing military and law enforcement officials to catch up with them and thus force them into any such battle.

And maybe for a time Pizaña, de la Rosa, and their small army of rancheros thought that they were winning. By the end of September many Anglo farmers and ranchers had sent their families away, either to nearby cities such as Brownsville and Corpus Christi, where the raiders posed no real threat, or to San Antonio and other cities out of south Texas altogether. Those who remained traveled only when armed and made sure that their trusted workers also went armed. Ranch hand Warnock remembered being baffled by a mysterious, extremely heavy box that he was sent to town to pick up in the fall of 1915. His puzzlement vanished when his boss opened the box, revealing a package of expensive rifles. The foreman "gave us each one of these high-powered Krag rifles and 400 rounds of ammunition," Warnock remembered, "then he put a six-shooter on everyone too. He told us, 'Don't ever be caught without these guns. Have them at night where you can just grab them, reach down on the floor at anytime and just pick them up. When you come in for meals, set those rifles behind you where you can just turn around and get your hands on them.'"[63]

The raids spread terror among the Anglo farmers whom the Sediciosos held responsible for their dispossession. In particular, the murder of the Austins shocked neighbors and acquaintances. The lives and activities of the two men who met horrible ends resembled those of numerous other recently arrived white farmers. The Austins had come to south Texas in 1909. They bought a forty-acre farm and rented approximately thirty more acres to farm, and they sold livestock feed and operated a corn sheller for nearby farmers. Many of these farmers fled after the raid. Ruth Schultz lost almost all of her business from the small store that she ran out of her farm. Schultz's farm "remained uncultivated for several years following the bandit raids," recalled a neighbor, "for the reason that most of the people of this vicinity became frightened away, and there was no one to whom the farm could be rented." Sebastian's justice of the peace similarly remembered that "there was practically no business at Sebastian for a year or more after these raids. . . . People were afraid to live in that section until conditions became quiet again."[64]

If Pizaña and his compatriots knew of the labor problems that their raids created, then they had yet another reason to feel satisfied with the progress of their insurrection. In late August, for example, a rancher some thirty-five miles south of Hebronville requested that a detachment of cavalry be stationed at his ranch. "The trouble alleged," wrote a military commander in Rio Grande City, "was the appearance of a band of Mexicans at the ranch who had ordered the ranch hands off the ranch with threats to kill them if they returned." This was no isolated incident: a week later J. J. Sanders, a Texas Ranger on patrol in Cameron County, noted that the threat of raids was costing several large ranches substantial portions of their labor forces. "Everything is quiet at Norias just now, but the families of all Mexicans employed on the ranch have left again, the last one on the evening train yesterday. They have undoubtedly had information of some kind which caused them to leave." A foreman and his crew at a nearby ranch "were frightened away from the place they were branding calves. His hands refused to go into the brush, saying they were afraid, and when they heard shooting near their camp they all left for Raymondville."[65]

The Sediciosos' Tejano enemies fared no better. The September attack on his store forced Florencio Saenz to shut it down and transfer his goods to Mercedes. Although he hired a private security force to defend his vast estate, the frequent raids forced most of his tenants and the nearby population out of the area for the better part of three years. "Consequently," as his heirs later wrote, Saenz "was unable to operate his fields and ranch properties at Toluca, as it was impossible to get employees to live near the river and operate these properties. . . . [T]he fields were abandoned, grew up in brush and will . . . have to be opened up and cleared at a large expense." Indeed, so many fled the Progreso area that Saenz judged it unwise to reopen his store even after the "bandit troubles" ended.[66]

In light of such troubles, the complaint of a San Benito resident to his congressman (and future vice-president) must have reflected the sentiments of many south Texas landowners. "Now, Mr. Garner," wrote J. L. Crawford, "this disturbance is ruining this country and we are going to have to get the thing stopped."[67]

The Mexican Revolution and the Plan de San Diego

Since 1910, the distant thunder of the Mexican Revolution had rolled across Texas, bringing rumors of battles, coups, and intrigue. At first the news was hopeful—the country seemed to unite behind Francisco Madero, and Porfirio Díaz's resignation appeared to signify a peaceful and orderly transition to democracy. But it was not to be: the assassination of Madero pitted the remnants of the old order against the revolution, plunging Mexico into mass warfare. In 1914, the United States occupied the port of Vera Cruz, raising the prospect of a full-scale invasion and the dismemberment of Mexico.

When the cavalrymen of Pancho Villa destroyed Mexico's ancien régime, choking it in the dust of their horses in critical battles in 1914, hopes again flared that the nation's turmoil was over. But instead the one revolution became many revolutions, as different factions and leaders struggled to exert control over Mexico and to command the loyalty of its citizens. Three factions were the most powerful. The Constitutionalist forces, led by Venustiano Carranza, sought to restore the liberal and moderate government of Carranza's old friend,

Francisco Madero. Pancho Villa and Emiliano Zapata, more enthusiastic about the mobilization of peasant armies, formed a weak and generally uncoordinated alliance that, on paper, controlled most of the country. Local warlords and political factions controlled other regions and states, shifting their loyalties as the fortunes of the larger coalitions ebbed and flowed.[68]

The revolution deeply influenced Tejanos such as Luis de la Rosa and Aniceto Pizaña, providing them with hope that ordinary people could overthrow their oppressors and regain their land. But the appreciation of the two leaders of the uprising was more direct and immediate, for they had benefited from the direct assistance of the Constitutionalist forces in control of the section of Tamaulipas directly across the Rio Grande.

As the Sediciosos basked in the warm glow of their victories, they had reason to boast of their military prowess, of their intimacy with the Valley's fields, chaparral, and waterways, and of the solidarity among so many of their fellow Tejanos. But they knew that their greatest asset was the international border, for it allowed them to find safe haven from the burgeoning number of posses and U.S. army patrols in south Texas. Indeed, the commanders of these patrols traced most of the attacks to specific border crossings. Even raids that began in Texas generally ended with retreats across the Rio Grande. Without such a refuge, the tens of thousands of regular U.S. soldiers and the hundreds of Texas Rangers, sheriffs, and vigilantes would have had a much easier time preventing such a concentrated string of attacks.

Constitutionalist support was not limited to providing this safe haven. Some of the faction's soldiers directly participated in raids in August and September. One officer apparently joined the attack on the Norias Ranch house, for example. It also appeared that a Constitutionalist commander had initiated several raids of his own, nearly provoking a direct clash with U.S. military forces. In early August, a month after the initial flurry of Sedicioso attacks, Lieutenant Colonel Z. Vela Ramírez sent several of his soldiers to the Isla de Morteritos, a small island in the Rio Grande, with orders to return with as many cattle as they could round up. Irate U.S. citizens—including some Tejano ranchers—complained to Constitutionalist authorities, pointing out that Carranza himself had agreed that the island belonged to the United States. Vela Ramírez brushed off the charges, damning the Tejanos involved as "anti-patriotic . . . renegades to our country . . . who have had the right to live off of the product of our suffering people temporarily taken away." Some two weeks after the incident on the island, about ten of his soldiers again crossed the river, stealing new mounts before being chased back by the U.S. cavalry.[69]

The support of Tamaulipas Constitutionalists for the Sediciosos baffled those familiar with the course of the Mexican Revolution in the state. The commander based in Matamoros, Emiliano Nafarrate, had shown no particular concern for the sufferings of Tejanos. In fact, the previous December he tried to enlist Texas Rangers in the formation of a de facto border patrol to harass the opponents of Carranza and to disrupt their political activities. As Brownsville's Constitutionalist Consul José Z. Garza reported to his superiors, "[W]e [Nafarrate and Garza] have organized a very effective vigilance service, which includes two Texas Rangers . . . in order to tenaciously pursue all of the violators of neutrality laws, with the capacity to . . . make arrests, and use armed force, when they deem it necessary, without seeking written authorization from civil authorities."[70]

Neither was Nafarrate an agrarian radical, moved by the dispossession of rancheros north of the Rio Grande and their struggle to regain their land. In fact, he and other Constitutionalists opposed radical land redistribution of the sort contemplated in Pizaña's and de la Rosa's manifestos. A year before the Texas uprising, the most powerful Tamaulipan agrarian radical, Alberto Carrera Torres, proposed that the lands of adherents of Huerta, Felíx Díaz, and even of Madero be confiscated and distributed to the landless population. Constitutionalists established their own agrarian commission to provide irrigation and credit but warned the public not to heed Carrera Torres's call for land seizures and occupations. In May 1915, Constitutionalist units forced him to withdraw from the state capital, Ciudad Victoria. In September, while Nafarrate aided the south Texas uprising, Constitutionalist forces dealt Carrera Torres further defeats on the battlefield, all but eliminating his statewide power.[71]

Even Aniceto Pizaña was unsure why Nafarrate gave his forces tacit support. Before leading raids back into Texas, Pizaña stayed for a time at the house of a friend in Matamoros. A deputy of Nafarrate approached Pizaña with an invitation to meet with the general. During his audience, Nafarrate, whom Pizaña did not know, expressed his support for the uprising in Texas. He offered arms and ammunition to support it, joking that "don't you know that good weapons are like women—they need men?" In Pizaña's account, the general told the now exiled ranchero that "we have to take from the damned gringos all the territory that Santana [Santa Anna] pawned."[72]

Perhaps Nafarrate viewed Pizaña and other rebellious Tejanos as useful vehicles to express widespread Mexican anger at the United States. The military occupation of Vera Cruz the previous year raised the prospect of a full-blown invasion from the north, deeply troubling Mexicans of all walks of life. The Sediciosos publicly appealed to this inflamed nationalism, linking it to the resentment of the poor treatment of Tejanos. If such appeals garnered significant support in northern Tamaulipas, then Nafarrate might have feared the consequences of not aiding Pizaña. He certainly had his own resentments: the decision of U.S. military authorities to allow the transport of wounded Villista soldiers onto Texas soil after their unsuccessful March 1915 attack on

Matamoros convinced him of America's hostility to the Constitutionalist cause. Pizaña, no great lover of the Stars and Stripes, was struck by Nafarrate's "anti-American" views.[73]

Constitutionalist support for the Sediciosos raised deep concerns among U.S. officials. The knowledge that Tejanos were responsible for the raids initially tempered military commanders' anger at Nafarrate and Carranza. But American military leaders nonetheless feared that the south Texas border would become the site of heavy bloodshed in the event of a larger conflict between the two nations. "I invite the attention of the Secretary of War to the urgent military necessity of giving General Funston [in command of units stationed in the Rio Grande Valley] ample warning of any step intended to be taken by our Government which may result in hostile acts on the part of Mexican forces on or near the border," wrote the army chief of staff to the secretary of war in August. "I consider it easily possible that a reckless and desperate Mexican military commander, whether acting under instructions from his chief or whether merely animated by a desire to wantonly provoke a conflict, may cross the Rio Grande and cause great damage and loss of life with consequent humiliation to our government," he warned.[74]

Such reactions gave Constitutionalist authorities their own grave concerns. The raids from Mexican territory seemed to offer the Colossus of the North the perfect excuse for an all-out invasion. Yankee soldiers had left Vera Cruz just two years before, and any future such occupation was likely to be much more protracted. And Carranza had higher hopes than simply avoiding invasion: the formal diplomatic recognition of the U.S. government would allow him to gain much easier access to international credit to fund his armies' offensive against the forces of Villa and Zapata. It might even result in the American government closing the border to arms shipments to his opponents.

So with good reason Constitutionalist diplomats sought to deflect blame for the uprising. "Some political leaders in Texas are credited with believing that if blame can be attached to soldiers of either Gen. Carranza or General Villa, armed intervention by the United States might be precipitated," a Constitutionalist press release stated in August. Publicly, Constitutionalist diplomats maintained that they had nothing to do with the disturbances in Texas and that they were in fact doing all they could to help the U.S. government to suppress them. "General Nafarrete is acting in combination with American authorities to destroy this lawless gang which is composed principally of ex convicts from Texas border jails," their spokesman attested in August. The following month, another Constitutionalist diplomat went to Washington to declare that Magonistas in the United States were responsible for "the troubles on the border."[75]

Behind their public facade, however, the Constitutionalist diplomatic corps became increasingly adamant that Nafarrate had to be removed. As the raids continued, and as Nafarrate proved himself to be either unwilling or unable to curtail them, the Constitutionalist hierarchy turned against their man in Matamoros. After receiving word of Vela Ramírez's own raid, Constitutionalist ambassador Eliseo Arredondo urged Carranza to give Nafarrate strict orders that his soldiers "abstain from committing actions that in these moments could bring international complications." Carranza's diplomatic corps in south Texas sent increasingly urgent warnings that ordinary Texans and army officers stationed along the border blamed the Constitutionalists for instigating the uprising. The Laredo consul flatly declared Nafarrate to be "a threat to international relations."[76]

Constitutionalist authorities did not trouble themselves with the implications of their stance for the well-being of Tejanos. That ethnic Mexicans were suffering across the river in the United States did not concern them; the thought that the Tejano struggle might have shared the same goals as their own did not occur to them. What mattered above all was the threat that the Texas uprising would interfere with their military and diplomatic strategy. "At this moment the only perturbation in the betterment for peace is the uncertainty of the press with respect to the disturbances on the Texas border, trying to involve and complicate our soldiers at the frontier in these disturbances," Arredondo wrote in September to a Constitutionalist supporter in the United States. "I am confident that in a few days the American government will be convinced that our enemies, the reactionaries, and some Texas citizens moved by selfish interests are provoking these troubles, as they are sure that their intrigues in Mexico have failed."[77]

Arredondo did all that he could to help the American government gain such confidence. A week later, at his urging, Carranza ordered one of his most trusted generals to go to Matamoros to determine Nafarrate's connection to the unrest and to consider his removal. By the end of September, even as his public statements continued to deny Carrancista involvement, Arredondo proposed to U.S. authorities a joint investigation to determine whether Nafarrate's subordinates were complicit in the uprising. The situation would be "promptly remedied," he promised, should such evidence emerge. On October 1, Carranza removed Nafarrate from his command at Matamoros.[78]

The transfer of Nafarrate initially appeared to deal the Sediciosos a serious blow. They mounted numerous raids each week in August and September, but only two relatively small clashes occurred in the first two and a half weeks of October. On October 9 an unidentified band fired on a cavalry patrol near the Mercedes pumping plant. One soldier was killed, and the assailants recrossed the river. Three days later, Texas Rangers clashed with a band near San Benito, apparently killing some of them. Apart from these encounters, small by comparison with the intensive military conflicts of August and September, army units reported no other combat—and no sign of raiding parties.[79]

But de la Rosa and Pizaña had become too powerful for a simple change in commanders to end their rebellion. Barely two weeks after Nafarrate's transfer, they mounted their most dramatic attack yet. In the early morning hours of October 19, approximately fifty to sixty men lay hidden in chaparral just to the side of the railroad, some twelve miles north of Brownsville, waiting for the early morning train out of Brownsville. Like all south Texans, they considered the train to be the most prominent sign of the changes brought by the last decade. Every day its engines towed car after car of vegetables, cotton, and corn grown on land that used to be theirs. And the men most responsible for this transformation often rode the passenger train. A wire had been roped around the track's west rail, which now lay unattached, the spikes that once held it to the wooden ties having been pulled loose and scattered on the rail bed. The man holding the other end of the wire heard the rumble of the train and saw the smoke from its engine. He waited patiently until the train was almost upon them, and then he pulled on the wire with all his might.

Inside the train, District Attorney John Kleiber felt several abrupt jerks as the train abruptly stopped. The passenger coach rocked back and forth but did not turn on its side, as he saw the engine and front-most cars do. Kleiber scrambled for cover as mounted men pumped volley after volley of gunfire into the coach, shouting "Viva Luis de la Rosa!" and "Viva Aniceto Pizaña!" The other passengers also sought safety; among them were four off-duty soldiers, former Texas Ranger H. J. Wallace, and Brownsville's quarantine officer, Dr. Edgar McCain.[80]

As the gunfire ceased, four armed men forced their way into the coach. They immediately took aim at the three soldiers in uniform, instantly killing one and seriously injuring the other two. McCain and Wallace locked themselves in the bathroom, but the Sediciosos fired repeatedly through the door. McCain sustained a horribly painful wound to his stomach, and he died the following day; Wallace suffered multiple injuries in his arms and hands but eventually recovered. The assailants robbed the other passengers, then quickly rejoined their compatriots and fled the scene before army patrols could arrive.[81]

Two days later, the Sediciosos mounted another large raid, returning to their favorite target at Ojo de Agua. Late the night of October 21, sixty to eighty men approached a sleeping cavalry unit in its bunkhouse. Part of the group opened fire on the soldiers, shouting "Viva Mexico y la Independencia de Texas!" as a trumpeter accompanied them with a battle song. At the same time, several dozen Sediciosos assaulted the nearby Dillard homestead. The

The wreckage of the train derailed by Sediciosos north of Brownsville, Texas, on October 15, 1915. Courtesy Runyon Collection, Center for American History, University of Texas at Austin.

raiders knew that the Dillards, a mixed Anglo-Tejano family, had cooperated with efforts to crush their uprising. The family had prospered by running improved cattle on their land on the Ojo de Agua tract. Their son, George, was an Hidalgo County deputy sheriff and worked as a scout after the raids began. For some time the Dillards feared that they might become the targets of further raids at Ojo de Agua. They requested special protection after the September clashes. "Several efforts were made to kill my son, George Dillard, by [raiders], as they resented his working with the American soldiers," recalled Manuela Dillard. "My son speaks perfect Spanish, and also speaks perfect English, and he was of great value to the Military forces in being able to mingle with the Mexican people and determine who were the spies who were improperly here from the Mexican side inciting trouble with the Mexican people on the American side." The night of the raid George was out scouting for another army unit. His absence may have saved his life. Calling out his name, the attackers surrounded the house and burned it down, running off the family's livestock as they left. Their compatriots killed three soldiers in their barracks before the arrival of reinforcements forced them to withdraw across the river.[82]

The train derailing and the Ojo de Agua battle embarrassed both the Constitutionalists and the U.S. government. President Woodrow Wilson officially recognized Carranza as the rightful head of the Mexican nation on October 19, the day after the attack on the train. Wilson hoped that Carranza's faction, bolstered by the benefits of diplomatic recognition, would reunite Mexico under one stable government.[83]

In the face of the seeming resurgence of the Sediciosos, both Carranza and Wilson took new measures to crush the rebellion. Carranza and Arredondo promised U.S. authorities that they would redouble their efforts. "Had conference with Arredondo regarding border situation," telegraphed the U.S. consul in Piedras Negras, "he will recommend sending one of their most experienced and dependable officers to Matamoros and a detail of their best secret service men to cooperate with the military in hunting down and bringing to justice any outlaws who may be using Mexican territory as a base or as a refuge."[84]

U.S. diplomat John Belt met directly with Carranza, with similar results. The Constitutionalist leader, according to Belt, "states he will personally investigate this situation, further that he shall remove from that section of the border any troops that may be inclined to instigate trouble, replacing them with soldiers to be relied upon.... He further assured me that he had ordered the arrest of De Larosa [sic]." Several days later, in a meeting with the U.S. consul in Piedras Negras, Carranza went even further, suggesting an "international agreement which would permit American armed troops to pursue outlaws into Mexican territory and vice versa."[85]

Carranza was true to his word. As he approached Matamoros on his tour of Mexico's northeast, his subordinates gradually but surely clamped down on the Tejano rebels. Repeated attempts to arrest de la Rosa and Pizaña failed, probably because of the significant local support that the two men enjoyed. But they did force the Tejano rebels to withdraw their forces from the immediate vicinity of the Rio Grande, instead grouping them in more discreet and defensible camps farther from the border. The "bands of Pisano [sic] and de la Rosa heretofore camped opposite Capoto and Jardin de Flores," reported a U.S. army commander in Mission, "have seemingly disappeared, probably due to patrols of Carrancista soldiers reported in those regions."[86]

And so while occasional sniper fire and small acts of theft still occurred in Cameron and Hidalgo counties, for the most part army patrols and civil officers reported general quiet. The Sediciosos were too busy avoiding the Constitutionalist regulars to continue their campaign in Texas. "Situation is better here now than at any time since bandit troubles started last July and steadily improving all the time," noted the commander at Mercedes. Other officers and diplomatic officials echoed his report.[87]

The Constitutionalists subjected the Tejano forces to continued pressure. "It is reported on reliable authority that no organized bands now exist in the Mexican territory opposite this district and that all Mexicans not belonging to the Carranza forces are being disarmed," wrote an army commander in Rio

Grande City in mid-November. A former officer in Porfirio Díaz's national
police force reported to an Hidalgo commander that "all bands of bandits
have withdrawn to the foot-hills." Two other U.S. officers reported that Carrancista officials had arrested several members of the Tejano forces and had executed at least two. "The names of these men," wrote the cavalry officer at Mission, "correspond to names appearing on lists of bandits in our possession."[88]

"Business here is getting better," wrote the U.S. consul in Matamoros,
"and I hope in the course of a few months that there will be a decided change
here for the better. The farmers are at work and the crops are fairly good." As
the calm lasted, U.S. military officers' confidence in their Constitutionalist
counterparts grew. In December, the commanding officer at Mission asked
Secretary of State Lansing to pressure Carranza to keep his commander at
Reynosa. "We know that there has been a remarkable and most satisfactory
change in conditions—vigorous patrolling has evidently had the desired effect
and bandits have either been executed or driven out of the locality," he opined.[89]

As he completed his tour of the northeast, which included a three-day
visit in Matamoros, Venustiano Carranza also finished the task of asserting
Constitutionalist power over the Sediciosos. He appointed new commanders
in both Laredo and Matamoros, actions that U.S. officials viewed favorably.
Pizaña and de la Rosa did not mount another major military incursion into
Texas for the next eight months, until June 1916. While Carranza's turning
against them curtailed their plans, events in Texas in the fall of 1915 posed an
equally serious obstacle.[90]

5
Repression

By August 1915, Anglos in south Texas felt threatened nearly everywhere. The Sediciosos killed those from different walks of life and attacked all manner of targets: the homes of families such as the Austins and Stanley Dodds in the new farming settlements; ranches, including the King Ranch itself, still the region's single most powerful institution; the railroad that had made farming in the Valley so lucrative in the first place; and the soldiers who had been sent to quell the violence. The raiders, whose precise identities and motives were not always clear, continued their attacks despite the concerted efforts of local law enforcement officers, the Texas Rangers, and the national government and its army.

Events clearly had spiraled out of control. But who was to blame, and what was to be done? Killing local Mexicans known for their "bad character" was one easy and immediate response. "The known bandits and outlaws are being hunted like coyotes and one by one are being killed.... The war of extermination will be carried on until every man known to have been involved with the uprising will have been wiped out," observed the *Lyford Courant* six weeks after the start of sustained raids. Indeed, from the uprising's beginning,

Anglos did not merely strike back at those Tejanos they suspected of involvement; they also seized the opportunity to punish any Tejano against whom they bore a grudge. Anglo south Texans, recalled Brownsville Independent Party leader R. B. Creager, "had a practice of making what they called I believe Black Lists. . . . I have seen a list and I know that they had them . . . and the name of any Mexican who was suspicioned by any men of standing in the valley or even [partial] standing who would report the fact that a certain Mexican was a bad Mexican would be placed upon one of those lists." "[I]t was a common rumor and report, and it was true that in most instances that Mexican would disappear. If he would learn that his name was turned in his course of course would be to take refuge across the river. If he did not learn it—he was usually—he would disappear some other way."[1]

Ethnic Mexicans were not alone in their vulnerability. The summer's tumult allowed for the violent settlement of disputes between Anglos as well. Shortly after the raids began in July 1915, for example, Rangers and other law officers intervened in a dispute over water rights between rancher Virginia Yeager from the San Diego area and her neighbors. Yeager leased her water to a nearby landowner but closed the gates when he discontinued payment. She recalled being alone when "Rangers came into my home . . . with this man who was a Sheriff of another county. . . . [T]hey . . . frightened me and one of them came and told that I would be . . . always mistreated if I did not do what this man said for me to do, that was to give him my water—the only bit of water for about forty miles around."[2]

But most Anglos found that pursuing private vendettas was not an adequate response. Anglo newcomers were convinced that there was more behind the raids than the ill will of disgruntled "Mexicans." Farmers living in the heart of the raided areas expressed "an absolute lack of confidence in the honesty and integrity of the local law officers," reported army officials shortly after the uprising began. The coverage in the *Lyford Courant,* as staunchly anti-machine as its readers, reflected this suspicion. The paper mixed its enthusiasm for lynching ethnic Mexican suspects with hints that the machine's coddling of criminals was an inducement to further violence. "The widespread belief that criminals are being shielded for political motives is very demoralizing. . . . [T]hat both officers and courts have been too lax in bringing petty criminals to justice there can be little doubt," it opined.[3]

It was not just that the machine was too corrupt and dependent on the "Mexican vote" to stamp out the uprising. Many newcomer Anglo farmers expressed even stronger suspicions. Four residents of Raymondville, stunned by the killing of the Austins, informed Bureau of Investigation agent R. L. Barnes that they suspected machine involvement in the raids. Accusing deputy sheriffs of deliberately avoiding the pursuit of raiders, and even of hampering such efforts by providing posses with false information and unfulfilled promises of mounts and provisions, the informants asked that their names be kept confidential "for fear that they may be shot down on sight by Mexican tools of certain parties hereafter mentioned." Machine boss James Wells and his compatriots, they felt, "probably incited certain Mexicans to organize the present uprising for purposes of his own and probably those of his political, fraternal or other associates in this district and county and has at least protected and abetted said Mexicans indirectly." Those behind the "bandits" had singled out people such as the Austins precisely because they opposed the machine. One of the informants went so far as to accuse Leon Gill, a Cameron County deputy sheriff, of fomenting the attacks. He "thinks it possible that Leon Gill has been engineering the operations of these bandits, especially during the early stages of this affair," reported Barnes, "[and] that their object has not been to rob and steal except incidentally and from certain parties, but has been for the purpose of killing certain individuals and terrorizing others and that all people living here who desire to see order established fear to exert themselves in any manner under penalty of being killed." The Lyford man attributed the murders of so many Tejanos to the fact that "Gill and his accomplices are now in favor of killing all Mexicans who are known to be concerned so as to effectually hush up any connection he may have with the affair." Recent Anglo arrivals also were deeply suspicious of Cameron County sheriff W. T. Vann, whose vigorous campaign for sheriff had presented the machine as a bulwark against Anglo segregationists.[4]

Even law enforcement officials suspected one another's motives during the first several months of raiding. After the clash at Aniceto Pizaña's ranch, for example, Brownsville deputy sheriff Mike Manahan expressed his belief that Emilio Forto was involved with the rash of theft and raids. Manahan owed his appointment to the 1914 victory of the anti-machine Independent slate in Brownsville, whereas Forto was a fixture of Jim Wells's machine, having served terms as sheriff and judge of Cameron County in the 1880s and 1890s. "I have always thought that old man Forto . . . was giving this band aid but have not secured much direct information to sustain this belief," Manahan informed the Department of Justice. "It is significant enough though that one of his henchmen . . . gave the bandits a calf and a goat and otherwise rendered them assistance when they were camped in his vicinity . . . another henchman of Forto is known to have harbored these bandits." Moreover, Forto had personally misled the military authorities. According to Manahan, he hired an automobile and showed an army colonel around the area, convincing him "that there was no organized movement[,] that it was not uncommon in this country to see a Mexican with a 30/30 [rifle] strapped to his saddle and that whatever exploiting was being done was a matter for the State authorities to handle."[5]

Not all machine figures came under such suspicion. Nobody accused W. T. Vann's counterpart in Hidalgo County, political boss and Sheriff A. Y. Baker, of involvement with the Sediciosos. Baker not only pursued the raiders with a vengeance but also killed numerous prisoners and other Tejanos. Adam Medveckey, an army soldier who stayed and settled in south Texas, described Baker's conduct years later. "Mr. Ramos, I hate to say this thing," Medveckey told his student interviewer: "I had a run-in with Mr. A. Y. Baker to this extent, after I witness him killing three guys, three Mexican fellows, in cold blood. I says, 'man, you're heartless.'" Medveckey concluded that "[t]hat's the kind of man A. Y. Baker was. He was killing Mexicans on sight." Lloyd David, a Hebronville resident who helped pursue raiding parties with the Texas Rangers in 1915, had similar recollections of Baker's conduct. During the uprising David was a member of a posse that captured an unidentified Mexican traveling through the countryside with a Winchester rifle. Baker told the group, "Well, boys, I've had that man in jail more times than I've had fingers and toes. Every one is just like ya'll have got him now: no evidence against him. I don't want to ever see him again. Go on out and leave him wherever you want to."[6]

Officers who owed their positions to the political machine, in turn, resented those who charged that they ignored or even supported the raids. Brownsville resident Frank Pierce implied that the opportunism of anti-machine politicians hampered the effort to contain the raiding. "Had Sheriff Vann . . . been given proper and patriotic support by some of his constituents who figure prominently in the political affairs of this region," Pierce argued during the high tide of the Sedicioso raids, "the situation could not have become so acute." Those removed from these factions found the recriminations extremely frustrating. "If it were possible to deport all the bad Mexicans along the border, guaranteed 'bad' by any leading representative of one political party," wrote an exasperated army officer, "one half the Mexicans along the border would be deported; then if all those declared 'bad' by a representative of the other political party were to be deported, there would be none left."[7]

Anglo Solidarity

If the onset of the raids exposed the differences among Anglos, then the continuation of the uprising created a powerful incentive for them to overcome their differences. Pizaña and de la Rosa struck at the economic basis of both the machine and insurgent farmers. Major landowners and businessmen constituted the bulwark of the machine's strength, and indeed machine players such as Florencio Saenz and the King family numbered among the raids' victims. Similarly, Anglo farmers formed the electoral mainstay of the anti-machine forces, and they too were attacked, along with the railroad and irrigation works that made their livelihoods possible. Soon enough, the need to stop the raiders made new allies out of old enemies.

Even some of those initially worried about the potential for massive racial violence came to endorse it. In late September, after nearly three months of attacks, Samuel Spears wrote to General Frederick Funston, commander of the U.S. forces stationed in the Valley. He began by describing the work-ings of the south Texas machine to the general and then implied that its long toleration of crime was partially responsible for the growing anger among the Anglo population: "[F]or some years our ranchmen and farmers have been continuously losing property by theft, and have been unable to apprehend and convict the thieves, though in many instances the thieves were well known." As a supporter of anti-machine politics, Spears might have dwelled on the weakness or even on the complicity of the machine in the violence. Instead, he commended both the Rangers and the county officers for the manner in which they had "vigorously taken the situation in hand." Although in early August he warned Department of Justice officials of the potential dangers of Anglo vigilantism, six weeks later his anger at the raids overshadowed his concern for restraint and due process. "All things considered," he told Funston, "these officers and rangers have proceeded with commendable discrimination. Much more has been said about killing innocent Mexicans than the facts, as I have them, justify." Indeed, Spears now had only harsh words for the critics of lynch law: "The people who most loudly criticize these occurrences [lynch-ings], have [the] least to say about the eleven white men who have been killed. In my judgment it is better by far to make this kind of mistake than to have our own people killed."[8]

Spears was not alone in his journey toward racial solidarity. On Octo-ber 24, at the invitation of Brownsville's mayor, more than two hundred men from across the Valley gathered in the city to develop a coherent response to the continued raids. The train derailing occurred only four days earlier, and there was no evidence yet that the Constitutionalists were willing or able to move against the raiders. The assemblage approved resolutions to lobby in Austin and in Washington, D.C., for the deployment of more armed forces in south Texas. The four men elected to spearhead the effort were an im-probable combination of bitter political enemies. Machine boss James Wells was joined by his friend, client, and close political ally, King Ranch manager Caesar Kleberg. Wells's former legal associate and ex-state senator D. W. Glasscock of Mission, and Falfurrias's Ed Lasater, perhaps the leading anti-machine politician in the Nueces Strip, rounded out the delegation. The rest of the lobbying committee included numerous anti-machine figures, including developer Lon Hill and landowner and factory operator A. A. Browne.[9] The newcomers and the old guard had come to realize that their disputes were trivial in the face of an aggressive ethnic Mexican insurgency.

Vigilantism

Tejanos paid a high price for the newfound unity of Anglo south Texans. Just as most Anglos came to think of the rebellion and the need for its defeat in racial terms, so too did Tejanos experience a hardening of racial boundaries.

At first, despite the Plan's racial rhetoric, the violence did not follow a particularly racial pattern. The raiders, to be sure, were ethnic Mexicans, and most of their targets were Anglos. But they did attack Tejanos as well. Moreover, some of the early violence between Tejanos had little to do with the Plan de San Diego or the tensions that had spawned it. Just as Anglos used the chaos as an opportunity to even old scores, so too did Tejanos. For example, the family of Carlos Esparza, a Cameron County deputy sheriff who was killed in early July, had a long-running feud with the Escamilla family, members of which joined the Sediciosos. A similar resentment may have been at work between Sostenes Saldana and his illegitimate son, Sostenes Saldana, Jr. The elder Saldana served for many years as Cameron County deputy, working actively in 1915 and 1916 to stop the raids. His son described himself as "a big man among the bandits ... [and] urged all the Mexicans to join in the movement." The younger Saldana was killed in October or November of 1915.[10]

But what Tejanos might have to fear from one another soon paled in comparison to what they had to fear from Anglos. Those suspected of joining or supporting the raiders constituted the most obvious of targets, as they had from the uprising's beginning. Ethnic Mexican suspects were lynched after nearly every major raid in 1915. Shortly after the attack on the Norias ranch house, for example, unknown assailants killed three Tejanos, Abraham Salinas, Eusebio Hernández, and Juan Tobar, presumably for suspicion of aiding or participating in the attack. The Texas Rangers who had arrived after the fight might have been responsible. In any event, the Rangers' actions encouraged such measures: the next morning, they posed with their lassos around the three corpses, and the picture soon circulated as a postcard. Several weeks later, as the raids continued, Ranger captain J. M. Fox wrote to the commander of the force to describe another thinly disguised execution of a suspect: "Yesterday we caught a Mexican by name of Tomas Aguilar one of the 3 that robed [sic] the Depot at Combs and sit [sic] the R.R. bridge on fire to which he admitted and was also in the killing of Mr. Austin & Son of course he tried to make his escape but we killed him." A similar event occurred on September 10, after raiders attacked the Galveston ranch some twenty-four miles west of Brownsville, killing two U.S. soldiers and injuring two more. "During that

Texas Rangers pose with corpses after Sedicioso raid on the Norias division of the King Ranch. Courtesy Runyon Collection, Center for American History, University of Texas at Austin.

day the soldiers arrested five Mexicans living at the ranch," wrote Franklin Pierce. "They were taken to San Benito, turned over to the deputy sheriff, and placed in jail. That night at about 9:30, the deputy sheriffs took three of them out of jail and started on the Harlingen road. Next morning these three Mexicans were found dead, having been executed."[11]

Landowning Tejanos, regardless of whether they aided in the raids, were particularly at risk of vigilante violence. The murder of Antonio Longero, for example, ended a major lawsuit against Hidalgo County developer S. W. Seabury. "[H]e was one of the principal witnesses and parties, he and his father-in-law," recalled James Wells, "a very well known Mexican who owned a ranch out there." Shortly after the trial began, "the attorneys came and said they had just heard that Antonio and his brother and his father-in-law had been killed out on the ranch." Deprived of his witness, Wells postponed and eventually dropped the case for lack of evidence. Although Longero, a former county commissioner, was a well-connected and reasonably prosperous ranchero—"as good a Mexican as there was in the Rio Grande Valley," according to a description by a prominent Anglo from Mission—in the end that status did him little good. Although Longero was never named or suspected of involvement with the Sediciosos, Rangers under the command of Captain H. L. Ransom killed him.[12]

Longero and other rancheros had particular reason to fear Lon Hill, who used the tumult to kill and expel those whose property he coveted. Hill and his friends Bert Carr and Jeff Scrivener (Aniceto Pizaña's neighbor) "seemed to have made up their minds to terrorize Mexican inhabitants so that they would leave the country and sell what they had for a song to Anglo-Americans," complained one Tejano to a Bureau of Investigation agent. Because it "simply confirm[ed] considerable data along the same lines," the agent reported, the matter "was not followed deeply." After driving Tejanos from their land, reported the Constitutionalist consul in Brownsville, Hill would send agents across the river to Tamaulipas to buy it from them at a drastically reduced price. Though his brutality was legendary, the consul said, only Frank Pierce and Emilio Forto had the courage to confront him about it.[13]

Tejanos equally had to fear mass lynchings. On September 28, for example, Rangers clashed with about forty raiders near Ebenoza, Hidalgo County. The victorious Rangers took a dozen or more of the raiders prisoner and hanged them. "The Rangers say little about what happened[,] they never talk but you can always tell that they were there," wrote army scout John Peavey. He saw the bodies later that same day. "The Military District Commander from Fort Brown and I were on our way to Fort Ringold at Rio Grande City," he remembered, and "when we arrived at the Tower road near [Ebenoza] we saw the Mexican bandits hanging by the neck I didn't count them, but there must have been at least 10, the Colonel remarked as much as I would like to hang some of them bastards, we as soldiers cannot hang a prisoner." The bodies remained in the open for months. James Wells remembered coming across the decomposing bodies as he saw buzzards circling overhead and smelled something foul. Another description of bodies "with empty beer bottles stuck in their mouths . . . near Ebenezer" likely referred to the same victims. "I saw the bones about five or six months afterwards, the skeletons," recalled Mercedes farmer J. J. Bushby.[14]

The executions near Ebenoza were not an isolated event. On October 1, army troops near Lyford came across the bodies of eleven ethnic Mexicans who were murdered presumably for their alleged complicity in nearby raids. After the derailing of the train on October 19, Rangers and civilians detained about ten ethnic Mexicans whom they found in the vicinity. "Ten of those Mexicans," recalled railroad developer J. L. Allhands, "immediately paid for the crime with their lives; four of them were corralled and executed by hanging on trees; the others were shot down by their captors." Sheriff W. T. Vann pointed the finger of blame directly at Ranger Captain Ransom. "[T]he morning [of the train derailing] we came out there and arrested these four men,

Captain Ransom had them and walked over to me and says, I am going out to kill these fellows, are you going with me? I says no, and I don't believe you are going. He says, if you haven't got guts enough to do it, I will go myself. I says, that takes a whole lot of guts, four fellows with their hands tied behind their backs, it takes a whole lot of guts to do that, and I went up the road four or five miles [in search of other suspects]." The sheriff returned to find that "Ransom had killed [the] men, and I told my deputy, you take these [other] men and put them in the car and carry them to town. . . . Ransom says he is going to kill them too. I says, no they are my two, he hasn't enough Rangers here to kill my two at all, and we carried them and put them in jail and they proved to be innocent." [15]

Vann's insistence that the due process of law be used to sort the guilty from the innocent proved to be increasingly rare among law enforcement officers. If the many Tejanos with ambivalent or even hostile feelings toward the uprising initially hoped to escape the reprisals, that hope dimmed over time. The Rangers and local vigilantes exerted little effort to distinguish between loyal and rebellious Tejanos. Anybody who looked "Mexican" was vulnerable.

Tejanos whose relatives or friends had joined the uprising—or were believed to have done so—knew that they were particularly at risk. Such was the case, for example, with Manuel Robles, a Sebastian-area ranchero whose nephew may have joined the rebels. In late October, "a party of five Americans (they were not soldiers, rangers or sheriffs)" approached his house, reported a Bureau of Investigation agent, "and called for the man by name. . . . Robles came to the door and was taken a short distance from the house and riddled with bullets." [16]

Even living near the sites of raids could be fatal. The men who raided rancher James McAllen's house on September 24 stopped at a nearby rancho to regroup, tend to their wounded, and feed their mounts. "Those Mexicans took them in. . . . If they hadn't, the bandits would have killed them," recalled Roland Warnock, an employee on rancher Sam Lane's nearby property. The Rangers who responded to the raid saw things differently. They determined from inspecting the tracks and blood that the neighboring Tejano ranch had taken in the wounded men. The Rangers stopped at Lane's house, where many of them fell asleep on the porch. Later they observed two men, Jesús Bazan and another whose last name was Longoria, approach Lane and confer with him for several minutes. The Rangers watched as Bazan and Longoria rode toward the Tejano ranch. Realizing that the two lived where the raiders had taken refuge, the Rangers' commander, Captain Ransom, decided to kill them. Sam Lane, an ex-Ranger himself, protested. Lane enjoyed cordial relations with his Tejano neighbors, several of whom recently had ridden more

"Four Dead Mexican Bandits who have been dead for days." Remains of some of the many killed by vigilantes and Texas Rangers. Courtesy of the Hidalgo County Historical Museum.

than fifteen miles to warn him that "bandits" intended to attack his ranch and steal his horses. Lane secured a promise from Ransom not to kill his friend, the sixty-eight-year-old Bazan.[17]

"These two Mexicans pulled over to the side of the road to let [the Rangers] pass, and when they did, the Rangers just shot them off their horses, turned around and went back to the ranch and went back to sleep," recounted Warnock. The bodies putrefied in the sun. "About two days later we could hardly sleep because of the stench. Human scent is the worst in the world. We went over there and found the bodies still lying where they had been shot. We buried them the morning of September 29, 1915. Their horses wandered back to their farms, and when the families found out what had happened, they pulled up everything and left, never to come back." The graves of Bazan and Longoria can still be seen off the side of FM 1017, in Hidalgo County, several hundred yards from the Guadalupe Ranch headquarters.[18]

Anglo ineptitude with Spanish surnames and enthusiasm for killing on the flimsiest of evidence gave Tejanos further reasons to fear for their lives. On September 17, for example, Rangers killed Refugio Pérez in Hidalgo County, thinking that he was Jesús Pérez, whose relative was killed during the fight at Ojo de Agua earlier that month. Sometime that same fall, a young man whose hand was in a sling got off the train in Mercedes for an appointment with the doctor treating his injury. Rangers, who were looking for somebody shot in the hand during a recent raid near Mercedes, arrested him, and he was found dead several minutes later. "The incident was so notorious," J. T. Canales remembered, "that the doctor himself stated at the time that they had killed the wrong man because he was not wounded but he had a tumor in the hand and [the doctor] was treating him." [19]

Living with Terror

By early fall, the signs of the vigilantism were inescapable. It was not just that Tejanos knew of friends and relatives who were dealt summary justice and could speculate about the chances of meeting such a fate themselves. The violence directed at them had clear public manifestations in the piles of bodies left to rot in public. Dorothy Pope, at the time a young child living near Alamo, remembered later that "[s]everal bandits were killed in Alamo and people passing south of the highway could observe the bodies lying there for several days. Donna residents on their way through Alamo were shocked to recognize some of the dead as being from a camp a half mile near their home." [20]

Yet those who yearned to bury their loved ones were often too afraid to do so. The Rangers and vigilantes targeted relatives of alleged bandits, and so to bury a friend or relative was to court death. One instance in 1915 left a particularly strong memory with Cameron County coroner H. J. Kirk. "One afternoon about two o'clock a party came to me and said that there was dead bodies in the neighborhood and they were so offensive that they wanted them disposed of and wanted to know why the authorities did not take action," he later described. "I didn't know anything about it before, and a little later on a man . . . asked me if I would go out there with him and relatives to bury these bodies. I asked him why don't you go out and bury them yourself? He said he was afraid to go, and I asked him why, and he said he was afraid that the Rangers would shoot them." If burial was too dangerous, however, then grieving survivors often took the lesser risk of erecting groups of wooden crosses to honor their dead. [21]

The ongoing sights were enough to convince any Tejano that there was no refuge in south Texas. In mid-September, for example, someone traveling from San Benito to Edinburg might well have seen what a New York reporter witnessed: "The bodies of three of the twenty or more Mexicans that were locked up overnight in the small frame jail at San Benito were found lying beside the road two miles east of the town this afternoon. All three of the men had been shot in the back," he wrote. "Near Edinburg, where Octabiana Alema, a mailcarrier, was shot and beaten by bandits whom he came upon accidentally in the brush, the bodies of two more Mexicans were found. They had been slain during the night. During the morning the decapitated body of another Mexican roped to a large log floated down the Rio Grande. Soldiers removed the body from the river at Fort Brown."[22]

Tejanos also knew that their persecutors made deliberate efforts to terrorize those whom they did not kill outright. After the September 21 battle at Ojo de Agua, for example, local Anglos gathered together the bodies of slain raiders. "Their bodies were placed on a pile of wood, saturated with gasoline and burned. The following day people from the upper Valley towns came down to see what had happened at Ojo de Agua," remembered Maude Gilliland, a resident of a nearby ranch. Others also recalled instances of burnings. Interviewed by his grandson nearly sixty years later, Francisco Sandoval emphasized that the Rangers killed people simply for the pleasure of it, adding that "they burnt them, they burnt them alive." Reynolds Rossington, who as a young man lived in Hebronville, recalled seeing Rangers bring wounded suspects to the lumberyard of the Henry Eads Company in Hebronville. "[T]hey came in every morning and they brought these desperados in, the ones that were part dead, they just built up a big fire and burned them up in a brush pile behind this lumber company," he said.[23]

After awhile the sheer number of lynchings may have inured residents, especially Anglos; terror and fear had become part of daily life. The "finding of dead bodies of Mexicans, suspected for various reasons of being connected with the troubles, has reached a point where it creates little or no interest," reported a San Antonio newspaper in September. "It is only when a raid is reported or an American [i.e., white person] is killed that the ire of the people is aroused." No doubt many Anglos shared the experience of Brownsville lawyer J. C. George, who commented in early 1919 that "[t]here have been lots who have evaporated in that country in the last 3 or 4 years. I am not in the attitude of inquiring into and was not when I heard of their evaporation but it would be talked around upon the street the next day."[24]

As such "evaporations" continued, some horrified observers attempted to make accurate counts of those killed. Any Tejano could likely name dozens of acquaintances or relatives who had fallen, and it was clear to even casual Anglo observers that the death toll reached well into the hundreds by the end of the year. Frank Pierce, who would later publish numerous works of local history, could identify one hundred and two victims by name, based almost entirely on his own investigations in southern Cameron County. An appalled Pierce labeled the Rangers' campaign "a systematic manhunt" and was told by numerous civilians and army officers that "at least 300 Mexicans were so killed." Other south Texans made somewhat lower estimates. Independent leader and Brownsville resident R. B. Creager stated that "conservatively one hundred, maybe two hundred Mexicans [were] killed." But three hundred seemed to be the consensus number for federal officials, repeatedly cited by Emilio Forto and General Funston. Some were sure that this count was low, however. In early October, *Regeneración* reported that the Rangers had already killed hundreds, often burning their homes and destroying their crops in the process, and that the pace of killings had increased in the last weeks of September. By the following April, the paper had raised its count to fifteen hundred.[25]

"How many lives were lost can not be estimated fairly," wrote army scout Virgil Lott, "for hundreds of Mexicans were killed who had no part in the uprisings, their bodies concealed in the thick underbrush and no report ever made by the perpetrators of these crimes." With reports such as the *New York Sun*'s terse statement in September that "[t]hirty dead Mexicans have been found within the last twenty-four hours near San Benito, Mission, Progreso, Chapin, and Mercedes," most south Texans shared Lott's uncertainty as to the exact death toll.[26] (So did later historians. Walter Prescott Webb, the first such professional to examine these events, offered as his best estimate the wide range of five hundred to five thousand killed. Later research has been unable to arrive at a more specific conclusion. While several dozen Anglo soldiers and farmers perished in clashes with the Sediciosos, hundreds of names of murdered Tejanos have been documented, often cited by multiple witnesses apparently independent of one another. The challenge in calculating a death toll remains as difficult as it was during the events: what portion of the killed do those specifically named represent? The fragmentary nature of the surviving accounts and the discovery of skeletons even decades later suggest that a number in the low thousands is probable. If this is in fact the case, then several percent of the population of deep south Texas died during the Plan de San Diego uprising, for the 1910 census counted about forty thousand in Cameron and Hidalgo counties. Even a lower death toll would mean that a Tejano in south Texas was more likely to "disappear" than a citizen of Argentina during that country's infamous "Dirty War" of the 1970s.[27])

Flight and Dispossession

It was not the past, but the present, that so concerned Tejanos in the fall of 1915. As they were forced to wonder if they would soon meet the same fate as the rotting corpses and charred bodies of their friends and relatives, they also saw signs that Anglos meant not only to crush the rebellion, but also to establish their permanent dominance over south Texas. Tejanos watched the racial lines harden as the violence continued and Anglos armed themselves. A "[r]egistry of all Americans who have arms and will be ready to respond to a call and repel invaders in case of trouble . . . has been completed in Brownsville and other border cities," reported a newspaper in mid-September. Anglo militias were not organized "in fear of an invasion from the Mexican side," wrote another reporter, "but against Texas Mexicans."[28]

At the same time, many Tejanos were forced to give up their own weapons. Tejanos living in San Benito, reported an army officer in September, relinquished "all their fire-arms; the Mexicans in return to receive receipts for same to be held by them as evidence of their good conduct and intentions." It "is expected that the search of Mexican homes and the confiscation of their arms and ammunition will be extended to the towns and cities," reported a New York journalist later the same week. Canales recognized that this was not a good time to be unarmed. "[T]he River was low and the bandits and thieves across the river who were hungry would come and steal the very things and the property of . . . Mexican tenants and farmers along the river, and they had no arms to protect them . . . they were between the devil and the deep blue sea. . . . They intended to disarm because they thought . . . in that way they would establish order, but the reverse was true."[29]

Thousands of Tejanos concluded that the only sensible response to continued Sedicioso raids, vigilante killings, and their own disarmament was to flee from their ranchos to Brownsville, or even into Mexico. In late August, border observers began to note large numbers of Tejanos who were fleeing, often with many of their household possessions in tow. "Large exodus of Mexicans with household goods to Mexico continues," wrote a Brownsville military commander in September. Specific threats prompted at least some of them to leave. "A great many families continued their migration during the week. In some cases they reported that they had been given several days notice to leave their places in the United States," reported an officer upstream from Brownsville. Tejano refugees made a visible impact on Tamaulipas border cities. "Every day I see Mexican families moving over here from the Texas side," wrote the U.S. consul in Matamoros, "leaving their homes where many of them have lived all their lives on account of the troubles in the Valley."[30]

Such flight left large areas of the countryside almost entirely depopulated. In mid-September, Captain Ransom of the Rangers noted this during a scouting excursion in northwest Cameron County and northern Hidalgo County. In the process of riding two hundred miles, he visited numerous ranches and small towns, finding "some territory entirely deserted." The same week, Donna resident Ireneo de la Garza, Jr., wrote to Brownsville consul José Garza that "all the towns of the Valley remain empty of Mexican people" due to the killing rampage. De la Garza told the consul that he feared being declared a bandit himself and thus refrained from further investigating the scenes of fights and killings. Several weeks later, George Martínez told Bureau of Investigation agent J. B. Rogers that most of his neighbors had fled "because they were afraid of the Rangers." Though they "have no work in Mexico and their families are

Tejano refugees flee to Mexico in the fall of 1915. Courtesy Runyon Collection, Center for American History, University of Texas at Austin.

suffering," they would return only "if the Rangers were not here." By early November, after the raids had ceased, Rogers himself reported that "two thirds of all the Mexicans mentioned in this letter have gone into Mexico and only one fifth of them remain at Los Indios [the balance had moved to Brownsville]."[31]

Those who fled to Mexico were truly desperate, for they knew the conditions that awaited them south of the river. They had seen thousands of Mexican nationals coming through the Valley, driven from their homes by extensive warfare and the collapse of both the agricultural and industrial economies. Tamaulipas, they knew, was no exception to this pattern of misery and emigration. Hunger and disease stalked the land. Warfare, most notably between the armies of Francisco Villa and the Constitutionalists, had disrupted the planting season in 1915. Moreover, "[t]here is an epidemic of small-pox on the Mexican side and a strong quarantine has been established in this county," wrote a U.S. army officer in Hidalgo County. "[T]he people on the other side are evidently beginning to suffer from hunger," he reported, and "they come down to the river and beg to be allowed to come over."[32]

Under such circumstances, it took even more than the vigilantism and raids to force Tejanos from their homes and across the river. Rangers, other law officers, and private citizens launched deliberate campaigns to remove them from large portions of the Valley. An army patrol in mid-September found an "[e]xodus of Mexican Texans from . . . about twelve miles east of Harlingen. . . . Civil officers of Texas sent these people out in order the better to find the bandits in the brush thereabouts." Three weeks later, the refugees still had not returned, and the cleared area had in fact increased. Justice Department Agent J. B. Rogers, driving through the same region, noted that Los Indios "is abandoned except by the soldiers. I noticed that all the houses were vacant, some of them very nice homes." At nearby Rio Hondo, where Luis de la Rosa may have served as a deputy sheriff several years earlier, "there remain nine families out of fifty or more. . . . This is the condition as I see it all over the rural section here," Rogers concluded.[33]

Many Tejanos found the Texas Rangers to be particularly adept at such expulsions. Captain Ransom, responsible for the executions after the train derailing and for killing Longoria and Bazan near the McAllen Ranch, made a habit of running Tejanos out of their homes as he patrolled the south Texas countryside. On a scouting ride in September in south Texas, he cheerfully reported back to the head of the Ranger force that "I drove all the Mexicans from three ranches. Rancho Leona, Rancho Nueva, and Rancho Viejo."[34]

Private citizens followed Ransom's example. Many Tejanos were fired wholesale from their jobs. "Hatred for all Mexicans along the river was manifested in demonstrations to-day when even Mexican employees at some of the ranches were driven out," reported one newspaper in late September. Such removals could be profitable, as the "general exodus of Mexicans is furnishing a field for rich profits for persons desiring to buy cheaply the property of these refugees," according to another newspaper.[35]

Proposals for a more systematic and formal ethnic cleansing accompanied the de facto effects of these private and extralegal efforts. In late November, King Ranch manager Robert Kleberg proposed the establishment of martial law in south Texas. He argued that authorities should "require every person to give an account of his coming and goings" and that "such as were unable to, he would gather in concentration camps along the river from Rio Grand City the Gulf about 100 miles." To stifle the raids, Kleberg argued, the concentration camp residents should be given "employment in clearing a zone a mile wide from the river northward," and a road should be built "along the edge of the clearing for the use of the military." Kleberg felt that such a plan would also protect Tejanos from arbitrary violence. "One injustice which is done to Mexicans," he stated, "is to assume that guilt runs in consanguinity. When a certain man [who] is discovered to have taken part in a bandits' raid is captured or killed in such a raid, his brothers, half-brothers, and brothers-in-law are assumed to be guilty and are immediately arrested or killed."[36]

Tejanos would have recognized Kleberg's consideration for their welfare, odd though it may have been in the context of putting many of them in concentration camps, as a reflection of the traditional relations between elite ranchers and their employees. Though doubtless horrified by the substance of his proposal, they also would have shared his sense that the old system of paternalism, which had constrained racial violence for almost seventy years, was shattered.

Had they known of another, more extreme proposal, Tejanos would have had yet another reason to believe that the violence had irrevocably changed their world. "During those troubles, one good citizen—a lawyer who had held high places in the judiciary of Texas—suggested to me that we ought to compel all Mexicans resident on the Border to go across the river until the troubles were over, and then go out and shoot all that were left," recalled Canales's friend Harbert Davenport. "The mere fact that a larger proportion of those he proposed to exile were born here and were the children of parents who were born here, and that they would be no safer on the Mexican side of the river than he or [any] member of his family simply did not register."[37]

Tejano Politics Under Siege

In the midst of such extreme adversity, Tejanos found themselves as divided as Anglos had become united. Even as the fury at the dispossession and murder of their kin drove more Tejanos to join the uprising, others, such as Florencio Saenz, found themselves among the rebels' leading targets and joined Anglos in naming suspects and thereby exposing them to vigilante wrath. Still other Tejanos continued to work loyally for the machine in positions such as deputy sheriff and thus numbered among both the raiders' victims and pursuers. Rather than muting their previous economic and political divisions, as Anglos did, Tejanos who had walked different paths in the decade before the uprising became outright enemies. Large landholders and businessmen such as Deodoro Guerra and Florencio Saenz had profited from the Valley's agricultural development even as Pizaña and other rancheros suffered from it. Now Saenz and Guerra were at war with Pizaña and his compatriots, joined in their efforts to crush the rebellion by the Tejano deputies who still served the machine.

Tejano Progressives found themselves in an awkward and in-between position. On the one hand, they wanted little to do with any violent upheaval or radical overthrow of established economic power. By the time of the Mexican Revolution, the Idars had broken with the Flores Magón brothers, charging that their efforts to create a "socialist utopia" would in the end "give no more result than the loss of another piece of Mexican soil" and earn the brothers the "very deserved title of traitor."[38] The Sediciosos' attacks on the railroad and the farmers affronted the Progressive support of economic development in general, and of south Texas's agricultural boom in particular. But on the other hand, the Progressives abhorred the growing vigilantism. The events of 1915 and 1916 confirmed their worse fears of the powerlessness of Tejanos in the face of Anglo racism. And the machine's inability or unwillingness to limit such violence reflected their judgment that it held little promise for the betterment of Tejano lives.

Because no raids had yet occurred near Laredo, the Idars did not directly have to confront these tensions in the fall of 1915. Canales, on the other hand, was caught in the middle of them. His family's land (which included five discrete ranches at the time), his own enthusiasm for agricultural development, and his on-again, off-again partnership with the machine made Canales a staunch opponent of the uprising. He proved to be an active one as well. Although not part of the Brownsville meeting held to coordinate a response to the raids—perhaps because his ethnicity made him suspect—Canales chose his own method of action. He organized a regular patrol of like-minded Tejanos who assisted the army's efforts to turn back all raids at the river. "A system of patrolling along the River bank with Mexicans has been in operation for two days," wrote the army commander at Los Indios in late October. "If properly supplemented with observation posts along the River, it is thought this would practically prohibit the bandits from crossing or operating in this sector." Canales poured an enormous amount of time and energy into organizing this service. "Mr. Canales virtually closed his law office, as I recollect it, two or three weeks, and got in his Ford and rode all up and down the river helping organize that scout movement," recalled his law partner Oscar Dancy. "I will say further, he did it at the risk of his own life, and perhaps risked capture and torture."[39]

Canales's efforts bore fruit. In late October a cavalry officer informed his superiors that timely information from a Tejano scout enabled him to stop a border crossing. "The most reliable Mexicans living along the River have been selected and they work in pairs in the sectors assigned to them in the vicinity of their homes," he telegraphed. "They are required to make a report at least twice a day to the nearest detachment. . . . There are about 30 of these men in this sector. Mr. Canales, a lawyer in Brownsville, and who has represented this district in the State Legislature, has rendered valuable assistance in organizing the secret service."[40]

At the same time, Canales also made efforts to stop the vigilantism. Convinced that rancher Jeff Scrivener orchestrated the attack on Aniceto Pizaña's ranch to satisfy a personal vendetta, Canales did what he could to help the ranchero's family. When Aniceto's brother Ramón was charged with attempted murder for his role in the fight, Canales served as his legal counsel, ultimately winning his acquittal on the grounds of self-defense in an appeals court. On at least one occasion Canales secured the release of Tejanos detained for suspicion of involvement with the uprising. When the vigilantism grew more extreme in the fall of 1915, he spoke out publicly against the Texas Rangers' brutality. "I have heard Mr. Canales from the platform in public speeches in Cameron [C]ounty condemn the Rangers and their conduct . . . [in Spanish and English for] . . . Mexican audiences and American audiences," remembered Independent politician R. B. Creager. In 1919, again a member of the state legislature, Canales launched an investigation into the conduct of the Rangers that would document the worse of their crimes (see chapter six).[41]

Although Canales's opposition to both the rebellion and the repression that it prompted left him in a difficult position, the U.S. army's split with Texas officials and citizens responsible for the vigilantism made it more tenable. Tejano Progressives had long noted the gulf between the highest principles of the American political system and the segregation practiced in Texas. The differences between federal and state authorities, which broadened even as local Anglos set aside their differences, struck the Progressives as confirmation of their position.

Federal officers and the army took a dim view of vigilantism. Because it generated support for the uprising among both the local Tejano population and some of the Constitutionalist forces across the river, such violence made the government's goal of restoring order more difficult. Consequently, army officers did not engage in arbitrary executions, killings, or removals. As Tejanos knew, some even attempted to prevent Rangers and civilians from doing so. "The Department of State would very greatly appreciate your co-operation, with the view of quieting border conditions in the district of Brownsville," Secretary of State Robert Lansing told Texas governor James Ferguson as the mass executions began. "The Department feels assured that a solicitous word from you to state and county officials in that district would prove most efficacious in allaying race prejudice and in restraining indiscreet conduct." Lansing concluded with the argument that Texas authorities and citizens would refrain from inflaming racial animosity and engaging in "indiscreet conduct"—presumably an oblique reference to lynchings—"if they should realize the responsibility they are unconsciously imposing upon the National Government by failure to give consideration to the seriousness of the situation."[42]

Military authorities were more adamant in asserting that the lack of restraint on the part of state and local forces simply exacerbated an already bad situation. In mid-September, General Funston bitterly complained to Governor Ferguson that his soldiers witnessed three Cameron County deputies and a Brownsville policeman firing across the border at nothing in particular. The conduct enraged Funston, who several weeks earlier had ordered that all civilian lawmen be placed under military command and that patrols not fire across the river even if fired upon themselves. The general told Ferguson that, despite eyewitness corroboration of only this one incident, he had received numerous reports "that on other occasions civilians have opened fire across the border with the apparent intention of drawing a return fire and then involving the troops in the fight." Such conduct by "peace officers who are such scoundrels" was foolish. "It is easy to see that in the present excited state of the Mexicans across the river a repetition of such conduct could easily involve us in a long and bloody war," he warned. While puzzled by "how the people on the border who would be heavy sufferers in the event could deliberately provoke such a calamity," Funston threatened that "unless these violations can at once be stopped I shall feel compelled to recommend that the President of the United States place the counties on the lower river under martial law in its' [sic] severest form."[43]

Funston was even more appalled by the mounting number of vigilante killings. His repeated complaints prompted the Texas adjutant general and Governor Ferguson to issue formal orders to Ranger officers that they "prevent the execution of all Mexicans except by due process of law," warn "county and city officers and citizens generally that any unlawful execution of Mexicans will be at their peril," and report all civilian casualties and the names of witnesses to the adjutant general's office.[44]

Such federal interventions were hardly effective—Rangers, including officers such as Ransom, would continue their reign of terror for more than three years—but they did make Tejanos aware that the United States as a whole had not cast its weight behind their brutalization. Indeed, Tejanos, particularly Progressives such as Canales and the Idars, sought to use the differences between state and local officers to their own advantage. They often asked for army units to be assigned for their protection. On September 17, for example, the town of San José, about twenty-five miles upriver from Brownsville and "composed exclusively of Mexicans," asked for and was assigned a unit. "San José men," reported the *New York Tribune*, "say that they were all 'good mexicans' there and need protection as much or more than Americans." Army field officers happily honored such requests, and some even went out of their way to offer protection, as did a commander at Los Indios in mid-October. Noting that "[s]ome of the Mexican families are known to have returned to their former homes in Texas" after fleeing to Mexico, the officer instructed a subordinate to "get word to any Mexican families that they would be protected."[45]

The extent to which at least some Tejanos came to rely on such protection was evident. The "Mexican population seems to be considerably exercised over rumors current to the effect that a withdrawal of the troops was being contemplated," reported the Los Indios officer in October. "They fear that, if the troops are suddenly withdrawn, former conditions of outlawry will be resumed, vengeance being meted out against those Mexicans who have been friendly to, or have been employed as scouts or spies by, the Americans; that the Rangers will return, killing innocent as well as guilty; and that the Mexicans' only recourse will be an exodus en masse to Mexico."[46]

Canales also enlisted the aid of army units to protect Tejanos. Assisting in reconnaissance near the San Pedro ranch, Canales pointed out the large number of Tejanos preparing to flee from the area. "If those men are going to leave their homes and go into Brownsville and Mexico, the source of our information is gone," he told the major in command. The officer took his soldiers to the Tejano encampment and, with Canales as his translator, promised them that "these soldiers are here to protect [you], not only from Mexican bandits across the river, but from American bandits. . . . I am in command of this force over this ranch, the San Pedro, clear to the headgates of Mercedes, and I am giving instructions to my officers that not a Ranger shall come within ten miles of the line, and if they do they will all be put in the guardhouse and we will stop this thing." Trusting this promise, as Canales remembered, the residents "went back with their goods and lived peaceably in their homes."[47]

Beyond the Valley

While south Texans had come to live with fear—the fear of arbitrary arrest and murder, of being attacked and killed by strangers, of losing a beloved farm or ranch—both Anglos and Tejanos living beyond ground zero of the Plan de San Diego also had reason to worry. The Plan, after all, called for a rebellion across the Southwest. Ethnic Mexicans lived in other places—their numbers, in fact, were growing by the year as more fled from Mexico—and were rarely treated with respect by Anglos. Could the uprising in Cameron and Hidalgo counties spread? Would Anglos have to confront uprisings elsewhere? Would ethnic Mexicans have to face the same kind of vigilantism that Tejanos did in south Texas?

Anglo residents of areas with significant Mexican populations were particularly nervous about the prospect of wider rebellion. Requests to the state for officers and weapons poured in from towns west of the Nueces River. "[W]e feel that we are in danger and have been threatened," stated a typical plea, this one from forty miles north of Laredo, asking for Rangers to aid in the "protection of Asherton, Crystal City, and Carrizo Springs and one hundred fifty miles of border adjacent to these towns, all of which are in striking distance of river, each having a population of one thousand, sixty percent Mexican and each of said towns being on west side of the Nueces River." Most requests for state aid mentioned not only a potential threat from Mexico, but also home-grown threats from Tejanos—the "disorder or lawlessness likely to occur among the Mexican population during the present trouble," as a message from north of Corpus Christi put it.[48]

Anglos throughout Texas paid much closer attention to the behavior of ethnic Mexicans. Those purchasing arms came under particular scrutiny. In early September, for example, a federal agent in Fredericksburg, fifty miles northwest of San Antonio, reported widespread alarm that "all the Mexican cotton-pickers in that vicinity were going to town and buying all the guns and cartridges they could and an uprising was feared." The county sheriff "disarmed all the Mexicans and ordered the dealers . . . not to sell them any more arms or ammunition." Similar reports of arms purchases prompted Alonzo Garrett, the fretful U.S. consul in Nuevo Laredo, to write that "[h]ardware dealers along the border, and as far inland as Austin, state that there has been a noticeable increase in the demand for arms and ammunition by Mexican residents of Texas during the past ten days." Garrett was nervous enough to urge that "the whole Mexican border . . . be placed under modified marshal law, so as to permit the Military Commanders, to search for and seize arms from Mexicans suspected of complicity with the so called revolutionists on the American side and, if it is possible, to prohibit the sale of arms and ammunition to Mexicans until this trouble is settled." The management of the King Ranch must have held similarly deep fears, for by the end of September the ranch headquarters in Kingsville was equipped with two cannons and a powerful searchlight mounted on its roof. All of its Anglo employees, according to a newspaper account, "go armed all of the time."[49]

Under the cloud of such fear, Anglos often saw the potential for a conflagration even in isolated acts of theft or muddled reports of odd behavior. "Two of our houses at the dam were burglarized yesterday," wrote a panicked agricultural developer southwest of San Antonio. "We are going to have some trouble with Mexicans who are being encouraged to rob and steal by bandits from across the border and by inflammatory Mexican papers published in this country." A federal agent in Houston received frantic reports that local Mexicans were recruiting for some sort of armed camp. Despite their considerable anxiety, his informants' only concrete suggestion was to keep an eye on Juan Mercado, a high school Spanish teacher (and, apparently unbeknownst to either the agent or his source, a friend and political compatriot of the Idar family). Mercado frequently gave sermons at a Methodist church, during which he "talked in a general way, about what the Americans have done to Mexico, and also referred to the murders on the border. He did not propose that anything should be done, but his talks had the effect of arousing resentment against Americans."[50]

Amid the paranoia that would lead federal agents to pass along the contents of Methodist sermons, Anglos did receive credible indications that some

Tejanos were in fact interested in a wider rebellion. In late September, for example, San Antonio officials intercepted a letter, sent to a man in Hidalgo County, that contained the admonition to be "prepared for the day, as the recruiting is progressing, and they continued to come in[,] [that] this land will soon be ours." They arrested a man named Pietro Garcias on charges of sedition and issued warrants for some fifty other suspects.[51]

Other reports suggested that ethnic Mexicans were approaching African Americans to enlist them in a prospective uprising. Federal agent Howard Wright, stationed in Austin, collected rumors that "Mexicans living near Austin were endeavoring to persuade and induce negroes to join them in an effort to make Texas a part of Mexico." The most credible such report came from a black informant living six miles outside of the city. "These Mexicans told me that they really owned Texas; that they owned all the country from the Rio Grande to the Red River and that the white Americans didn't own none of it," his contact told Wright. "They said that the white folks can't fight . . . and that they wanted the niggers in Texas to join them against the Texas white folks."[52]

Authorities grew similarly concerned over events in Eagle Pass and San Marcos. In September, during the high point of the Plan de San Diego's military successes, the Bureau of Investigation uncovered a letter indicating that an armed group had formed in San Marcos, about thirty miles south of Austin. The letter asked a local man for help in acquiring dynamite. "The first ones that we should get rid of are those Rodrigues," it stated, referring to a family that, according to the investigating agent, was "friendly to the sheriff in San Marcos and [had] been giving him information and assistance." The U.S. consul in Piedras Negras, Eagle Pass's twin city, observed similar organizing. At a ranch a few miles north of Eagle Pass a man named Domingo Peña held a recruiting meeting that was attended by "a number of prominent Mexicans from both sides of the border." The consul feared that Peña was likely to find a receptive audience. "Since the publication of a picture by the *San Antonio Express* showing American Cowboys carrying off dead Mexicans for burial at Brownsville, Texas, tied with ropes, there has been considerable anti-American talk among the peon class in this vicinity," he wrote. Moreover, "Americans living on the out lying ranches say that after seeing the above mentioned pictures the Mexican laborers on the ranches have openly expressed their desire to join the bandits or followers of the Plan de San Diego."[53]

While the regional and multiracial uprising advocated in the Plan never came close to materializing, officials did receive reports that people recruited for the Plan hundreds of miles away from south Texas. In late December, Bureau of Investigation officers began searching for Teofilo Flores, a resident of Baytown, a small city thirty miles east of Houston. Flores's wife claimed that "he went to Brownsville and joined the bandits there and was killed in one of the battles near there." Although the agents could not find Flores or confirm that he had been killed in south Texas, they did learn that he "was known in Bay City as an agitator among the Mexicans, and had urged them to take up arms in behalf of the Plan of San Diego." The same month, army officials reported that a black medical doctor, Jesse Mosley, "spent about three months in Texas and Oklahoma trying to enlist negroes to join in an uprising against the Government of Texas, joining with the Mexicans." Their informants also stated that Mosley was paid by Constitutionalist General Luis Caballero for his work, and that he has "been heard to say that they could enlist in their cause a large number of Germans and German-American, also Japanese . . . [and] that several platoons of Negro soldiers had agreed to desert the U.S. Army and join their cause."[54]

Many federal and state authorities were wary of reports of impending mass uprisings. Such scenarios as a black doctor conspiring to unite Mexicans, Japanese, Germans, and black soldiers struck them as improbable, owing more to the fears of Anglo observers than to any real plan afoot. The very real uprising in south Texas and the increasing likelihood that the United States would enter the war in Europe against Germany had fueled fears beyond the point of reason. "I deem it only fair to state that most of the reports [of German backing of a rebellion across the Southwest] which have come to me," wrote the U.S. consul in Monterrey in early 1916, "have been brought to me by persons strongly pro-Allied and it is possible there was some exaggeration."[55]

Anglos and American authorities were not the only ones to wonder about the larger future of the Plan de San Diego. Ethnic Mexicans living beyond the Valley conducted often intense debates about the origins of the Plan and the prospects of its expansion beyond deep south Texas.

The Mexican exile press generally avoided participating in this discussion, or did so only to dismiss the Plan as a ploy of Venustiano Carranza. Such was the attitude of Antimaco Sax, a pro–Porfirio Díaz exile living in San Antonio. Writing in 1916, Sax alleged that Carranza fomented the uprising to gain U.S. diplomatic recognition, jeopardizing Mexico's national sovereignty by courting an invasion. San Antonio's influential La Prensa, also published by pro-Díaz exiles, accused the Flores Magón brothers of being the "intellectual authors" of the uprising.[56]

If conservative Mexican exiles tended to dismiss the importance of the Plan—a small affair caused by the worse sort of refuse washed up from Mexico—then others were keenly interested, damning the violence as a result of Anglo racism and thus part of the abuses to which the United States was subjecting Mexican people. The San Antonio newspaper La Época, for example, published an editorial cartoon that featured a spider named "Revolución de Texas" dangling over a bowl of soup about to be eaten by "Tío Sam" [Uncle Sam]. The drawing accompanied an editorial written to protest the Texas Rangers' recent killing of former Maderista general Pascual Orozco in west Texas. "It is necessary that this people, whose governors boast of being just and altruistic, open their eyes to the light of reason and abandon the bad road that they take out of their hatred and contempt for those of our race," the editors wrote of Americans. "It is said that the revolution of Texas, which already costs the American government some dead, was born of an injustice committed against a Mexican and friends in Brownsville," they continued, "and the death of Pascual Orozco, if it becomes clear that it was during an ambush, could create even more serious unrest in the territory."[57]

The Flores Magón brothers similarly linked the uprising to the oppression of Mexicans in the United States. In the pages of *Regeneración* they deflected attention away from the regional secession and revolt envisioned by the Plan de San Diego, stating that "there is no such thing as the Plan de San Diego nor partisans of that class." They admitted that "[i]n the Revolution of Texas there are anarchists, our compatriots," but, perhaps to avoid being implicated in the violence themselves, insisted that "they obey no command, for in so doing, would cease to be anarchists." Instead, they argued that the uprising "is a movement of legitimate defense by the oppressed against the oppressor," aimed at "making themselves safe from the threats that people of our race are so frequently the victim of in this country." The economic conditions of south Texas created popular support for the rebellion: "[T]ired of offering their arms to the bourgeois who exploit them . . . they encountered in the attitude of the rebels a good opportunity to wrest themselves by force from the hands of the capitalists who deny them and their families a livelihood." The violent retaliation by the Rangers and others simply exacerbated the situation, argued the Flores Magón brothers. The expulsion, general harassment, and killing—"the Mexican is killed wherever he is found"—turned a few skirmishes into a revolution.[58]

Texas's voice of agrarian radicalism, the *Rebel*, initially paid little attention to the uprising. In early October it briefly mentioned that the press and some officials blamed the "border trouble," which it did not really describe, "on the IWW [the labor union Industrial Workers of the World] and indirectly the Socialist Party." It went on to say that "all of this sounds very harmless, but it isn't as a good many innocent people—most of them Mexicans—have been killed." Events soon forced the paper to become more interested, however. In late October San Antonio authorities arrested Land League organizer J. A. Hernández and charged him with inciting sedition during a public speech he delivered. The *Rebel* protested Hernández's arrest, arguing that leading politicians in San Antonio and south Texas feared that his courageous words would deprive them of the Mexican vote. After the Socialist Party posted his bail, Hernández planned to attend an upcoming party convention. "[T]he welcome he will receive from his American brothers," the paper argued, "will convince him that the work he is doing to lead his Mexican brethren into the light of truth and out of the grip of the rotten Southwest Texas political rings is appreciated and that he will not be deserted in his hour of need."[59]

Hernández himself offered more commentary on the Plan de San Diego than did his white agrarian allies. The struggles and sufferings of Tejanos to the nearby south directed his attention and aroused his passion. "These fellows on the border are our brothers and are being killed and it is no harm for us to kill an American or a German," he declared in a speech in San Antonio's main plaza, just a stone's throw from the icon of Anglo conquest, the Alamo. Hernández, much like the Flores Magón brothers and Aniceto Pizaña, thought of the rage of Tejanos in the larger context of worldwide revolution and warfare. "The new continent begins its dark marriage with the nations of old Europe," he wrote in a San Antonio paper in reference to the prospect of U.S. and Canadian involvement in the Great War. He criticized U.S. intervention in Mexico and economic dominance of Latin America: "[I]n the midst of this iniquitous concubinage . . . the [Colossus] of the North threatens with its thirst for dominion the sovereignty of the Spanish-American countries." Only one force could stop Yankee imperialism and domination of the Western Hemisphere: "[T]he fierce north wind that announces to the world the close of human exploitation . . . [f]rom Alaska to Louisiana, from Florida to the Rio Bravo this specter is rising, it is the proletariat, it is the enfuriated [sic] people that threatens to destroy the empire of the Yankee colossus." Thus for Hernández the fact that "South Texas is on fire" meant that "the moment of decapitation has arrived for the country of the dollar." Criticizing press accounts that blamed the uprising on the Flores Magón brothers, he instead concluded that "it is the social revolution which breaks, it is the history of humanity reproduced in Texas, it is the cry of the Social Emancipation."[60]

The Silence of the Sediciosos

"Social Emancipation" seemed increasingly distant with the arrival of spring 1916. If ethnic Mexicans, whether immigrants or Texas-born, shared the resentments of Anglo racism and segregation felt by the followers of de la Rosa and Pizaña, they didn't show it by starting their own rebellion. Hernández must have hoped that Partido Liberal Mexicano (PLM) *grupos,* widely dispersed throughout the state and much of the rest of the Southwest, would provide the seedbeds for a wider uprising, just as many members of Pizaña's grupo had taken up arms. To be sure, he knew that some parts of Texas would be less fertile ground for the gospel of revolution. Anglos dramatically out-numbered ethnic Mexicans across the state, but there were enclaves—the city of San Antonio, and almost all of the border area—where that was not the case.

Perhaps Hernández recognized that distinct characteristics of the Valley made it the only place able to support a sustained uprising such as the Plan de San Diego. Even as they lost enough ground to breed resentment, more Tejanos remained landholders in the Valley than anywhere else except for the ranchlands from Laredo to Rio Grande City. And that area, so similar to the Valley in terms of its history, racial composition, and political order, experienced neither a meteoric agricultural development, a huge influx of Anglos, nor an uprising. And finally, if Hernández knew of Emiliano Nafarrate's aid to the Sediciosos, he had an additional reason to understand the difficulty of extending the uprising to other regions.

Even in the Valley, so well suited to foster an armed rebellion, the Plan de San Diego had petered out. The last identifiable raid had occurred in No-vember of 1915, and as 1916 stretched on and spring arrived without a resur-gence of the uprising, residents of south Texas began to wonder if the worse was past. Some even dared to act as though that was in fact the case. "Valley dwellers were beginning to breathe freely again," wrote army scout John Peavey in early 1916. "Land men started new colonization projects. The cities began to hum with industries that had been dormant." People returned to a semblance of their previous lives: "Farmers began to expand their fields, not fearing to poke their heads into the brush lands bordering their citrus orchards and the isolated ranches were populated again by returning refugees."[61]

The flight of ethnic Mexicans from south Texas stopped, and it even reversed as early as December 1915. From then on, those crossing into Texas from Mexico heavily outnumbered those heading south by as much as twenty, thirty, or even forty to one. Some of this migration was due to the circumstances that drove so many to flee Mexico during the revolution. "The majority of these aliens are coming from the interior of Mexico, and have never lived in the United States previously," wrote the commander at Mission in December 1915. "Without exception they report that working conditions in Mexico at this time are very bad. . . . All provisions are very high and it is hard for them to make a living in that country." The recovery of the Valley's economy meant that some of these immigrants chose to stay, at least for a time. "There is a big demand for farm laborers in this valley now, and laborers arriving find work immediately," the officer concluded.[62]

Some Tejanos who had fled the uprising and vigilantism also began to return. On New Year's Eve of 1916, a Brownsville officer noted that a "num-ber of families who went over into Mexico with their furniture, stock, and other belongings during the height of the bandit trouble, have returned to this side with their belongings. From all appearances, conditions have assumed their normal state along the border." Many of these Tejanos could not bring themselves to share the officer's confidence, instead choosing to cautiously investigate the circumstances in their old haunts. "They have brought little or no household goods," noted another official of the Tejano returnees, "and have probably come back to examine conditions on this side."[63]

Perhaps the increasing Tejano willingness to trust the army had something to do with their decision to return. "Since the last bandit troubles," wrote a commander in Brownsville in March 1916, "the Mexicans on this side of the river have gradually been acquiring a feeling of respect for the troops on this side and realize that they will not only be fairly treated but protected from any unfair treatment such as they have been subjected to in the past by local authorities."[64]

There were, to be sure, signs that the troubles might resume. In early February, a small band again raided Florencio Saenz's ranch and apparently made off with some personal property. Less than two weeks later, unidentified assailants fired on a U.S. patrol near Ojo de Agua. On March 7, two "bandits" killed a ranchero near Edinburg. In early April, A. Y. Baker's deputy Filigonio Cuellar was killed. About a month later, approximately three unidentified men killed Curtis Bales near his farm outside of Mercedes. Investigators could find no clue as to the identity, motive, or whereabouts of the perpetrators of the first three instances, but the killings of Cuellar and Bales seemed suspiciously connected to the tensions of the uprising. Locals stated that Antonio Rocha and Aniceto Ramos, who had been involved in numerous raids the preceding fall, were responsible for killing Cuellar. Bales's killers "stated to one Mexican of this vicinity that their intention was to kill certain Americans, among them the sheriff of Hidalgo County," according to an army officer who directed patrols in the area.[65]

These incidents, together with the vivid memory of the recent violence, tempered the fervent hopes that the raids and reprisals had come to an end. The Tejanos who returned remained extremely cautious, as did Anglos. In March 1916, for example, the mayor of Mercedes warned the state's adjutant general not to draft men from the border into the national guard. Should the government take "all them away from this section we would be helpless indeed." Border Anglos, he said, "would gladly serve the National Government in case of war elsewhere, [but] they feel that their first duty is to protect their homes, which is [sic] seriously threatened by a barbarian nation, fully organized and equipped with American guns and ammunition." Neither was the American army confident that the troubles were over. The secretary of war rejected suggestions that troops be withdrawn from the now-quiet lower border.[66]

Exactly what had happened, Anglos and Tejanos alike wondered, to Luis de la Rosa and Aniceto Pizaña? Why had they halted their raids? Would the rebellion return, stronger than ever, or had it been defeated for good? As rumors that the two men were raising a huge army circulated throughout the region in late 1915 and early 1916, the scarcity of raids for months on end must have puzzled the south Texans who had endured so many earlier. It wasn't that the Rangers or soldiers were turning back incursions, overmatching the Sediciosos on the battlefield; there simply wasn't any organized rebellion in the first place.

Pizaña and de la Rosa weren't puzzled, but they were frustrated. If the flight of many Tejanos from south Texas made it harder for them to find shelter and sustenance and to receive information about the whereabouts of their pursuers, then at the same time the vigilantism that precipitated the flight gained them scores of recruits. "[T]housands of Mexicans and Mexican-Texans crossed from the Texas side to Mexico seeking safety and refuge," recalled Frank Pierce of Brownsville, and "[m]any of these joined the raiders and bandits." Moreover, the outrages in Texas only deepened their support in Mexico. "The effect [of the killing of Tejanos] was that immediately every relative of that Mexican would go to Mexico with his tale of woe, and it aroused a strong feeling between them and the bandits instead of being minimized," concluded Canales in 1919. "That feeling increased [to the] alarming extent . . . that practically the Mexican border on the other side was at war with us, sympathizing with the relatives of these men that had been wrongfully killed."[67]

It was the Constitutionalist forces that were the real problem for the Sediciosos, preventing them from drawing on their base of popular support to rejoin the battle. Intensified Constitutionalist pressure had led to the halt in raids in the fall of 1915. Continued scrutiny and arrests prevented their resumption. In late December 1915, Carranza's general in charge of the Mexican northeast promised Carranza and Governor Ferguson that he would arrest de la Rosa, whom he referred to as "an American citizen." Carranza himself gave orders to the governor of Nuevo León that "those individuals responsible for the revolution in the State of Texas" were to be arrested.[68]

The Sedicioso leaders were difficult to capture, but they did feel the pressure nevertheless. Gathering their followers to cross into Texas proved impossible. And soon enough they fell into the hands of the Constitutionalists. In early February 1916, Maurillo Rodríguez, a Constitutionalist based in Monterrey who apparently had supported de la Rosa and Pizaña, was imprisoned. A week later, multiple sources reported that soldiers under General Alfredo Ricaut had arrested Pizaña in Matamoros.[69]

The backers of the Sediciosos were infuriated by the reports of Pizaña's arrest. How could Carranza, who claimed to be liberating Mexicans from the despotism that had for so long immiserated them, turn on such a champion of Mexicans in Texas? Aniceto Pizaña, wrote the editors of *Regeneración,* should be known "not as a criminal, but as a victim of the unjust persecutions of the two tyrants who today shake hands: Woodrow Wilson and Venustiano Carranza." Tejano radicals made their own protests. Marcos Mendoza, a resident of Guadalupe County east of San Antonio, wrote to Carranza directly to demand "the immediate and absolute liberty of Aniceto Pizaña," lauding him as a revolutionary hero and concluding that "if for you he is a criminal for us the disinherited he is a hero and martyr." Thirty members of the Hondo, Texas, PLM grupo wrote, "Those who sign below belong to the disinherited class, and believing our comrade Aniceto Pizaña to belong to the same class . . . we protest with all of our energy . . . against this infamous crime."[70]

What made the arrests even more galling to those who had supported the Texas rebellion was that Wilson and Carranza seemed to have formed an unholy alliance. Carranza happily sacrificed the interests of Mexicans in Texas to gain Wilson's cooperation in ridding some of his most prominent critics of their freedom. Eight days after Pizaña's arrest, federal marshals entered the Los Angeles offices of *Regeneración,* beat Enrique and Ricardo Flores Magón, and hauled them off to jail. The federal government charged the two with mailing obscene material, citing their articles on the Plan de San Diego, which Carranza's secret service had drawn to their attention, as particularly offensive. (At their trial, visiting anarchist Emma Goldman was struck by the devotion that ordinary Mexicans had for the brothers. "An impressive scene took place," she wrote. "The chamber was full of Mexicans, and when the judge entered, none of them stood, but when the Magóns appeared, all rose from their seats.") The brothers were convicted and sentenced to prison, to the benefit of both Carranza and Wilson. When the U.S. Senate demanded that Wilson show how his recognition of Carranza's government had protected American lives and property, he could point "to the fact that since assurances in this respect were given to this government . . . the disturbances along the border have in a large measure ceased." The solidarity of the oppressed envisioned in the Plan de San Diego was no match for the solidarity of their oppressors.[71]

Pershing and Villa

Wilson's confidence soon proved to be disastrously overstated. In the early morning of March 9, 1916, less than a month after Wilson gave his assurances to Congress, Pancho Villa led hundreds of his men across the border and into the town of Columbus, New Mexico. Though a sharp defeat in military terms—Villa's force lost over one hundred fifty men, his adversaries fewer than twenty—the attack prompted a substantial military intervention into Mexico, which might well have been Villa's intention in the first place. Wilson, stung by mounting criticism, decided that he had no choice but to respond. Six days after the attack the U.S. government sent a "punitive expedition" under the command of General John Pershing with orders to eliminate Villa as a military force and to capture him if possible. Pershing's expedition began with forty-eight hundred men but soon reached more than ten thousand. These troops were to spend the next ten months in Mexican territory in vain pursuit of the rebel leader.[72]

With such a force on Mexican soil, the stakes for controlling the Texas *Sediciosos* were even higher. Carranza and his subordinates knew that the cost of allowing a resumption of the raids in south Texas might be a full-scale invasion. "Our enemies . . . have continued to organize bands on both sides of the boundary line for the purpose of attacking American detachments and towns in an endeavor to provoke an international conflict," Carranza wrote to Eliseo Arredondo in early May. The Constitutionalist leader stressed the importance of controlling the border. United States authorities similarly valued control of the border and viewed controlling de la Rosa and Pizaña as an important part of that task. "In view of the importance of removing these two outlaws from the border," the secretary of war told Secretary of State Lansing, "it is requested that steps be taken to impress upon the de facto government of Mexico that the continued presence of these bandits near the border is a menace to the peace and security of American citizens living on the border."[73]

Despite their shared desire to prevent raids such as Villa's or the troubles in south Texas, Wilson's and Carranza's governments were at loggerheads. The punitive expedition was simply unacceptable to Carranza, as it was to the vast majority of Mexicans. They had fought to see their country redeemed from its corrupt despotism and would not stand by and see it subjected to American rule instead. It was difficult for them to believe Wilson's declarations that the United States had no interest in waging war against Mexico, especially when General Pershing was calling for the occupation of their entire nation, and his deputy George Patton dismissed their very capacity to govern themselves. "One must be a fool indeed," he declared, "to think that people half savaged and wholly ignorant will ever form a republic. It is a joke. A despot is all they know or want." The Wilson administration, for its part, refused to be burned for a second time. Carranza had proved himself incapable of protecting the border, so the American military would have to do so.[74]

When negotiations between the two governments broke down after several months, the prospect of war seemed increasingly likely. Eliseo Arredondo deemed the punitive expedition an "invasion of our territory by American forces contrary to the expressed wish of the Mexican Government." It is Mexico's "duty to request, and it does request, of the American government, that it order the immediate withdrawal of these new forces, and that it abstain from sending any further expedition of a similar nature," he concluded. While stressing his hope that there would be no clashes between the two armies, Arredondo stopped just short of threatening a defensive war: "The Mexican Government is aware that in case of a refusal to retire these troops, there is no further recourse than to defend its territory by appeal to arms, yet at the same time it understands its duty to avoid, as far as possible an armed conflict between both countries."[75]

To the Brink of War

The possibility of an all-out war between the two nations—actually endorsed by Texas governor Ferguson, who called on the U.S. government to invade Mexico and establish a stable government, even if it required an occupation of several decades—thus loomed as Pizaña and de la Rosa made their last effort to restart the uprising in south Texas.[76]

Conflicting reports of de la Rosa and Pizaña's whereabouts and activities circulated through the press and the United States intelligence network alike. Some had the two under arrest and awaiting execution, while other contacts swore that they were actively training hundreds of soldiers. Although PLM members in the United States assumed that Pizaña had in fact been arrested, they could not verify this. The lack of organized raids seemed to confirm that the Sediciosos were being restrained, but who could say for sure?[77]

Whatever had in fact happened to them, in June the Sedicioso leaders regrouped their forces and again threatened south Texas. Even as the firing at a train conductor near the Norias ranch house drew some attention to the Valley, a large group of armed and mounted men camped at a ranch about thirty miles southeast of Nuevo Laredo, waiting for someone to guide them across the river. This new military mobilization seemed very different from the rebels' tactics the previous year. Whereas they had practiced small hit-and-run actions in their bases of greatest support in Cameron and Hidalgo counties, now they seemed to be massing for a larger assault farther upriver near Laredo. The "party consisted of four hundred men under the personal command of Luis de la Rosa . . . [and] 200 men were sent at the same time toward" the nearby border, reported one U.S. army officer to General Funston. Funston in turn warned the secretary of state that "having been recruited[,] organized[,] and armed," the Sediciosos "are now approaching our border about four hundred strong but we cannot tell where in a distance of a hundred and fifty miles they may attempt to cross river."[78]

Many shared Funston's sense of alarm. On June 10, wealthy ethnic Mexicans began fleeing Laredo for Corpus Christi and San Antonio in anticipation of a raid. Bank withdrawals in the city were much heavier than usual all week. Reports that a Constitutionalist commander had detained more than one hundred armed men heading upriver toward Laredo provided yet another indication that the number of Sedicioso fighters was greater than ever.[79]

The fears of Laredo's elite proved to be well founded. The Sediciosos struck the following day. On the morning of the eleventh, some twenty miles north of Laredo, more than a dozen men descended on a ranch, scattered its employees, and rounded up scores of its horses. The raiders fought both a civilian posse and U.S. soldiers as they headed toward the river and retreated into Mexico. One of the three raiders captured by the army claimed that he had been forced to serve as guide. Pointing to a red and white flag and a flask of kerosene as evidence, he stated that the attackers intended to join about thirty men already on the U.S. side and burn railroad trestles and destroy track. According to a Tejano who spoke with one of the raiders, "[I]t was the purpose of the party to invade the United States and to damage the . . . [r]ailroad by burning culverts [and that] besides themselves they had several other parties along the border near Eagle Pass, Del Rio, and below Eagle Pass, that their purpose in crossing was to make as much disturbance as possible and advertise their presence, this all with the view of raising an insurrection in Texas, New Mexico, and Arizona." One of the ranch's Anglo employees, who was briefly held captive when the raiders took the horses, reported that the band's leader "claimed to be of the de la Rosa faction and to have previously operated around the Brownsville district."[80]

The next day, June 12, thirty mounted men attempted to burn a railroad bridge. Carrying a red flag with a white diagonal inscribed "Equality, Independence, Liberty," the men cut telegraph lines and were about to ignite the bridge when an army patrol came upon them. The ensuing skirmish resulted in the death of two of the raiders and the capture of two more. Several witnesses implicated local Constitutionalist commanders in the assault. Simón Solis, a Tejano arrested later the same day just outside Laredo, testified that the band was led by a Lieutenant-Colonel Villareal and a man who called himself General Maurillo Rodríguez. Four days before the effort to burn the bridge, Solis stated, Villareal imprisoned him and forced him to be a guide. He escaped shortly before the band reached the bridge. Norberto Pezzatt, captured at the bridge itself, demanded to be treated as a prisoner of war, stating that he was following the orders of regular Constitutionalist officers. Pezzatt later wrote a letter to General Alvaro Obregón, Carranza's leading general, protesting that his government had abandoned him.[81]

Early the morning of June 15, three days after the clash at the bridge, a larger party, estimated at sixty to one hundred men, crossed the river about forty miles south of Laredo at San Ignacio and attacked two U.S. cavalry troops. The party killed four soldiers and wounded six others, retreating across the river after six of its men were killed and three others captured. U.S.

soldiers reported that the well-armed and well-provisioned band was commanded by a regular colonel in the Constitutionalist army and led into battle
by Major Cruz Ruiz, one of the those killed in the conflict. Moreover, the soldiers recovered thirty-two bombs, forty-five pounds of dynamite, and various
firearms and mounts.

The Carrancista officer in charge of the opposite side of the border,
according to his U.S. counterpart, "expressed his desire to cooperate and reported later that he had captured eighteen of the bandits, three of whom were
severely wounded.... They will be forwarded to Monterrey via Nuevo Laredo
for trial." Nevertheless, American authorities were convinced that regular Carrancista officers led the raid. The captured men, José Antonio Arce, Vicente
Lira, and Francisco de León, protested that they were soldiers and had simply
followed their superiors' orders. They maintained that they joined the attack
"pursuant to a council of war held at Monterrey" attended by at least five Constitutionalist officers. (An appeals court found the evidence convincing enough
to overturn the men's conviction on the grounds that they were regular army
soldiers following orders in a time of de facto war between Mexico and the
United States.)[82]

As if the strong evidence of the involvement of his officers in the clashes
at Webb and San Ignacio were not trouble enough for Carranza, combat also
resumed in deep south Texas. On June 14, the night before the attack at San
Ignacio, a band of twenty or so men crossed the Rio Grande about ten miles
west of Brownsville. An army patrol encountered them near San Benito. One
of the raiders died in the ensuing battle, and several U.S. units gave pursuit.
In the early morning hours of June 17, still in hot pursuit, about fifty soldiers
crossed the river. They soon clashed with the raiders for the second time, this
time killing two of them. About eight hours later, another hundred or so soldiers crossed, taking with them motor trucks and a machine-gun troop, and
they camped for the night just seven miles outside of Matamoros.[83]

The resulting tense situation contained all the ingredients for a full-
scale war between the United States and Mexico. Not only had the raids into
Texas resumed, but the United States now had two bodies of soldiers on
Mexican soil, both threatened by Constitutionalist generals. Also on the seven-
teenth, General Jacinto Treviño threatened to attack Pershing's forces if they
headed in any direction but north. The U.S. consul in Tampico similarly reported that General Nafarrate "sent me to-night official notice that entrance
into Mexico of any more American troops or sailors will be considered act of
war ... and would oblige his forces to wage war without quarter."[84]

Despite the withdrawal of the U.S. troops from near Matamoros the
next day—during which Constitutionalist forces fired on the last retreating
unit—observers in both countries predicted that war would break out. President

Wilson called up numerous state militias to be stationed on the border. "Belief general here that state of war exists. . . . Official newspaper to-day although suppressing mention fighting plainly indicates seeming certainty war," reported the U.S. representative in Mexico City. Many in Piedras Negras shared his belief: "Many of people and large part of soldiery left last night for south fearing intervention . . . [t]he belief of all is that intervention is only a course of a few hours [away] and people are leaving town by the hundred," telegraphed the U.S. consul. Secretary of State Lansing reiterated a threat apparently made earlier that year to the effect that "Mexico would find in Tamaulipas another punitive expedition similar to [Pershing's]" if the raids into Texas continued.[85]

To make matters worse, on June 21 a U.S. army captain entered the town of Carrizal, Chihuahua, in defiance of General Pershing's specific orders and the warnings of the local Constitutionalist commander. Mexican forces killed the officer and six other soldiers and took twenty-four prisoners in the ensuing battle. President Wilson privately began drafting a declaration of war that emphasized the failure of Carranza to secure the border. The secretary of war granted General Funston permission to declare martial law when and where he saw fit. "Never before since the beginning of the Mexican revolution has there been such a general belief among Mexicans and Americans alike that war between Mexico and the United States was a surety, as there has been in the past week," wrote the Piedras Negras consul. He reported that the local Constitutionalist commander, with whom he was on good terms, informed him "that he expected to receive a frank notice from the American Commander before any action would be taken by him in case of war between the two countries." While the officer was aware that "he probably would not be able to offer resistance . . . he could assure me before evacuating Piedras Negras the town would be totally destroyed and his march to Saltillo would be a repetition of Sherman's march to the sea."[86]

Ultimately such measures were not necessary. Carranza soon released the U.S. soldiers taken captive at Carrizal. Most important, no further raids into Texas occurred. Although the Sediciosos had proven their ability to gather large numbers of men in coordinated attacks—and apparently to convince some local Constitutionalist officers to join their efforts—their new strategy failed. The raids took place outside the major base of support for the rebellion and did not appear to garner local support near Laredo, as their earlier raids had done in the Valley. Indeed, the gathering of larger bodies of soldiers may have been the undoing of Pizaña and de la Rosa. Reports suggested that Carranza's loyal subordinates had little difficulty in arresting Sedicioso leaders and dispersing their followers. General Ricaut may have succeeded in arresting de la Rosa as early as June 14, the day that U.S. soldiers crossed near Matamoros. Newspaper reports claimed that de la Rosa was imprisoned in Monterrey. Ricaut told the American consul in Matamoros that he had arrested de la Rosa and forty of his men, and that Constitutionalist soldiers had "instructions to arrest all parties who could not give good account of themselves."[87]

In early July, barely two weeks after the uprising's brief renewal, U.S. army commanders on the south Texas border reported that all was quiet, that they had no evidence of bands—much less raids—forming across the river, and that the nervousness of their Mexican counterparts was also declining. "It is reported by parties coming from Monterey, Mexico, that the followers of De La Rosa and Pizaña became disappointed and disagreed on account of the failure and defeat at Webb Station and San Ignacio and decided to quit them. It is believed that the De La Rosa band has been dissolved," noted an officer in Laredo. The next week, General Ricaut told the Brownsville commander that he had arrested several more Sediciosos.[88]

The Plan de San Diego had ended.

6
Citizenship at War

By 1916, Tejanos had seen much of what they once held slip from their grasp. More than a decade of intense agricultural development had forced many to surrender ranches to the tax collector, to somebody with deeper pockets, or to simple thuggery. Unlike their predecessors, the thousands of Anglos drawn by the promise of agricultural bounty showed little interest and less respect for Tejano customs. Would their new neighbors learn Spanish? Only enough to supervise their farmhands. Would they look for marriage partners among the daughters of Tejano ranchers and merchants? Not likely.

Although it appealed to some Tejanos, the Plan de San Diego only deepened their losses. If many joined in the Sediciosos' sense of triumph at the vengeance meted out to farmers like the Austins and at the attack on the hated railroad, then many more soon came to regret the price exacted for these fleeting victories. The foolishness of their friends and neighbors in launching the rebellion played right into the hands of the most hostile of Anglos. The Texas Rangers and vigilantes not on the state payroll accomplished in months what it might have taken years of economic pressure and more sporadic violence to wrest from Tejanos.

The abandonment of beloved ranches for the relative safety of Brownsville or the other side of the river, the loss of a brother, father, or husband, and the swelling choruses for the absolute disenfranchisement of "Mexicans" were the most obvious signs of how much the Plan de San Diego had cost its intended beneficiaries. But something else had been lost as well, choked in the dust of desperate flights and the mounting fear of men with guns. It was not that Tejanos looked back to 1914, before the uprising, or to 1903, before the railroad, as some sort of golden age. But amid the more immediately pressing worries of death and dispossession, many may have taken the time to reflect that they had once been able to grapple with the challenges that faced them, to grope their way toward shaping their own destinies. Those worried about losing their land could scour the pages of *La Crónica* for advice and discussion of how their people might avoid complete pauperization, deciding for themselves whether Progressive educational and political proposals were up to the challenge. The angrier program of the Flores Magón brothers was also available, whether through the pages of *Regeneración* or the meetings hosted by PLM loyalists such as Aniceto Pizaña. The early stages of the revolution only added other voices to this conversation, bringing representatives of most of Mexico's vast political spectrum into Texas.

Now that the uprising was over, only the scattered and private fragments of this once-vibrant political culture remained. Ranching families were too busy fleeing or seeing to their own defense to deliberate about what the future—if they had one—might hold. The economic hardship and dislocation brought by the rebellion made the orderly dissemination of newspapers difficult, if not impossible. Key political figures such as J. T. Canales and the Idars were consumed with helping to end the uprising and with protecting as many Tejanos as they could. And perhaps most insidiously, the chance that a neighbor might view the rebellion in a very different light—might, in fact, count his fellow Tejano as an enemy—made the political deliberation of the previous decade impossible to sustain.

And some people wanted it that way. The fabric of Tejano society was intact enough to offer some pointed and public criticism of vigilante terror. Such criticism, however, was promptly stifled, no matter its source. In Laredo, the newspaper *El Progreso* continued much of the work of *La Crónica* after the latter ceased publication shortly after Nicasio Idar's death in 1914. Jovita Idar was a reporter for *El Progreso*, which was run by Leo Walker and Emeterio Flores. Flores was an appropriate heir to the Idars' paper. He served several terms as a commissioner for Webb County, headed the now-defunct Mexican Protective League, and helped lay the groundwork for the Primer Congreso Mexicanista. He and Walker continued the Progressive tradition in the pages of *El Progreso*, supporting the Carrancistas against radicalism and reaction alike. They also paid considerable attention to events in Texas, condemning the intensified racial violence directed against ethnic Mexicans during the Plan de San Diego.

In August 1915, shocked by the initial wave of vigilantism, Walker and Flores urged ethnic Mexicans to defend themselves. *El Progreso* ran several articles of Mexico's Constitution under the heading "IF YOU ARE A MEXICAN, READ," and it included the statements, "It is the obligation of every Mexican to defend the independence, the honor, the rights and the interests of the fatherland," and "It is a prerogative of the Mexican citizen to take up arms in the army for the defense of the republic or its institutions." But, true to form, Progressives did not wholly identify the interests of ethnic Mexicans in Texas with the redemption of Mexico. After the June 1916 clashes in the Laredo area, local and federal authorities needed a reliable Spanish-speaking witness and translator to deal with the captured raiders. Court documents name a "C. N. Idar" as a witness to the statements of three men captured after the Webb Station raid on June 12. Clemente Idar copied and translated the letter from one of the prisoners to Constitutionalist leader Alvaro Obregón. Moreover, when it looked as though the Sediciosos would extend their campaign to the Laredo area in May and June 1916, he also served as an agent of the U.S. Department of Justice, passing along information about the Webb Station raid.[1]

Laredo's political establishment showed little appreciation for the merits of this stance. *El Progreso*'s articles enraged District Attorney John Vals, who attributed their publication to the machinations of Laredo's Constitutionalist consul. "I have warned, I have entreated the Mexican consul and Emeterio Flores to stop the libelous and incendiary editorials which continually appeared in *El Progreso*," Vals later wrote. But, "the editorials increased in virulence and animosity against the United States . . . [and they] tended to incite one race against the other especially at a time when the relations between the two governments were so delicate and strained."

Time made *El Progreso* only more adamant in its rejection of arbitrary violence, whatever the source. In May 1916, Leo Walker criticized Tejanos such as Florencio Saenz for their complicity in the reprisals in Cameron and Hidalgo counties. Vals promptly arrested him, releasing the editor only after securing a bond of five thousand dollars, subject to forfeiture if he again printed such articles. An undaunted Walker refused to change his editorial stance. As another Sedicioso raid loomed in June, some "citizens of Laredo escorted Leo Walker to the bank of the river," a pleased John Vals related, "and after explaining to him the necessity for such action ordered him to cross into Mexico and not return . . . [and they] informed him this action was taken because they believed a continuation of his conduct would lead to race riots and bloodshed." Emeterio Flores also fled across the river shortly after his colleague's expulsion. Although Vals was a bit defensive to state authorities about these expulsions, he refused to condemn such vigilantism. "The guilty fleeth when no one pursuer [*sic*]: probably fear induced by the lash of conscience impelled Emeterio Flores to depart from Laredo," he explained. "While I am a firm believer in the principle that every accused is entitled to a trial according to the law of this land," he concluded, "yet, nurtured as I was in the purest principles of American liberty, I do not admit that my fellow citizens committed a grievous wrong in the Walker incident."[2]

In Kingsville, Anglos and Tejanos appalled by racial violence made similar protests, and with similar results. Although the Plan de San Diego made even less headway near Kingsville than it had near Laredo, the Rangers were intent on eliminating any public criticism of their conduct. In May 1916, fearing a renewal of the uprising, local law enforcement officers imprisoned the editor of the local Tejano newspaper along with two men, José Morin and Victoriano Ponce, whom they believed to be planning raids. After the intercession of a Tejano pastor and the Anglo lawyer Thomas Hook, the editor was released. Morin and Ponce had no such luck. Several days later county sheriffs removed them from jail and turned them over to Texas Ranger captain J. J. Sanders. The two men were never heard from again, and rumors and local press reports concluded that they had been killed. Sanders denied the charges, but he was unable to say where they were or what had become of them.[3]

This pattern was all too familiar. The editor and his friends conferred with Thomas Hook and asked him "if it would not be proper for them to petition some authorities for the protection of their lives." Hook, believing "it was a good opportunity for the good element among the Mexicans to get in closer touch with the government and the government in closer touch with them," assisted in preparing a petition to President Wilson and Governor Ferguson. The petition began by noting the apparent execution of Ponce and Morin and then argued that such conduct imperiled the lives of all those of Mexican descent: "[Y]ou see that we have reason to believe that our liberty and even our very lives are menaced. One or more of us may have incurred the displeasure of some one, and it seems only necessary for that someone to whisper our names to an officer, to have us imprisoned and killed without an opportunity to prove in a fair trial, the falsity of the charges against us . . . some of us who sign this petition may be killed without even knowing the name of him who accuses. Our privileged denunciators may continue their infamous proceedings—answerable to no one."

Using classic Progressive rhetoric, the petitioners invoked their loyalty and rights as U.S. citizens to protest such conduct. "[L]et us point out," they wrote, "that the great majority of the people of the Mexican race living in this city and county, are honest, law-abiding and peaceful citizens, who labor for good order, community betterment, and culture within their modest sphere." They concluded that "[i]t is the right, guaranteed under the United States of America constitution, to life, liberty, and the pursuit of happiness, that each of us ... expected. It is those rights which have been ruthlessly and violently denied. And we look to you, the constituted authority, the custodian to whom is entrusted the safe-guarding of such rights to all, to safeguard such rights to us."[4]

This appeal to citizenship rights provided Thomas Hook with no more protection than Leo Walker or Emeterio Flores had; neither Wilson nor Ferguson replied. Shortly after sending the petition, however, Hook encountered Captain Sanders in the Falfurrias courthouse. After an acrimonious exchange of words, Sanders pistol-whipped the lawyer in the hallway. "Mr. Hook writes in the local papers ... as to the brutality of the Rangers and the way that they were treating the Mexicans," Sanders later stated, "and he was accusing the Rangers and officers generally of being cut-throats and murderers and everything of that kind." Future Ranger adjutant general W. W. Sterling, then an Hidalgo County rancher, later portrayed Hook as a dangerous agitator who deserved what he got for crossing the race line. He was a "religious fanatic," Sterling concluded, who "objected from the first time he got there to the way Mexicans were treated there, that was long before the revolution or the bandit troubles. . . . [He] would go around and get up these land titles, these old Mexican heirs and everything, he was a kind of title jumper, they called him I believe . . . when people were charged with anything he would not look to see if they were guilty, but just defend them because they were Mexicans."[5]

The Clouds of War

The United States as a whole would soon undergo something resembling the lower border's experience of violent political suppression. For several years, Americans' concerns about revolutionary Mexico were joined by worries about the course of a major war in Europe. Although the early stages of the Great War made the slaughter in the Old World seem thankfully remote to the interests of the New, by turns America found itself more and more drawn into the conflict. Though deeply divided over the wisdom of joining the European conflict, the country joined the war in April 1917.

The domestic measures taken in the name of the war would affect Americans—including Tejanos—more than the fighting itself would. The ethnic and political divisions that had kept the United States from entering the fray for more than two years did not simply vanish once Congress had acceded to the president's request. Many of the nation's ethnic communities, and much of organized labor, deeply opposed the war, and its advocates knew it. The

Wilson administration, fearing that such opposition and reservations would hamper the war effort, mounted an enormous propaganda campaign to insure "loyalty" and supported measures to prosecute "disloyal" left-wing and pacifist groups. Within months of the American declaration of war, Congress made it illegal to "obstruct" military operations. This effectively criminalized open criticism of the war, and the postmaster was granted the power to ban the circulation of antiwar material via the U.S. mail. Socialist leader Eugene V. Debs was sent to federal prison for publicly opposing the war, winning nearly one million votes for president while still imprisoned during the 1920 campaign. The war to save democracy abroad left it in shambles at home.[6]

The politics of the war were so divisive largely because they exacerbated the nation's deep ethnic tensions. Roughly one of every three Americans was either an immigrant or the child of one or more immigrants. Nearly a third of these had close ties to Germany and its allies. The diversity and size of this immigrant contingent had given rise to a vigorous debate over immigration and ethnicity in the prior decade, one that helped the Idars and other Tejano Progressives imagine a place for themselves as respected members of the national community. While some argued that new arrivals from southern and eastern Europe would deracinate the nation's essentially Anglo-Saxon democratic character, others insisted that the United States was better off for the presence of diverse ethnic communities. As the country drew ever closer to entering the war, the Wilson administration became increasingly convinced that ethnic pluralism posed the greatest domestic threat to a successful prosecution of the war.[7]

The government therefore subjected ethnic minorities to particularly harsh scrutiny. Indeed, President Wilson had warned of the threat of what he called "hyphenated Americans" even before he called for a declaration of war. "There are citizens of the United States, I blush to admit, born under other flags but welcomed under our generous naturalization laws," he told Congress in 1915, "who have poured the poison of disloyalty into the very arteries of our national life. . . . Such creatures of passion, disloyalty, and anarchy must be crushed out [and] the hand of our power should be closed over them at once."[8]

Although the president's warnings were most directly targeted at European ethnics living in the East and Midwest, his "hand of power" encircled ethnic Mexicans as well. On March 1, 1917, a month before Wilson's request for a declaration of war, newspapers reported the interception of a telegram from German foreign secretary Arthur Zimmermann to the German ambassador in Mexico. Zimmermann offered Mexico the prospect of regaining New Mexico, Texas, and Arizona in exchange for its joining Germany in war against the United States. The proposal held little interest for Venustiano Carranza's government, and revolutionary Mexico was in any event hardly in a position to threaten its northern neighbor. But by linking Germany with U.S. troubles regarding the Plan de San Diego in south Texas and Pancho Villa's raid in New Mexico, the telegram ensured that many Americans would perceive "Mexicans" as part of Germany's threat.[9]

Ethnic Mexicans were under few illusions as to what this combination of wartime hysteria and nativism spelled for them. "A good many mexicans with their families have been crossing into Mexico," reported an army officer in Brownsville just two weeks after the United States entered the war. "Some of these have been living in Texas for some time, and are reported as being good working people," he added. Thousands more crossed back into Mexico in May and June. Another Brownsville commander attributed the continued flight to "malicious reports that all Mexicans would be drafted into the United States military service, and that a large force of rangers were to be stationed along the border." Though he did not speculate on the source of the rumors, he did state that some fellow officers are "of the opinion that the trouble was brought about by certain malicious persons, with the intention of acquiring the property of these poor and ignorant people for practically nothing."[10]

To many Tejanos, the war mobilization looked suspiciously like the deployment of security forces in the region during the Plan de San Diego. "Since it has been made known to the Mexican population of our border, that the Legislature has passed the law, giving you authority to increase the Ranger force in this State," wrote Starr County tax assessor Adolph Oosterveen to the governor, "we have had an exodus of Mexicans through all border ports, some of them selling their belonging very cheap and others leaving them in charge of their compatriots, fearing that their lives are in danger, expecting (without any foundation) the repetition of what had happened during the bandit raids two years ago." Oosterveen emphasized that Starr County "has never suffered from any raids," but that fear of the Rangers was so great that nevertheless "scores of Mexicans have left and are still leaving, although the military authority, as well as our Sheriff and myself, have explained matters to them but without avail."[11]

For many of those happily unfamiliar with the law-enforcement techniques of the Rangers, the draft alone was reason enough for flight. By mid-June immigration officials were reporting that families from interior Texas were crossing, and in early August a Laredo officer noted that "[t]rains arriving in Nuevo Laredo are bringing large numbers of Mexican laborers from Kansas, New Mexico, and Texas, en route to Mexico for fear of being drafted if they remain in the United States." Like other residents of the United States, many Mexicans found the aims of the war to be too removed from their own lives to be compelling. Besides, they had good reasons to not fight for the United States. As one

Mexican-American soldier recalled, many Mexicans and Tejanos "had enough experience to feel, with just resentment (naturally due to the harsh racial prejudice that they had seen), the small social and political consideration that we had." For those with such bitter experiences of segregation and lynchings, to "speak of symbols, rights, privileges, democracies, . . . to be told to fight for the flag of the Americans" would simply have evoked the response, "That I have to fight for the flag of the gringos—they can defend theirs, and I will defend mine!" This soldier had a particularly vivid memory of one father telling his sons, "You are Mexicans, your country is that of Juárez and Cuahtémoc, and better dead than sign some [draft] registry!"[12]

At the outbreak of war, U.S. law provided that aliens would not be conscripted unless they had begun the naturalization process. Nevertheless, ethnic Mexicans' fear of the draft was well founded. The government mandated the registration of most males of fighting age and in practice did in fact enroll tens of thousands of aliens into the army. In the first draft round, for example, more than 76,000 of the 123,277 immigrants drafted had not taken steps toward naturalization. In any event, the distinction between conscription and registration may have been lost on many Mexicans, and for good reason. An army proclamation directed to "The Mexican Citizens Residing in the States of New Mexico, Arizona, Oklahoma, and Texas" is a good case in point. Although the general who authored it blamed German propaganda for arousing unfounded fears of mass conscription and urged Mexicans to remain at their jobs and homes in the United States, his legal advice for gaining exemption from the draft was hardly reassuring. "All that is necessary for a Mexican Citizen to do to secure exemption," he wrote, "is to establish his Mexican citizenship." Specifically, this meant that "those who can do so should have with them their birth certificate. In the event that this certificate is not at hand, it is suggested that you secure affidavits from two reliable witnesses concerning your birth place or such other evidence as is available."[13]

With the burden of proof squarely on their shoulders, and possessing generally poor documentation and few political connections in the United States, many Mexicans responded to the general's words by voting with their feet. They may well have shared the sentiments articulated by a Mexican woman to her son in an anonymous letter found at the time on the streets of Brownsville. Even if her son could make much more money in the United States, the troubled mother urged him to flee the draft and not return, as "your life is worth more than money."[14]

The process of draft registration in south Texas made the war appear much more like forced labor recruitment than it did the glorious defense of democracy that it was supposed to be. One veteran recalled that, in Duval County, armed Anglos simply went around and rounded up ethnic Mexicans to register them: "[A]t the point of a carbine, like criminal bandits, they were brought walking to sign a registry that they did not understand." Such "registration" looked suspiciously like the violence of the previous two years. As some south Texans had suspected, the Rangers provided good reason for border Mexicans to fear the conscription and registration laws. "[T]here had been a great exodus of Mexicans down there across the river," Canales later recalled, "owing to the fact that these rangers would go into a man's ranch . . . into a man's house and among his laborers and arrest those ignorant Mexicans to get the $50.00 reward for failing to register. . . . [These] citizens of Mexico are scared and will go into Mexico . . . because some of them that have registered can't prove . . . their [place of] birth because of conditions in Mexico[,] where many of the certificates have been destroyed."[15]

Flush with their new powers and the lure of the fifty-dollar bounty, the Rangers went to little trouble to check citizenship documents. In one case, the Rangers' arrest of a young man who lived on a ranch near San Diego appalled an Anglo neighbor, who attempted to help. His status was uncertain, remembered the neighbor, Virginia Yeager, as "he had been examined Friday and it was Sunday afternoon and he wanted to know what they were going to do with him, if he was to be sent immediately or if he was to be permitted to finish his work on this road. . . . [The young man and his mother] did not speak English, and their ranches were near mine, and the local boards did not give them very much encouragement about answering questions." While Yeager was driving him to the local induction center, pursuant to the advice of the county sheriff, Rangers under the command of Captain Sanders stopped the car at a narrow bridge, "came in front of us very quickly . . . and they did not open the door of the car but they took [the young man's] wrists and jerked him over on his head," placing her friend under arrest for the violation of registration provisions. Yeager complained bitterly to the governor about the incident, stating bluntly that the Rangers "terrify the whole SouthWest Tex[as]. That is why 15,000 people had left . . . any of them would go to war but [for] the brutality of these creatures who respect no law nor individual."[16]

Ethnic Mexicans found little more consideration from local draft boards, even though they were run by civilians. The war's arrival found a young man named Gustavo Durán working as stenographer for Canales to support his physically disabled father, his mother, and his five younger brothers. Initially classified 1-A, the most subject to immediate draft, Durán appealed to Canales for help. Canales persuaded the board to put him in Class 3. But several months later, Cameron County agricultural developer C. L. Jessup, the board's chair, reclassified him as Class 1-A, stating that the armed forces needed more men from his district. Durán fled the country, despite Canales's advice to stay and seek employment as a stenographer for the army. The family of Maximiliano

Gonzáles of Martindale, south of Austin, endured a similar ordeal. The local draft board called up both sons, the sole source of support for Maximiliano, a blind seventy-year-old. Despite the family's repeated efforts to secure an exemption for at least one of his sons, both ended up fighting in France. Maximiliano died shortly after their departure, a death that friends attributed to his sons' absence.[17]

Perhaps as a result of such practices, south Texas saw high rates of draft avoidance. According to the Texas adjutant general, by the war's end Cameron County saw over 6,700 registrants, with the 432 men in active service outnumbered by 757 "delinquents and deserters." Webb County reported similar numbers of 225 and 495, respectively.[18]

Resistance, Weakened

As stories spread of the plight of the Gonzáles, Durán, and other families, Tejanos looked for any possible assistance. But who could help? Even their most powerful allies, such as Canales, proved unable to protect those closest to them from the thuggery of the Rangers and the farmer-dominated draft boards. No political party represented their interests, and the mouthpieces of dissent, such as *La Crónica* and *El Progreso,* had been silenced. Fleeing to Mexico or otherwise eluding the draft seemed the only responses available.

That Tejanos had so few options reflected not only the return of the Rangers to south Texas, but also the larger currents of wartime politics. The "hand of power" invoked by Woodrow Wilson held millions of Americans in its grasp, preventing them from challenging the war and its justification. In the rest of Texas, local draft boards often made special efforts to draft African American farm owners so that whites could claim their land. Some black Texans alleged that draft agents impressed as many blacks as they could to avoid drafting whites. The disproportionate percentage of blacks in Texas's conscripts —they comprised 16 percent of the state's population but 25 percent of its draftees—seemed to support his allegation. Black newspapers such as the *Crisis* and *Chicago Defender,* analogous to *La Crónica* and *El Progreso,* loudly criticized such discrimination and urged blacks to escape Jim Crow by moving north. The postal service used the war to justify keeping these publications out of circulation. Central Texas's German community, one of the nation's largest, was also subjected to harassment, intimidation, and occasional violence.[19]

Anglo voices questioning the war were no less immune to persecution, as Texas's agrarian radicals soon discovered. In May, scarcely a month after the declaration of war, Texas Rangers stormed *Rebel* editor Tom Hickey's farm, kidnapping him and holding him incommunicado for two days without filing any charges. The next issue of the *Rebel* damned the government for its actions. It was the last issue of the *Rebel* ever to be published. U.S. postmaster general Albert Sydney Burleson promptly banned the publication from the mail during the war—the first such interdiction in the nation. Burleson held that the paper "breeds disloyalty" with its arguments "that this government is the tool of Wall Street or munitions-makers." Burleson's action may have been less than altruistic, because Hickey had recently criticized him for replacing numerous tenant farmers with convict labor on his four-thousand-acre Texas cotton farm.[20]

If those clearly recognized as Americans—including those whose whiteness and native-born status were beyond question—were so vulnerable, then what could ethnic Mexicans hope for from the U.S. government? The assault on ethnic difference and political dissent seemed to confirm the Flores Magón brothers' dim view of the United States, not the sunny-eyed optimism of the Progressives.

But at the same time, the Magonista hope that a redeemed Mexico could embrace its lost children seemed more and more remote. If Mexicans could expect little from the United States, they couldn't expect much more from their own supposed homeland. Those fleeing the draft, for example, found little help from Mexican authorities. Carranza's government, intent on escaping the cloud of suspicion created by the Zimmermann telegram, often assisted in the enforcement of American draft regulations. "The co-operation of Mexican military commanders . . . with the officials of the United States Department of Justice in the capture of escaping Germans and the return of soldiers who have deserted into Mexico," wrote a U.S. army officer in Laredo, "indicates a strong desire to be on friendly relations with the United States." He approvingly noted that "[n]otwithstanding attempts on the part of those who are taken into custody to bribe their captors to release them, they are promptly turned over to United States officials."[21]

Although rampant brutality and racial chauvinism had pushed many into rebellion not even two years earlier, by 1917 armed struggle held little appeal for even radical ethnic Mexicans in the United States. The leading apostle of such struggle, Ricardo Flores Magón, was rotting in Leavenworth prison, in increasingly poor health. A few years later, knowing that death was upon him, he reflected on the ironies of his position. "My comrades," he wrote, "are now generals, governors, secretaries of State, and some have even been presidents of Mexico. They are rich, famous, and powerful, while I am poor, unknown, sick, almost blind, with a number for a name, marked as a felon." Resigned to his fate yet steadfast in his beliefs, he could not help but conclude that his high expectations for humanity had not borne fruit: "They have been the ant and I the fly; while they have counted dollars, I have wasted time counting the stars. I wanted to make a man of each human animal; they, more practical, have made an animal of each man, and they have made themselves the shepherds of the flock. Nevertheless, I prefer to be a dreamer than a practical man."[22]

Insurrectionists less well known than Flores Magón shared his realistic appraisal. The irredentism of the Plan de San Diego was moribund on its home ground of south Texas. Even those sympathetic to its aims had grown cynical and bitter about the prospects for any such uprising. In August, less than two months after the Webb Station raid and the apparent dissolution of de la Rosa and Pizaña's forces, Bureau of Investigation agent Manuel Sorola went to San Diego itself to see if he could interest likely followers in resuming the uprising. His most sustained discussion took place with Rafael Ramírez, a still-loyal follower of the late Catarino Garza. Sorola described Ramírez as "very anti-American." "I asked him if the men here in San Diego would join in an uprising," Sorola reported. Although he estimated that 90 percent of the men would support such a rebellion in their heart of hearts, Ramírez was certain that even the angriest of Tejanos recognized that their hopes would never be realized. Mentioning the lynching of Ponce and Morin in Kingsville, he told Sorola that "[t]here is no chance, to get anywhere without being caught. I know I've been in the game, nobody can tell me anything about it. . . . I am an old man with experience along this line and I want to advise you. You better drop that idea right now in time to save your life. If this thing leaks out, you are gone."[23]

The former leaders of the Plan de San Diego appeared to share Ramírez's pessimism. Military intelligence officers successfully tracked the whereabouts and activities of de la Rosa, Pizaña, and some of their most loyal followers in November 1916. They concluded that, despite some occasional travel around Matamoros and Monterrey, "the leaders in this movement continued to be inactive." In early December 1916 one officer managed to introduce himself to Basilio Ramos, the man whose arrest some two years before had first brought the Plan to light. "[Ramos] told me that the revolutionary movement, on his opinion, is about to end as everyone is disappointed, and the men could no longer be held together because the leaders were without funds," the agent wrote. In a subsequent conversation in Monterrey several days later, "Ramos stated that, being unable to do anything else, he was going to Laredo to see his family." The next week a former confidant of de la Rosa informed the officer that the Tejano rebel was imprisoned in the barracks in Monterrey under the orders of General Eugenio López. Finally, at the end of December the informant found several of Pizaña's former followers, who told him that "the revolution had completely fallen through; that for a long time they had been held together merely by promises, and [that] in course of time . . . the majority of them had gone their [separate] ways."[24]

The rampant disillusionment of potential rebels did not mean that all was quiet in south Texas. Some raids and thefts did occur after the collapse of de la Rosa and Pizaña's forces. In July 1916, a small party attacked the San Pedro Ranch, which bordered on the Rio Grande itself. The assailants captured an ethnic Mexican inhabitant of the ranch and his son. The two made their escape during a fight between their captors and U.S. soldiers, during which one raider was killed. More than a year later, in June 1918, a small band attacked the Escobas Ranch in southern Zapata County, taking clothing, firearms, a saddle, and some two hundred dollars in cash. The investigating army officer suspected local involvement. October saw two more ranches attacked. J. A. Champion, a rancher of mixed Anglo and Mexican descent, reported that valuable horses and ranch equipment worth more than fifteen hundred dollars were stolen from his Hidalgo County ranch by men whom he believed to be Constitutionalist soldiers. That same month, Mission area rancher T. C. Gill reported that unknown thieves had made off with eight of his most valuable cattle. An attack in December resulted in higher casualties. Four unidentified men held up two Anglo guards carrying the payroll of a Cameron County sugar plantation, killing one of the guards. A cavalry unit soon captured four suspects, injuring two in the process. Several days later the commanding officer received a rumor that local authorities had executed the captured men.[25]

Although the identities of most such raiders were usually completely unknown, army officers sometimes suspected former Sediciosos. This was the case in a December 1917 incident, when a cavalry unit near Harlingen shot at five men attempting to cross the Rio Grande. They killed one of the men, who, an officer stated, "may be one Mariano Casarez, wanted by civil authorities for charged of banditry . . . connected with de la Rosa and Pizaña in their raids of 1915."[26]

Two somewhat larger attacks occurred in March 1918, both apparently involving local Texas-Mexicans. On March 3, a group of about thirteen Tejanos and Mexicans held up a ranch belonging to a man named Tom East about thirty miles from Hebronville. The raiders took over one of the ranch buildings and then waited for the East family, capturing them on their return. They forced East to open his ranch store, from which they removed more than twelve hundred dollars in goods. "The Mexicans could all talk English and said they were Texas Mexicans," East recalled. "We recognized three men in the bunch. They were all young men from 21 to 30 years old. They were very polite to the ladies and did not hurt them in any way, but punched the men around with their guns." Two days later a company of Texas Rangers clashed with the raiders, who had apparently also robbed a nearby ranch in the interim. The Rangers dispersed the band, killing at least two and forcing them to abandon many of their stolen goods. The second incident took place two weeks later, near Brownsville, when more than forty head of cattle were stolen from the Piper Plantation and an adjoining farm. Both the farm's owner and the managers of the Piper Plantation suspected the same group of recently dismissed employees.[27]

These raids were too infrequent, unconnected, and dissimilar to signal the resumption of an organized rebellion. But those familiar with the events of 1915 and 1916 surely recognized a clear pattern in the simultaneous killing and harassment of a number of deputies and collaborators. From October 1916 to January 1918, at least eleven former army scouts or deputy sheriffs were killed, injured, or threatened. Resentment over collaboration with the forces that crushed the Plan de San Diego clearly motivated some of these acts. For example, a party of men identified only as "bandits" broke into Hidalgo County deputy sheriff Amado Cabazas's home and "choked and threatened him until he promised to resign his commission." Similarly, two men, Pilar Rostra and Caustolo Mendoza, identified by an army officer as "two notorious Mexican bandits," shot and wounded former army scout Maximiliano Benavides. Sostenes Saldana, another army scout, may have avoided injury or death by not being home when four former Sediciosos came to his ranch and ransacked his house in search of weapons.[28]

The reasons for other murders were not so clear. Memerto Rosas, Maximiliano García, and Benifacio Gonzáles were also killed by Tejanos during this period, though no media accounts offered explanations. The reasons for the killing of Frank Martin, deputy sheriff and King Ranch foreman, at a party in Raymondville in late November 1917 also remained shrouded. Two Tejano brothers who lived nearby killed Martin at a party, injuring another Anglo deputy in the process. They then fled to Mexico. Although their motives were never known, somebody who was both a deputy and an important operative for the King Ranch would have been an obvious target for those who had supported the Plan or who resented the brutality of its suppression. A federal agent saw enough of a pattern in these events to alert his superiors that "a large number of known and suspected participants in the raids of 1915" were involved in the killings of the former army scouts. Now that the once-fearsome uprising was no longer able to offer hope to even the most disaffected Tejanos, all that remained was a long list of grudges and a small set of assassinations.[29]

Wartime Accommodation and the Progressive Tradition

Some of those who advocated political reform and ethnic heterogeneity anticipated that the harsh "hand of power" that closed over outspoken newspapermen such as Tom Hickey and Emeterio Flores, and that gave the Rangers a renewed license for brutality, could have positive effects as well. Although many reformers, radicals, and intellectuals harbored deep fears about the war from its outset, others tempered their concerns with hopes that the national emergency would provide an opportunity for the expansion of democracy at home. Entering the conflict in Europe, it seemed, could renew a sense of national purpose, give the government enough power and legitimacy to address pressing social problems, and help to justify fighting for freedom at home as well as abroad. "We shall stand committed as never before to the realization of democracy in America," proclaimed the Progressive journalist Walter Lippmann. "We shall turn with fresh interest to our own tyrannies—to our Colorado mines, our autocratic steel industries, our sweatshops and our slums. We shall call that man un-American and no patriot who prates of liberty in Europe and resists it at home."[30]

And perhaps, some leaders of ethnic and racial minorities hoped, the need for unity could lead the country as a whole to address its most marginalized members, to give them something in return for their willingness to sacrifice for the greatest good. African American intellectual and activist W. E. B. DuBois, for example, urged black Americans both to fight for the United States abroad and to "marshal every ounce of our brain and brawn to fight a sterner, longer, more unbending battle against the forces of hell in our own land." Black Texans, particularly returning war veterans, heeded his call and organized new branches of the NAACP to fight racist violence and segregation. Thirty-three branches were founded across the state, with total membership tripling from 1918 to 1919.[31]

Some aspects of the mobilization for war suggested that these hopes— or at least a part of them—might be realized. The federal government and Anglo leaders in Texas wanted to enlist minorities in the war effort. The support of loyal African Americans, German Americans, and other groups, they felt, would reduce draft evasion, marginalize the war's opponents, and avoid disruptive labor strife. Thus, little more than a year after the U.S. entry into the war, the Texas State Council of Defense urged its county organizations to form black auxiliaries. "We think the time has now arrived when you should organize the Negro population of your communities into auxiliary Councils," its memo read. The exigencies of war demanded this inclusion: "It is the purpose of our government to organize every force in the United States and it is therefore apparent that the large negro population in this state should be mobilized and put in a position for work in every line of war activity in which it will be necessary for all people to work together." Of course the government intended such efforts to mute social conflict, especially labor unrest, by monitoring and acculturating subordinate groups. The Texas Council pressed county affiliates to insist on the use of English at all public occasions, making exceptions only for the private conversations of those unable to speak the language.

But this incorporation nevertheless indicated the government's need to secure the loyalty of millions of ethnics.[32]

The government similarly softened its nativist stance when dealing with American soldiers. Nearly a fifth of the U.S. army was foreign-born, and perhaps as many as one in four soldiers could not speak English, so the military had a strong incentive to acknowledge the legitimacy of ethnic pluralism. And it did. English classes, for example, were complemented with translations of rules and regulations and with orders forbidding the use of ethnic slurs. The armed forces made an "attempt at instilling patriotism along with a demonstrated sensitivity and respect for the immigrants' culture."[33]

Tejano Progressives saw opportunities for Texas-Mexicans in the war effort. J. T. Canales served as a "Four-Minute Man," that is, one of the patriotic speakers chosen by prominent community members to rally support for the war. He was the only Hispanic-surnamed speaker out of the fifteen speakers listed as the most popular and most frequently used by the chair of Cameron County's Defense Committee. Canales's numerous speeches in 1917 and 1918 urging ethnic Mexicans to stay in the United States, where their labor was needed to keep the army in the field, may have been part of his role as a Four-Minute Man. Canales also suppressed "disloyalty" on at least one occasion, reporting to authorities that several local priests made statements that he considered pro-German. Clemente Idar did similar work in the Laredo area. He served as the representative of organized labor on the city's community labor board, designed to contribute to the war effort by avoiding strikes and other disruptions. Although apparently not a Four-Minute Man himself, Idar nominated other Tejano orators to support the war effort. He also proposed that such speakers "make a tour of all the Southern States lecturing to Spanish-speaking audiences, so as to perfect the understanding of those people in reference to the great problems of the war and our participation therein." Idar hoped to extend such efforts across the border and thereby gain the support of Mexico as well as ethnic Mexicans in the United States. "I consider the mention of this subject as considerably important," he told a Four-Minute Man organizer. "Mexicans all along the South[ern border] are gradually becoming a useful factor more and more each day and in the Northern States of Mexico, this psychological influence of their own people residing among us, is being more strongly noticeable."[34]

Indeed, many Tejanos embraced the war. Many of Texas's Spanish-language newspapers joined prominent Tejano political figures in supporting the war effort and ran extensive coverage of the experiences of ethnic Mexican soldiers. Tejanos across the state participated in war savings drives. South Texas also saw some Tejanos join the war effort. The Laredo newspaper *Evolución* focused its coverage on the experience of the U.S. armed forces in

Europe—particularly Texas-Mexican soldiers—and portrayed the war as a principled struggle for democracy. Shortly after the declaration of war, Laredo politician Amador Sánchez urged Texas-Mexicans to follow the noble examples of such Mexican heroes as Benito Juárez and Miguel Hidalgo by enlisting in the army. In June 1917, a predominantly Tejano company formed in Brownsville.[35]

J. Luz Saenz offered the most complete and developed view of what the Tejano Progressives hoped to gain by their support of the war. Born in 1888 in the small town of Realitos in Duval County, Luz was the first Tejano male to graduate from high school in the town of Alice. By the time he enlisted in 1918 at age thirty, he had served as a school teacher in various south Texas towns for ten years.[36] Over the course of his service Luz both kept a diary and wrote numerous letters to friends and family. Much of his writing was published in Texas's Spanish-language newspapers at the time, and in 1933 he fulfilled a long-standing ambition to publish a consolidated version of his writings on the war, titled *Los México-Americanos y La Gran Guerra y Su Contingente en Pro de la Democracia, la Humanidad y la Justicia* (The Mexican-Americans and the Great War and Their Contingent in Defense of Democracy, Humanity and Justice).

Luz fervently hoped that the willingness of Mexican Americans to serve in the war would become a weapon in their fight for civil rights. "The opportunity presents itself to fight for the rights of oppressed humanity, to ask for justice for the humiliations and taunts that we so often receive by virtue of carrying the indelible marks of our race. Our intention is to show before the world our dignity as people," he wrote to his wife while traveling to the front for the first time. "[A]s long as the hateful historic and social prejudice in Texas for those of our race will not disappear, our contentment will never be complete," but he nevertheless considered Texas to be his home, and he dismissed as "unmanly" the idea of fleeing "from the state, where I was born and intend to die." He also wrote a letter "To Our Government" to be sent in case of his death. "We always had faith in the good intentions of our government to make all citizens enjoy equal prerogatives," he declared. "[T]here are many towns in Texas where . . . hostility is clearly shown, where we are denied any social consideration and decent schools for the education of our children. . . . Our sacrifice in this campaign is the last gesture of protest against that determined group of wretched citizens who have never been able to uproot [their] racial prejudice against our people."[37]

Luz's hopes for what the war could do for Tejano civil rights embodied much of the prewar thought of the Idars. Like his counterparts in Laredo, he had a nearly religious faith in the transformative potential of education. Unequal education or the outright denial of schooling troubled Luz more than any other aspect of Anglo racism. He described his work as a schoolteacher as a constant battle for the advancement of his people. As he left to enlist in the war he declared to his pupils that "until now I have waged my hard battles for the intellectual advancement of our people with pencil and pen," and he argued that his service in the army was a continuation of that struggle. Like the Idars, Luz could express frustration with fellow Tejanos whom he considered too backward to appreciate the need for education. While in France, Luz informally taught Mexican-American soldiers subjects ranging from writing and English to civics and math. Although some of his students made rapid progress, others, he said, "only come to free themselves from hard military chores. Great is my desire and enthusiasm to introduce new ideas into minds so thick and full of the ideas of the past." Similarly, while traveling through Houston on his return from the war, Luz could not help but observe that the large number of ignorant and slothful Tejanos who resided there reminded him of the pressing need for more racial progress. At the same time, however, he attributed such characteristics to racial discrimination and to Texas's refusal to educate all of its citizens.[38]

Unlike African American soldiers, who served in segregated units that were often relegated to manual labor and construction jobs, Mexican-American soldiers were integrated into the army as a whole. Luz's military service therefore exposed him to a wider range of American citizens than he had previously encountered. He recalled a long conversation with a Polish-American soldier from Minnesota who also took pride in both his American citizenship and his ethnic affiliation. After discussing the hardships faced by Poles in the United States, Luz realized that the other soldier's "fights, his moral sufferings, his hope that his race would find its place among the free peoples of the earth . . . are identical to mine."[39]

Luz's encounter with American Indian soldiers made an even greater impression. Visiting a nearby barracks of a group of these soldiers from Oklahoma, Luz was again struck by their mutual hopes for the war's results. "I soon came to know that their feeling is ours, in regards to their hopes for the future betterment of their people." And not only did both Mexican Americans and American Indians hope that their service would enable them to press their claims for equal treatment, but Luz also thought of himself as an Indian of sorts. "I am an Aztec from head to toe," he declared. Indeed, Luz initially thought that the Indians were Mexicans. When he learned that they were from Oklahoma he commented, "[W]ell, I'm from Texas, but we are the same, right?" Luz found himself drawing an insignia with a capital T and O incorporated into the design to embody "the brave representatives of the Oklahoma Indians and Texan Indians (the Mexican-Americans)." Despite his deep pride in his U.S. citizenship, Luz's writings about the Indian soldiers revealed that he also had an international consciousness that linked him to all Latin Americans. A victory in the war would leave the mountains and valleys of France forever haunted with the memory of "the silhouettes of the Mexican-Americans and the Indians of Oklahoma as the representatives of the aboriginal races of America in their first crusade to the new world in demand of justice."[40]

Despite this hemispheric racial consciousness, Luz's core belief was that his people were destined to become an accepted part of American society. Indeed, he was one of the first—if not *the* first—to regularly use the term *Mexican American* in this sense. He thereby turned his back on Mexican nationalism in a way that the Idars, whose politics were so similar to his own, had not. Where the Idars once thought that the Mexican Revolution held out the chance for Texas-Mexicans to return to a reinvigorated homeland, Luz understood himself as a member of an American ethnic group. Indeed, he speculated that Mexican Americans might someday serve in a war against the Mexican nation. "A war against Mexico," he reflected, "would be the greatest test that the American citizen of Mexican origin could subject himself to." Although Luz admitted that it would be tragic to arrive at such a necessity, he nevertheless emphasized that "to fight against Mexico would be no act of treason" and compared it to the service of American citizens of German descent in his own army unit.[41]

Luz knew that this attitude distinguished him from the many Tejanos who saw the draft as a crude impressment by an oppressive and racist government. His own support for the war did not blind him to the fact that others had very different goals. When an officer threatened to eliminate his classes, he wrote sardonically that "yesterday we were terrible, strong, valiant to rush at the enemy and make him respect the interests of the Morgans, the Mellons, and the Rockefellers, but if we hope to claim something for ourselves, we soon see that any ignorant and ferocious sergeant can quiet us." Luz attributed Mexican-American opposition to the war to the segregation and discrimination that Tejanos faced. He himself frequently encountered such racism in the army, and he felt compelled to distinguish himself from the "slackers" and otherwise "disloyal." The Plan de San Diego was a leading example of such disloyalty. Luz recalled that an Anglo officer pressed him about the details of the Plan. Although Luz told him that he knew nothing of it, the officer proclaimed that "I know these greasers well. We will never get anything out of them. Once a Mexican always a Mexican."[42] If Luz saw himself as an American citizen, others could see him only as a Mexican.

The South Texas Home Front

For the moment, the officer's disparaging sentiments were much more widely shared in J. Luz Saenz's home of south Texas than were the schoolteacher's. That some Tejanos had decided to join the army in the war for democracy did little to change the behavior of the Rangers, who continued to mete out brutal justice to those whom they deemed "disloyal." In September 1918, for example, Sergeant J. J. Edds and several other Rangers arrested Jesús Villareal, constable of the small town of Copita in Duval County. Based on the statements of several young men who had not registered for the draft, Edds suspected Villareal of smuggling draft dodgers to Mexico for money. "[T]hey got hold of me by my throat, mouth, and nose and they held me that way about five minutes," recounted Villareal, who denied the charges filed against him. "They told me to speak. I could not speak on account of my breath was about all out, you know. When I recovered . . . I told him . . . the boys were not going across the river but I was taking them to Roma. Then the cocked pistol was put into my mouth. They told me I would tell the truth or they would kill me." Edds gave a different version of the event, stating that Villareal "denied everything and acted very impudent and had been drinking . . . when we first went to search him he stepped back and when he did I shoved a pistol in his stomach and searched him and when I went and talked to these boys and they admitted that he had assisted to put them across the river we came back and talked to him again and he said that he wasn't no bandit, and ought not to be held up, that he was an officer of the law, that he was a constable of Duval County, and I told him, I said, 'Well, you are a pretty son-of-a-bitch to be constable, taking slackers to the river.'" Several weeks later, Edds killed a man named Lisandro Muñoz at his ranch near Rio Grande City while attempting to arrest another Tejano dodging the draft.[43]

Also reminiscent of the vigilantism of 1915 and 1916 were the swift reprisals against those suspected of property theft. In early April 1918, Rangers arrested Piper Plantation employee Florencio García on suspicion of horse theft, as the Cameron County enterprise's manager had requested. Some six weeks later García's father identified a body with three bullet holes as that of his son. The Rangers, under the command of Captain Charles F. Stephens, stated that they had released García unharmed. Another man, José María Gómez, who had been sought on suspicion of horse theft for more than six months by local law enforcement officers and Rangers, met the same fate. Two men working for a Jim Hogg County rancher apprehended him in September 1918. Captain Edds gave permission to ranch employees to take Gómez to the closest jail, which was in Hebronville. Gómez was found dead the next day. Even some of the Rangers recognized his death clearly as murder. "I believe the man was murdered because his body was found in the middle of the road, hand-cuffed and shot in the back," Ranger captain William Hanson later wrote. "I believe they simply shot him. . . . I further believe that the American citizens including the District Judge, of that District, believe . . . [they] did a good job in killing this man[,] for the District Judge, in the presence of [Ranger] Captain Wright, made such a statement."[44]

If Gómez's death was hauntingly familiar, Tejanos could also recognize something ominously new about this latest round of violence. Previously, those who held land were the most likely to be targeted for harassment, expulsion, or murder. Now, with so many Tejanos having lost their land, the violence seemed designed as a form of management technique to ensure their docility and availability as laborers. In August, for example, local farmers apprehended labor contractors Pedro Tamez and Arturo García near the city of Donna. Authorities jailed the men for speaking of moving to places farther into the United States with higher wages for agricultural work, and for encouraging others to do the same. Rangers and local law officers shot at the two men after they were released from jail, seriously wounding García in the leg. García filed a complaint with the Mexican consul in Brownsville, alleging that local farmers forced him into labor. Consul José Z. Garza, who several years earlier had notified his superiors of Lon Hill's personal campaign of terror, stated that "the Civil Authorities of Donna, Texas, demanded that he lend his services as a laborer in the fields of that district.... [T]he Consul suggested [to García] the advisability of his telling the said authorities that they had no right whatever to act as they did, and respectfully to beg them to let him return to Mercedes, Texas, where he lives. García did so and instead of yielding to his request they abused him for applying to the Consul for his protection, insulting him and speaking in disparaging terms of the Mexican government." Garza made an investigation of such instances and found "many cases of Mexicans who have been detained by the Authorities and compelled to work for much smaller wages than they pay in neighboring towns. All these men have been compelled to flee by night through the woods, as if they were criminals."[45]

The response of Rangers and local farmers to the accusation that they had mistreated Tamez and García confirmed that Valley farmers were resorting to armed force to secure their labor supply. "I find that the farmers in that section have large crops to harvest and they are not permitting anyone to interfere with their laborers," reported Ranger captain Hanson. "I do not believe that any one could be convicted in that county for preventing outsiders from coming in and disturbing their laborers," he concluded. Anglo farmers, according to Hanson, particularly detested contractors who "go into their country and quietly go among their laborers promising them fabulous prices to go somewhere else to work." Sam Bernard, a farmer living near Donna, confirmed Hanson's observations. "[A]bout a week before the detention of Arturo García ... the citizens of this community had a public meeting," Bernard recalled, "and at said meeting it was reported that certain people were in this community, contracting labor for Louisiana and other sections, and from reports received that day, a great many laborers had been shipped out of this country, thereby causing great damage to us and, indirectly, to our government. . . . It was agreed that day that we would not allow these labor contractors to further disturb our labor, or take them out of the country."[46]

The Politics of Disfranchisement

That Anglo farmers were in such dire need of laborers was one of many signs that the Valley's economy, seemingly derailed by the Plan de San Diego, was back in full swing. The cessation of the raids in 1916 and the continuation of high national crop prices returned the Valley's agriculture to boom times. "I never saw such development in my life in any section of Texas. This month there has been over 2,000 substantial farmers from the north in there and the great majority are buying land for actual settlement," noted a Ranger in early 1918.[47] The United States' entry into the war further spurred this settlement, sending grain prices through the roof. At the same time, the advantages of a terrorized labor force became all the more obvious. Tightening national labor markets forced agricultural wages up on plantations across the South. As the draft took nearly half of the nation's railroad workers, and several hundred thousand African Americans left the South for jobs in northern cities, the demand for Mexican workers only rose.[48]

The combination of an agricultural boom and a looming labor shortage led Anglo farmers to take vigorous measures beyond simply securing their supply of local laborers. For one thing, they sought to ensure a reliable stream of continued migration from Mexico. Ironically, this goal led them to oppose the more nativist changes in immigration law of the past few years. The Burnett Immigration Law in May 1917, which provided for a literacy test and an entry fee of eight dollars for all immigrants, was particularly worrisome. To be sure, Texas farmers fully supported the notion that America—particularly in the midst of war!—should not be taken over by a wave of ignorant and illiterate foreigners. But surely the country needed somebody to pick its crops. And so south Texas's new rulers took measures to ensure that the law did not apply to them. Just two weeks after its passage, one farmer wrote to the Texas State Council of Defense to complain. He argued that he was already facing a labor shortage due to the war and that the law would make his hiring of farm laborers even more difficult. The State Council agreed, sending telegrams to President Wilson and to the state's congressmen and senators, "urging the suspension of the Burnett Immigration Law as to the Mexicans and also advising the Mexicans that no conscription will be had as to them." Bowing to such pressure from agribusiness, the Wilson administration soon announced the relaxation of the law for Mexican immigrants, with the proviso that they could be employed only in agricultural labor.[49]

Valley farmers were even more adamant that local politics be shaped to their desires. That meant, above all, the end of the machine and its shameful reliance on the "Mexican" vote. A few years earlier, the threat of the Plan de San Diego had led to a temporary truce between newcomer farmers and the machine. But now that there was no concerted uprising, the old splits and rivalries resumed. This time, however, insurgent politicians could count on a new and powerful ally: the state government and its military arm, the Ranger force. William Hobby's 1917 ascension to the governorship after the impeachment of Jim Ferguson meant a decline in the statewide power of machine boss James Wells, who had remained a Ferguson supporter.

The results of this change in the power structure were not long in coming. The state legislature soon passed several measures to reduce the rate of Hispanic voting. Election judges were banned from assisting voters who had been citizens for less than twenty-one years in casting their ballots, and those immigrants who had applied for citizenship were no longer eligible to vote in primary elections. The first measure effectively stripped illiterate Mexican Americans of the vote—but not their Anglo counterparts, the vast majority of whom had been citizens all their lives—and the second prevented the machine from recruiting Mexican immigrants.[50]

The new governor also used the wartime mobilization against the machine. The war substantially expanded the Ranger force. Regularly appointed Rangers increased from seventy-three to more than one hundred and thirty, and legislation allowed the governor to appoint three "Loyalty Rangers" in each county to monitor "disloyal" activity. The reinvigorated Ranger service became one of Hobby's primary tools to defeat the machine. When his boss faced a challenge in the 1918 primary, Hobby loyalist William Hanson, now the Ranger force's inspector-general, threw the power of his position into the campaign. He urged that every Loyalty Ranger "be given a bunch of Hobby literature for distribution and that a letter be addressed to each one of them asking their opinion as to whether Governor Hobby will carry that county and further asking them for a full report of the county and their opinion as to how is the best way to carry it in case it is doubtful. There is nothing like keeping these men actively in the harness for the next thirty days."[51]

Hanson was quite serious about using the Rangers as campaigners. In August 1918, the captain of one of the Ranger companies informed the adjutant general that he had fired one man and suspended another for their insufficient support of Governor Hobby. "I have another man in my Company whom I suspicion of not being true to Gov. Hobby and I intend letting him out as soon as I can get a good man to replace him," he added.[52]

In south Texas, Tejanos experienced this politicization of the Rangers as an unprecedented assault on their voting rights during the elections of 1918.

In J. Luz Saenz's hometown of Alice, for example, the Rangers succeeded in cutting the total number of votes cast from some three hundred in the primary to only sixty-five. "The former large number of Mexicans who have voted in previous elections was conspicuous by their absence. They did not congregate at the polls, but up town they gathered in small groups and discussed among themselves this new thing of being watched by Rangers," one observer noted. "The town of San Diego was absolutely quiet throughout the day. It was the first time in the history of Duval County, as expressed by several Americans, that the town had not been run by Mexicans on election day," he added.[53]

As the Alice and San Diego elections suggested, in south Texas the Ranger force's new politics spelled a heightened level of harassment of politically active Tejanos. Outspoken leaders such as Emeterio Flores were not the only ones subjected to this treatment; any aspect of Tejano political representation was now a target. In 1918, Rangers disarmed numerous Tejanos living near the segregationist bastions of Lyford and Harlingen. They "took their guns away from them and went in their houses at night and scared the women-folks to death," one observer commented. Rangers were especially adamant about disarming and humiliating Tejano elected officials. Cameron County deputy sheriff W. T. Vann recalled a frightened deputy constable from Santa Maria who came to him after such an experience. "He said he had come down the road that day with his pistol on," Vann stated. "I knew he had been elected and qualified as a constable. He said he had met Captain Stephens and his men, and they had threatened him with violence." Similarly, Lyford area deputy sheriff Octaviano Narvaes reported that Rangers had hanged him by the neck twice during this time period.[54]

Deputy Sheriff Pedro Lerma, who had served as a scout for the army during the uprising, had similar complaints. Vann testified that "[h]e came to me very much worked up and told me that [while] he had been absent from home . . . some of Stephens' Rangers had come there and frightened his wife and daughters to death, went all through the house, broke open trunks and searched them and the room, and had taken away a lot of old firearms he had there . . . he wanted to know why he was treated so and wanted to know if I could not get the arms back and have it stopped." Santavo Tijerino, a relative of Canales, had a parallel experience with Rangers who arrested him while he was looking for his stolen cattle. Canales recalled that he told the Rangers "who he was and who his relatives were, and he was cursed and every relative that he mentioned were cursed. . . . [Tijerino] asked me to get him a passport so as to go into Mexico with his family, but he was born and raised here, his brothers and all the family lived here. I says, 'No, that is not good for you to do.' He says 'I believe those men mean to kill me.'"[55]

The Tejano deputies who complained to Vann and to Wells about their treatment frantically attempted to invoke the social accommodation that they had grown up with: "bad" Mexicans would get what they had coming, but those who understood south Texas surely had nothing to fear. If some of their kinsmen had turned against the machine, seeking either to overthrow it by violence or to replace it with a party of modernizing Tejanos, then had they not kept the faith with honorable men such as Wells? Had they not resisted the appeal of Progressives such as the Idars, and did they not help to crush the Sediciosos' rebellion? Surely they deserved more than to be cursed, disarmed, and spat upon.

Anglo machine leaders agreed and did their best to uphold their end of this old social bargain. Back in 1915 and 1916, Vann had privately objected to the lynchings of Tejanos. This time he went on the offensive. He arrested three Rangers—George Saddler, John Sitre, and A. P. Lock—for the murder of Florencio García, releasing them only after they had posted bond of three thousand dollars. He threatened to charge Anglos involved in the seizure of weapons with theft, telling one man that "you have no right whatsoever to go into those people's houses and take their guns, no more that you would have to take their money." Vann told Ranger captain Hanson that he would cooperate with Rangers only if they stopped their campaign of arbitrary detention and arrest. James Wells himself intervened, calling Hanson and several Ranger captains to his home to protest that they had been harassing and disarming Tejanos loyal to him.[56]

The Ranger force, which had once obeyed Wells's commands, showed no interest in honoring the commitments of the machine to its Tejano constituents. "I stated to [Wells] that the Rangers were disarming some of these suspicious Mexicans for the welfare and safety of the people," wrote Ranger captain Stephens. The practice of ethnic Mexicans holding office was simply unacceptable, as all intelligent white people had learned during the Plan de San Diego: "Judge Wells claimed that these were good Mexicans. I stated to him that all the serious raids that were made on the border were made by Mexicans mostly residents of Cameron Co. and most of the leaders of these raids were at one time either deputy sheriffs, policemen or some other kind of officers of Cameron County or Brownsville." Rangers mobilized their local supporters, the segregation-minded farmers intent on ending machine rule, to apply political pressure against Vann and Wells. Hanson met with prominent citizens of Brownsville and encouraged them to pressure Vann to end resistance to the Rangers. "They have an engagement with Sheriff Vann this afternoon," Hanson said, "and they are going to tell him just where to get off, and serve notice on him that he must get in line or they will not support him."[57]

Ultimately, Hanson's men were reined in, and their actions in 1918 never reached the level of savagery exhibited at the height of the uprising. But it was not self-restraint, nor the continued ability of Wells and Vann to live up to their commitments to Tejanos, that was at work. The only effective check on racial violence came instead from the farmers whose labor needs lay behind the resurgence of vigilantism. Still unhappy with what they perceived as a labor shortage, some farmers began to worry that the heavy hand of the Rangers contributed to their difficulties. Workers could still slink off in the night, slipping north or back into Mexico, or simply avoid the region altogether. If there was such a thing as being too nice to field hands, then it seemed that there was also such a thing as being too hard on them. Canales played on these fears, warning that a major exodus of Mexican laborers would occur unless one of the Ranger captains was replaced. Captain Hanson reported similar pressure, wiring to the adjutant general in late August that "[e]xodus of laborers on account of draft and other conditions very serious this section. . . . Am requested to attend meetings over county to reassure Mexican laborers of protection by Rangers and that no drastic treatment so long as they are right." Soon several Ranger captains found themselves addressing crowds of Mexicans across the Valley, promising good treatment if they remained in the area as laborers.[58]

Tejanos had hit the bottom of the Valley's new social order. They had not realized the ambitions of the Progressives or Sediciosos, nor even maintained their old power, but rather they only had the right to whatever treatment would keep them working in the fields that had once belonged to them.

The Canales Hearings

The split between the south Texas machine and the Hobby administration entangled the only systematic effort to hold the Rangers accountable for their actions from 1915 to 1918. In early 1919, state representative Canales abandoned his prior hopes that discreet back-channel communications could protect south Texans from the Rangers. Appalled by the force's wanton murder spree in 1915 and 1916, Canales initially opposed another appropriation for the Ranger force, but he withdrew his opposition when then-Governor Ferguson appealed to him to support the Rangers as a wartime exigency. Canales recalled the governor telling him, "We are just entering into war, I have reliable information that the Germans are making propaganda on the other side among Mexicans, you are an American citizen and I appeal to you as an American citizen not to make that fight, because it will imperil the property and the liberties of American citizens, but I will give you my word of honor, I will remove whatever undesirable men."[59]

After Ferguson's 1917 impeachment, Canales hoped that Governor Hobby would prevent further violence by disciplining or removing the worse Rangers. Indeed, as late as September 1918, Canales went so far as to laud Hobby's reform efforts publicly and express his confidence that he was improv-

Formal portrait of Representative José Tomás Canales for the 1919 Texas state legislative session. Courtesy of the Texas State Preservation Board.

ing the Ranger force. But the disarming and harassment of Tejano deputies and the killings of Florencio García and José María Gómez prompted Canales to turn on the Rangers with a vengeance. At the start of a new legislative session in early 1919 he introduced legislation that would have drastically altered the Ranger force. His bill provided for the elimination of the Loyalty Ranger positions and the reduction of the regular force to twenty-four men in ordinary circumstances and eighty during a declared emergency. It placed numerous checks on the remaining Rangers, who would be required to have two years of experience as law officers and to show proof from their local counties of a law-abiding past. They would also have to post a heavy bond (five thousand dollars for privates, fifteen thousand dollars for captains) to guarantee their good conduct. Moreover, the bill would subordinate Rangers to local officials. Rangers would have to deliver prisoners to the county sheriff and would be dismissed if the sheriff, county judge, or county commissioners filed complaints of maltreatment of prisoners. They would also be liable for civil suits for any abuse of their authority. In short, the bill provided the sort of state authority and local power that Tejanos might be able to secure to ensure that the previous four years of terror would never be repeated.[60]

The discussion of Canales's bill turned into a wide-ranging investigation of the Ranger force's conduct since 1915. In a series of hearings before a joint committee of state house and senate members, Canales filed nineteen charges against the Rangers and their superiors in the adjutant general's office. All of the charges related to conduct since Hobby became governor in 1917, although witnesses discussed many of the killings that occurred in 1915 and 1916. He charged Ranger inspector-general William Hanson and Adjutant General James Harley with covering up Ranger crimes and with using the force as a political tool. The hearings lasted for weeks, generating several dramatic confrontations and a transcript of some sixteen hundred pages. Numerous witnesses offered detailed evidence of dozens of instances of killings, torture, and harassment.[61]

Canales must have hoped that these hearings would bring a decisive showdown with the Ranger force and its backers in state government. For nearly four years, these men had cloaked themselves in the majesty of the law as they brought down a reign of terror on his homeland. Not only had their brutality spearheaded the unprecedented assault on his people's power, prestige, and very safety, but it had also exposed his own weaknesses to others and, perhaps, even to himself. Canales was born into power, surrounded since childhood by family friends, relatives, and admirers who looked to him for favors when times were good and who depended on him for protection when times were bad. He had what he needed—land, wealth, political connections—to meet these high expectations. What he was born into he then stamped with his own mark. Where others would have rested content with their status as local gentry, Canales had made himself into a beloved leader, a charismatic figure who both embodied and spoke for the goals of economic prosperity, cultural self-confidence, and political power. He had been powerful and smart enough to make even the Texas state political establishment respect his voice. And so his inability to curtail the Rangers not only refuted his political philosophy, it also threatened the self-image he had created. Passage of his bill would not only prevent a repeat of the Rangers' criminal rampage, it would also confirm that his public life was not in vain.

Canales faced formidable obstacles, and perhaps his familiarity and ease with power made him underestimate just how daunting they were. Governor Hobby and the directors of the Ranger force who served him had just as much at stake. They fought Canales tooth and nail not only because they were emotionally invested in the Ranger force, or because his bill would have prevented its future use to crush political dissidents, but they also believed that its implementation might well end their political careers. Hobby was in the midst of a fight with the partisans of former Governor James Ferguson for control of the Democratic Party—and thus of the state's government, since the Republican Party was an empty shell. The Ranger force was one of Hobby's principal advantages in this conflict. In south Texas the previous fall, in a closely watched state senate race between machine captain (and Ferguson supporter) Archie Parr and insurgent leader (and Hobby supporter) D. W. Glasscock, Hobby used the Rangers to reduce voting in Parr strongholds. The strategy seemed effective: the number of votes plummeted from the primary, when no Rangers were deployed, to the general election: from 1,366 to 843 in Hidalgo County, 865 to 499 in Nueces, 909 to 401 in Cameron, and 1,303 to 226 in Duval. In turn, Parr and Wells resorted to fraud of their own, discarding Glasscock ballots because of small misspellings of his name or other technicalities. The machine declared Parr the victor. Glasscock, backed by Governor Hobby, took his challenge to the state legislature, which began hearing the matter as Canales's investigation of the Rangers got under way.[62]

The timing of Canales's charges left him vulnerable to the allegation that he was merely protecting Jim Wells's machine. Their content put him at odds with the self-conception of much of Anglo Texas. The Rangers were not a mere state bureaucracy like the land office or the education board, or even just an important police force. They were an embodiment of the virtues of a tough frontier people who had carved out a place for their civilization, fighting every step of the way. It was one thing to find a few uncontrollable or needlessly brutal Rangers and dismiss them and condemn their excesses; it was another thing altogether to hamstring the entire force. Texas was a conquered land, many of those who spoke against Canales's measure asserted. Having been taken by force from Indians and Mexicans, it still had to be protected from them. The "three great monuments to Texas liberty" had to be remembered, insisted one representative from the Panhandle. The first was the "sacred" Alamo, "where Texas proved to the world that liberty was to be prized more dearly than life." Closely related was the battleground of San Jacinto, where the Texas army snatched freedom from the claws of Mexico with the battle cry "Remember the Alamo, Remember Goliad!" (The "palsied followers" of General Santa Anna, the legislator informed his colleagues, "fell prone on their faces with the cry, 'Me no Alamo, me no Goliad!'") The third was "a living monument so far as Mexican banditry is concerned . . . and it is nothing other than the brave, gallant, dashing and courageous Ranger organization!" The racial solidarity that underpinned this variety of Texas nationalism called for Anglos to set aside their petty factionalism in the face of a shared threat, much as their counterparts in the Valley had done in the midst of the Plan de San Diego uprising.[63]

The fact that Canales himself was a "Mexican" became a critical feature of the hearings, implicit in most of the discussion of his charges and often explicitly invoked by his opponents. The counsel for the Ranger force pressed Canales on his background, resulting in the following exchange:

"Now, Mr. Canales, you are by blood a Mexican, are you not?"
"I am not a Mexican, I am an American citizen."
"By blood?"
"Well, Mexican, you may call it, that's true, a Texas Mexican."

The counsel used the exchange to impugn Canales's loyalty. Because he was a Mexican, the lawyer argued, Canales could not see the matter clearly: "There is a saying that blood is thicker than water, and Mr. Canales has stated on the stand that he had a number of influential clients [and relatives] on the other side [of the border] through whom he could receive information. . . . I think it would have some influence upon the ordinary human mind as to whether unconsciously—I am not accusing the gentleman of consciously having motives that are not worthy—but I say that might unconsciously influence him in this matter." The defenders of the Rangers also pressed Canales on his own family's stance on the war, forcing him to admit that some of his relatives had fled to Mexico to avoid the draft.[64]

Canales's position was not entirely untenable, however. The crimes of the Rangers were just too outrageous to defend openly, and the adjutant general, who was the force's commanding officer, admitted that he had been forced to dismiss many of the authors of the most egregious. Canales found some support among his fellow legislators, including populist Anglos who resented the use of the Rangers to break strikes and disrupt political meetings of farmers and workers. Canales's reputation, record of legislative accomplishment, and cultivation of personal ties in his previous three terms in office all helped.

At critical points in the hearings, however, the usually brilliant and supremely self-assured lawyer from Brownsville faltered and seemed unsure of himself. He often appeared flustered and uncertain of where to direct his deep anger for how he had been treated, and of how to hold murderers and their commanders responsible for their crimes without descending into ad hominem attacks that would only discredit him. Canales failed to call key witnesses, and his occasional discourses on previous Rangers whom he had respected and aided were at best unconvincing, and at worse they undermined his call for a fundamental restructuring of the Ranger force.[65]

Perhaps Canales sometimes appeared uncomfortable partly because more was at stake than just his bill, or even his personal sense of achievement or his thirst for justice. Although he was a wealthy landowner, a respected member of the Tejano elite, and a state representative, Canales risked his life when he turned against the Rangers. In December, as he pressed the adjutant general, Canales encountered Ranger Frank Hamer in San Benito. When the hulking Ranger—Hamer's six-foot, three-inch frame gracefully supported his muscular two hundred and thirty pound body—commanded "Come here!" to the Brownsville state representative, he was already a legend in the making. His reputation as "The Angel of Death" in Texas was already well established, though it would not be until the 1920s, when he tracked Clyde Barrow and Bonnie Parker to their Louisiana hideout, resulting in the battle that cost the famous outlaws their lives, that Hamer achieved national fame.[66]

Hamer clearly had it in for the little man who challenged the Rangers. In front of a witness, he confronted Canales, cursing him for accusing the Rangers of brutality. "You are hot-footing it here, between here and Austin and complaining to the Governor and the Adjutant General about the Rangers," Canales recalled Hamer saying to him, "and I am going to tell you if you don't stop that you are going to get hurt." A shaken Canales asked Sheriff Vann for counsel. "My advice to you is, take a double-barreled shot-gun and I will give you a man and go over there and kill that man [Hamer]," an angry Vann suggested. "No jury would ever convict you for that." Canales declined to take such action, instead writing to Governor Hobby to recount the incident and ask for protection. Hamer nonetheless continued to stalk Canales, following him through the streets of Austin shortly before the hearings began. Canales family lore has it that his wife and a handful of friends in the legislature—including Lyndon Johnson's father—were careful to walk in front of him on the grounds of the state capitol so that he would be a more difficult target for assassination. Years later Canales wrote that his investigation "nearly cost my life."[67]

The governor's office and the state legislature crushed Canales's hopes for a drastic restructuring of the Ranger force. The committee approved a much weaker bill for the consideration of the entire legislature, one that reduced the size of the force but allowed the governor to expand it significantly in the event of an emergency. The revised version lacked Canales's provisions for bonding and local control. The committee did find that the Rangers broke the law repeatedly and engaged in unwarranted violence, concluding that "the Rangers have become guilty of, and are responsible for, the gross violation of both civil and criminal laws of the state." That was an unprecedented admission, but the committee softened it by also exonerating Harley and Hanson and praising their leadership of the Ranger force. Canales urged the House not to adopt the committee's report but lost by a vote of eighty-seven to ten.[68]

Captain Hanson declared "Vindication complete" in a telegram to a supporter, but the matter was not quite so simple. Though unsuccessful in passing his bill, Canales did put Governor Hobby and the leaders of the Rangers on the defensive, raising the prospect that further outrages might erode the force's political support. Shortly after the hearings, the adjutant general canceled the appointments of almost all of the Special Rangers "[o]n account of the serious objection made against Special Rangers by the Ranger Investigation Committee and other members of the Legislature." This step, and the disbanding of several companies of regular Rangers, suggested to some of the Ranger force's staunchest supporters that Canales had won something of a victory. "I went to Austin and untangled the fangs of Venustiano Canales from around your neck," wrote west Texas congressman Claude Hudspeth to the adjutant general, "and yet you fired all of your best captains, which included my friends."[69] Finally, the hearings' content reflected so poorly on the Rangers that the state house of representatives refused to print the transcripts, keeping them off-limits until the 1970s and thereby helping to bury the crimes that they so graphically documented.[70]

Any satisfaction that Canales derived from the new restrictions placed on the Rangers must have been tempered by fury at the treatment he had received. He defended his nation against the Plan de San Diego and pro-German conspirators, but when he turned to defend Tejanos against their fellow citizens, he learned that he may have just as well been another disloyal or rebellious Mexican. If a prominent, wealthy, powerful sitting member of the Texas House of Representatives was nothing more than the "greaser from Brownsville" to a legislative colleague, and could be stalked and threatened by employees of his own government, then what hope for decent treatment from the state could ordinary citizens of Mexican descent expect? With the machine in shambles, the Progressives in disarray, and the Sediciosos vanquished, there was no clear answer.

7
Legacies

J. T. Canales never returned to the state legislature. When his term ended in 1920, he returned to Brownsville and never again sought political office. No Mexican American would sit in the legislature again until 1956, when San Antonio voters sent future U.S. congressman Henry B. Gonzáles to the statehouse in Austin. Canales's withdrawal from electoral politics after the humiliation of the Ranger hearings seemed to fulfill a prophecy made at the start of the decade. "The newcomers," wrote the Idars in 1910, with their "new ideas, resources and lofty ambitions, will not hesitate to fleece us ... of the representation that we have collectively exercised for many years."[1]

By the 1920s, it was all too obvious to Canales and other Progressives that their people had indeed been fleeced. They watched with amazement as Anglo farmers resumed pouring into south Texas, as early as the 1916 hiatus in the uprising. Despite the killing of hundreds, possibly thousands, and the flight of so many more, the Valley resumed its growth, burying the signs of war under an avalanche of new farms and towns. At least ten thousand people moved to Cameron County between 1910 and 1920, increasing its population to thirty-seven thousand. More than twice as many came to Hidalgo County, meaning that almost two-thirds of its 1920 population of thirty-eight thousand were recent immigrants. These new arrivals—joined by Mexican immigrants, who accounted for more than a third of Hidalgo County residents and nearly a quarter of Cameron County's—made the Valley literally bloom. They cleared thousands more acres of chaparral and planted huge citrus orchards, cotton fields, and seemingly infinite rows of vegetables. As the backers of the railroad had intended, this was a modern and profitable business. The total value of farm property in Cameron County nearly tripled, and Hidalgo County's more than quadrupled. By 1924 Hidalgo County had become the highest-producing agricultural county in the nation, annually shipping more than $2 million in vegetables and fruits and $8 million in cotton.[2]

The defeat of the Plan de San Diego, which Canales welcomed, made all of this possible. For a brief time, it seemed that the rebellion would bring the region's growth to a screeching halt. The flight of Anglo farmers in 1915 and the fear of new raids a year later created significant cash flow problems for many land developers, threatening the land business that lay at the heart of the agricultural boom. James Wells, for example, found himself so behind on taxes and interest payments that he was forced to sell more than ninety thousand acres at a sharp loss. This move did not wipe out his debt, and he was threatened with bankruptcy until he died. Under such circumstances, the provisioning needs and spending money of the thousands of newly arrived soldiers were a godsend. P. E. Montgomery, then a small merchant in McAllen, recalled that the town "had been struggling along as best it could trying to forge ahead and grow into a city" when the soldiers' arrival inaugurated a boom "which might appropriately be designated as McAllen's Second Advent, or Birth of a Municipality. . . . The citizenship was outnumbered, ten to one, by the soldiery, and business establishments of every kind were swamped," he wrote. After the boom, "McAllen had grown to pretentious proportions and was launched on its way to its destined place in the sun." Not only did the soldiers' capital help revive the region's economy, but many of them also chose to stay and settle in the Valley. "Few of them came in contact with bandits but many fell in love with the country," stated the *Valley Morning Star* in commemoration of a forty-year reunion of servicemen sent to south Texas. "Cold, snowy winters never came and when they were mustered out they returned to the Valley in goodly numbers."[3]

Although Canales and the Idars had fervently hoped that agricultural modernization would help lead their people out of ignorance and backwardness, they instead had to face the bitter fact that the rulers of this agricultural empire wanted "Mexicans" as farm labor and nothing else. They had staunchly opposed the rebellion, but in hindsight it seemed that the defeat of the Plan de San Diego was the prologue for the wider erasure of Tejano power.

In the first place, the resumption of the farm boom toppled James Wells's machine. Anglo farmers who came after the uprising supported the Independent Party and other anti-machine forces. At the same time, Mexican immigrants were of little help to Wells and his compatriots. These arrivals generally worked in agriculture, lived on the road for much of the year, and did not have the long-standing patron-client ties that the machine relied on to deliver its vote. By 1920, the machine was doomed. Anglo voters, according to one account, "outnumbered the ring-controlled Hispanic voters by a majority of almost two to one." Wells lost most of his political power that year, failing to deliver the Valley for his preferred gubernatorial candidate and reelecting only four of thirteen major Cameron County office holders. He bitterly attributed his defeat to "the fact that the 'Snow Diggers' [newcomers from the Midwest] are in the majority, and fast increasing."[4]

The Progressives shed no tears for the machine itself. It had appealed to what they considered the worse aspects of Tejano culture—ignorance of the wider world, contentment with second-class status, and a near abject dependence on powerful Anglos. But the machine at least had a place for Tejanos; the same could not be said for the Valley's new rulers. Having toppled Wells, they subsequently used the poll tax, whites-only primaries, and other mechanisms to disfranchise Tejanos across much of south Texas. Whatever hopes the Progressives still harbored for Tejano revitalization—the dream that their people would progress along with the rest of the region, exchange their superstitions for modern education, and elect their own best and brightest to high office—ran headlong into their utter lack of political power.[5]

And it was worse than that. Canales and his compatriots watched the farmers create a virtual caste system, with "Mexicans" at the bottom. All that they had seen done to blacks and ethnic Mexicans in the rest of the state came to their own homeland. The signs of white supremacy were unmistakable. Klansmen paraded through Valley towns in the 1920s, and pro-Klan candidates for local and state offices easily carried Cameron County by large margins. Signs reading "No Mexicans Allowed" dotted numerous restaurants and other public accommodations. The Valley's new rulers thought it an indignity to send their children to school with ethnic Mexicans, so by 1930 some 90 percent of the region's school districts maintained separate facilities for "Mexicans" and whites.[6]

What particularly rankled Canales and others who had such faith in the benefits of economic progress was the modern look of segregation. It was not the heavy hand of the past that held them back, but the ambitions of the Valley's most educated and most energetic Anglos. The caste system became particularly rigid in the new towns given life by the agricultural boom, most of which had separate Mexican and Anglo quarters, often divided by the railroad tracks.

"American" and "Mexican" schools (above and below, respectively) in south Texas in the late 1920s. (Taylor, *American-Mexican Frontier*)

The towns along Highway 83—Weslaco, Donna, San Juan, Pharr, Mission, Mercedes—and the now-booming McAllen were among the first to implement school segregation. Some town governments used their legal powers explicitly to create and enforce segregation. Weslaco, for example, mandated that Anglos live and run their businesses south of the railroad, while heavier industry, warehouses, and ethnic Mexican residents and businesses were to be situated to the north. In other towns, such as McAllen, unspoken practices by real estate agents and land development companies yielded similar outcomes. As a result, these municipalities skimped on basic public services such as roads and sewers in the Mexican areas. Moreover, ethnic Mexicans were not welcome in such common areas as public swimming pools. Pharr resident Dellos Buckner's

1929 description of Anglo-Mexican relations revealed how much had changed since the railroad's arrival. "There is little culture in common with the two nationalities, therefore, they have but little social relationship," he wrote. "Communication between the two groups is very meager. Since they are economically segregated they have become socially segregated also."[7]

The wealthiest, lightest-skinned, and most influential of ethnic Mexicans could avoid some of this caste system. Much as they had forged alliances with incoming Anglos in the preceding generations, these elite Tejanos continued to enjoy social prestige and access to the Anglo-dominated world. In McAllen, for example, more than a dozen ethnic Mexican families lived in an exclusive and wealthy Anglo neighborhood in the 1940s. Such elite families were often able to send their children to Anglo schools, though not without some controversy. "It was not with little criticism that the school authorities of the Rio Grande Valley towns finally succeeded in educating the public enough so that some Mexicans were allowed to the American schools," Buckner remembered.[8]

There were other limits to south Texas's version of apartheid. In general, less-rigid segregation characterized cities such as Brownsville and Laredo, where ethnic Mexicans of all classes lived and where the interests of Anglo merchants in selling goods to "Mexican" customers ran at counterpurposes to the farmers' obsession with a controlled and cheap labor supply. While Tejanos living in the heavily agricultural areas that now dominated the south Texas economy were confronted with the most rigid segregation, those living in the now-peripheral ranching counties faced fewer indignities. Still more heavily Hispanic, the counties of Webb, Duval, Starr, and Zapata maintained unsegregated (if second-rate) rural schools. Beyond south Texas, the state's Anglo rulers were certainly not hospitable to those of Mexican descent, but neither were they as obsessed with their subordination as they were with keeping African Americans under the strictures of Jim Crow. For example, several dozen Mexican Americans from the Valley attended the University of Texas at Austin in 1930, a time when the state completely excluded African Americans from the university.[9]

Mexican American Politics in the Face of Segregation

If there were chinks in the armor of white supremacy, then most ethnic Mexicans were not in a position to appreciate them. They instead lived with the constant humiliations and absurdities of segregation. Even those who risked their lives fighting for their country were denied service at white funeral parlors and turned away from white cemeteries.

What could be done to combat such awful treatment? Just as they had done before the Plan de San Diego, Tejanos and Mexican immigrants debated this question. Cozying up to friendly Anglos, trading loyalty and service as a maid, field hand, or nanny for protection and something resembling economic security could work for some, but the larger incarnation of this strategy, the Democratic machine, was no longer powerful enough to offer such a bargain to many. And it certainly wasn't willing to openly challenge the racial chauvinism that lay behind the new segregation. Armed rebellion was out of the question —the spectacular failure of the Plan de San Diego made that all too clear. The Tejano Progressives' hope for a political and cultural revitalization appeared similarly out of reach. The indifference of the Mexican government, demonstrated so convincingly when it did nothing to stop the slaughter of 1915–16, denied them whatever protection that it might have been able to provide. The society north of the river was even worse. How could ethnic Mexicans expect education and prosperity when they were shunted into decrepit one-room schoolhouses and hired only for the most menial of positions?

There was no obvious answer to these questions, no clear way out of the maze of white supremacy. Perhaps the most appealing option was to avoid addressing them, to decline to grope for whatever solution might exist to such an intractable problem. Most ethnic Mexicans thus responded to segregation not so much by fighting it as by choosing to have as little as possible to do with the Anglos who so despised them. If they had to work for an Anglo farm owner, at least their co-workers were other Tejanos or Mexican immigrants, likely as not from their own family. If they couldn't send their children to a decent school, one where they would not be humiliated or beaten for speaking Spanish, then there were other ways for them to learn what they needed to navigate the world. They would be fine knowing only Spanish and would probably learn more about their history and culture by talking to a grandparent or family friend than from listening to a hostile and ignorant teacher. School authorities never enforced truancy rules for ethnic Mexican children vigorously, so parents could actually spend most of each day with their children, watching over them, working alongside them, following the harvest northward with the spring and summer. If a person didn't want to sit in the decrepit "Mexican" section of the theaters to watch a movie or hear a music recital, then his family or labor camp had its own bands and hosted its own dances. The chronic shortage of money was more difficult to finesse, but even here people could rely on their family and larger community, which could provide support when jobs were scarce. Some had special knowledge of medicine and herbs to help endure illnesses, and all would pitch in to make sure that a wedding or a funeral was a dignified affair. In short, if you stayed in Texas, especially in south Texas, you could live in a world inhabited, if not controlled, by people who were like you and who actually showed you respect.[10]

This strategy had its own shortcomings, however. Those who yearned to escape the never-ending drudgery of the fields, or low-level clerical jobs, needed more education than most of their schools would provide. A mother who hoped that her children would grow up to become lawyers or doctors —not to mention teachers or pharmacists—knew that somehow they had to get into college. People who couldn't stomach signs that read "No Mexicans Allowed" had to think of a way to make Anglos take them down. The vast majority who found their wages inadequate contemplated ways to make their employers raise them.

Some kind of political activity—agitating or suing the state for better schools, challenging segregation in the courts or the streets, or improving working conditions—was thus necessary for Tejanos and Mexican immigrants alike if they wanted to better their position. Those who chose formal politics had to grapple with the new and more virulent segregation. But at least they could draw on an old political culture. In 1921, eight Tejano men on a camping excursion near San Antonio decided to found an organization to advance the interests of Texas-Mexicans and established the Order Sons of America (OSA). Those who had avidly read *La Crónica* and followed the successes of leaders such as Canales easily recognized the mark of Tejano Progressivism in the new organization's purposes and outlooks, perhaps because J. Luz Saenz was one of the founders. Much as the 1911 Primer Congreso Mexicanista had drawn on fraternal and mutual aid societies, so too did the OSA offer straightforward economic benefits such as life insurance. But its orientation was forthrightly political. The organization worked to oppose the segregation of public accommodations and the exclusion of Mexican Americans from juries, providing those treated unfairly by the criminal justice system with legal and moral support. Despite the anger at the mistreatment by Anglos, OSA had a high estimation of the promise of American life. The charter proclaimed that its members sought only to "realize the greatest enjoyment possible of all the rights and privileges and prerogatives extended by the American constitution." Meetings were to be closed by the recitation of a prayer written by George Washington.[11]

The time seemed ripe for such an approach. By the end of the decade, OSA boasted chapters in Corpus Christi, San Antonio, Pearsall, Somerset, Alice, and Beeville. Canales tried, apparently unsuccessfully, to start a Brownsville chapter. Not everything was smooth sailing within the group, however. Personal tensions and the resentments of some OSA members over the political ambitions of others hampered the group's organizing efforts. Some became so disaffected that they left the organization, establishing the Order Knights of America in 1927.[12]

What sense did it make to have two virtually identical groups trying to represent the interests of Tejanos? With Anglos seeming to present a united front, many of the most politically active Tejanos felt that dividing their forces was sheer lunacy. Consequently, later that year several hundred gathered in Harlingen, the heart of the Valley's agricultural empire, to attempt to reunite the two organizations and join them with isolated local groups and individuals working for the benefit of ethnic Mexicans in Texas. The delegates created a new group, the League of Latin American Citizens, which they hoped would subsume its predecessors and enlist chapters across the state to advance the struggle for civil rights.

The delegates' hope was a return to the high expectations of the Primer Congreso Mexicanista, but significant internal obstacles had to be overcome. In the first place, too many of their fellow Tejanos seemed more interested in arguing with each other than with openly challenging Anglo repression. The OSA and Knights of America refused to incorporate themselves into the new organization, and so Tejano political power, not great to begin with, was now divided among three organizations. Eduardo Idar argued fruitlessly with James Tafolla, head of the OSA in San Antonio, that his support was necessary to unify Tejanos. "Our order was the first one to organize," insisted Tafolla, "and since its origin, others have arisen, with the same principles, with the same ideals, with the same purposes, and yet, KNOWING that there was already such an organization in existence . . . they get selfish, they get personal and go ahead and organize another society with the identical ideals and principles. . . . Who is it that cannot get together, those who remain loyal to their Order, or those who desert and organize another similar organization?" Idar insisted that "with three institutions in place of one we will never be able to do anything practicable," and, clearly exasperated, could not resist adding that "if we do not come to an understanding [it] is the reason that people of our race hardly can get together on anything."[13]

The continued division between the three groups was frustrating precisely because it did not correspond to any substantive differences of philosophy, membership, or approach. It was just petty squabbling. In addition, there was a second obstacle facing civil rights advocates: who exactly should these groups serve? Should they work on behalf of all those of Mexican descent, or just those born in the United States, or at least deeply rooted in Texas? This question threatened to be far more divisive. At the Harlingen convention, Canales, backed by Clemente and Eduardo Idar, proposed a motion that only U.S. citizens be allowed to join the League of Latin American Citizens. (This was consistent with the practices of the OSA.) Chaos erupted in the hall and the subsequent debate lasted for four hours. A political scientist who observed the event wrote of Canales, "[T]he meeting almost got away from him." When the shouting was over, according to this observer, the motion was narrowly passed after "a masterly speech" by Eduardo Idar. Many of the attendees then left the meeting in protest. The debate continued in the state's Spanish-language press, with San Antonio's Mexican consul and other Mexican figures damning the Tejano leaders as traitors to their race and their true country. Canales and his supporters were adamant that their approach was the best one, despite the high price that it exacted. Mexican Americans, they insisted, did have distinct interests from Mexican nationals. The opportunity to fight for rights as American citizens was too promising to ignore, and it did not mean that they had any less respect for Mexican culture and traditions.[14]

The League's architects could think of Mexican Americans as a distinct people in part because Texas-Mexicans had distinguished themselves culturally from Mexican nationals for several decades, using the term *México-Tejano* rather than simply *Mexicanos*. Cultural differences between Tejanos with deep roots in the region and recent arrivals from the interior of Mexico played a role in creating this separate identity. The impact of class differences was perhaps greater. The ranks of OSA, the Knights of America, and the League were dominated by the owners of small shops and by independent professionals such as lawyers and doctors, rounded out by several labor organizers (including Clemente Idar) and a handful of ranchers and farmers. This Mexican-American middle class was not large, but it was quite cohesive. And because it was based in the towns and small cities of the Valley—the heart of the region's new racial order—its members were both exposed to Anglo society and excluded from it continually.[15]

Few Mexican immigrants, in contrast, were middle class. Immigrant workers were much more likely to be Mexican nationals reliant on migratory agricultural work for their sustenance and thus, believed Canales and the Idars, to be less invested in the improvement of particular communities and less willing and able to fight for civil rights. (This was why OSA had limited its membership to United States citizens.) The attitude of some toward this population—particularly blue-collar Tejanos, whose feelings were similar to those of many Progressives—was tinged with an element of resentment: immigrants depressed wages and offered their sweat and toil to the very people who had taken control of the Valley from Tejanos. "Our people ... are poor; a great number are common laborers," wrote the Eagle Pass chapter of the League in the late 1920s. "[L]aborers residing in Mexico come over the river every day and work for what they can get and return at night," it complained, "apparently un-noticed by the Immigration authorities who seem bent on favoring the employers, with great damage to our resident laborers." Tejanos also had their elites—Canales was such a figure—but they were usually incorporated into the machine, or at least uninterested in the living circumstances of their more modest kinsmen. Wealthy Mexican immigrants were quite political, but they generally remained focused on Mexican politics, hoping for the ascension of a government more sympathetic to their interests.[16]

Limiting membership in the new organization to American citizens of Mexican extraction alienated some, but it also attracted others. Despite the controversy over citizenship, the League of Latin American Citizens grew rapidly, and by May 1929 it boasted chapters in eleven towns, including Brownsville, Corpus Christi, La Grulla, McAllen, and Edinburg. The same year, the OSA and Knights of America put aside their differences, joining with the new organization to form the League of United Latin American Citizens (LULAC). With this unification the nascent civil rights movement achieved a semblance of unity and power. LULAC had nineteen local councils by January 1930 and thirty-seven by February 1932. The local councils were most concentrated in the Valley, but they also represented San Antonio and a number of towns such as Hondo and Cotulla in the Winter Garden district between the city and the Valley.[17]

Progressivism Resurrected

LULAC was a decidedly optimistic organization, looking forward to a brighter future in which Mexican Americans freed themselves from both the racism of Anglos and the restrictive elements of their own culture, finally joining the triumphant chorus of American life. At the same time, however, the new organization drew heavily from the Tejano past to articulate this vision. Most of LULAC's platform and techniques had been anticipated by the Tejano Progressives in the decade before the Plan de San Diego. The Progressives were as intent on the modernization of their own people, the fitting of them with the skills and attitudes necessary to compete in the twentieth-century United States, as they were on confronting Anglo racism. So was LULAC. Earlier in the century, Canales, the Idars, and Luz placed many of their highest hopes on the transformative potential of education and thus singled out educational inequality and segregation as particularly offensive. So did LULAC. The Progressive current included politically engaged women and men who welcomed such activity. So did LULAC. The Progressives hoped that Mexican Americans would seek and gain political power on their own terms rather than on the machine's. So did LULAC.

It was no accident that LULAC resurrected much of the Tejano political culture of the early twentieth century. Former Progressives played a critical role in founding the new organization. Canales and the Idar brothers spearheaded the motion limiting membership to American citizens. Canales and Eduardo Idar joined Alice, Texas, native Alonso Perales in writing the organization's constitution (with input from Luz), and Clemente Idar was the primary author of its ritual book. In the 1920s, all of these leaders had been active in the political currents that eventually joined to form LULAC. "One generation visualizes that which another brings into practice," wrote Clemente Idar

Delegates to the 1929 LULAC convention in Corpus Christi, Texas. Courtesy of the Benson
Latin American Collection, University of Texas at Austin.

shortly after the new organization's founding. "In the history of all peoples,
that is exactly what human progress has brought about."[18]

Clemente Idar and the other founders of LULAC saw large obstacles
between them and "human progress" in south Texas. It wasn't only the hostility
of Anglos that so angered them, but also the passivity and ignorance of their
own people. Mexican Americans were just too willing to retreat into their own
world, or too ignorant of the possibilities offered by American citizenship, to
throw themselves into the fight against segregation. "[W]e Mexican-Americans,"
wrote Perales in a book he published 1931, "do not have a well-formed concept
of what is politics in the American sense." Political scientist O. Douglas Weeks,
who studied LULAC from its inception and who was present at the 1929
Corpus Christi convention, described the attitudes of other LULACers in
similar terms. Although LULAC wanted "to gain for the Mexican-American
equality before the law, equal facilities for educational and other forms of
improvement, and a reasonable share of political representation," the proto-
typical LULAC member, according to Weeks, "realizes full well that the greatest stumbling block in the way of accomplishing this end is the Mexican-

American himself, who possesses no very clear conception of the significance of the privileges and duties of his American citizenship." Perales lauded Weeks's article as "brilliant" and urged every Mexican American to read it; he also reprinted much of it in his own book.[19]

Little wonder, then, that LULAC devoted much of its efforts to attacking second-rate and segregated education, filing lawsuits against discriminatory school systems, supporting sympathetic school board candidates, and providing moral and financial support for Mexican-American children to stay in school and pursue higher education. This emphasis on education offered both an obvious way to attack the entire system of segregation and a better means for outfitting Mexican Americans for this challenge. "The public schools in the United States," wrote early LULAC leader Andrés de Luna, "always have been the melting pot where the dissimilar races of the world have been fused into one people, where children are suppose [sic] to learn to live together in peace and harmony, not by being kept in isolation from each other but by participating in common tasks." As segregated education was practiced in Texas, however, it had the opposite result. "Americanization," de Luna warned, "will take care of itself if we give these children the opportunity they need but Americanization without justice is a forlorn hope as injustice breeds antagonism and not loyalty." The flimsy and overcrowded schoolhouses that their children were packed into were the clearest sign that Anglos intended to visit the humiliations and outrages of segregation onto the next generation. Opening the much superior Anglo schools to their children would send the clearest message possible that Anglos were intent on equality and first-class citizenship. And better education would allow Mexican-American children to leave the fields and packing houses and join the merchants, clerks, small business owners, lawyers, and labor organizers that made up the bulwark of LULAC.[20]

Men dominated LULAC, accounting for all of its founders and first several slates of officers. At the same time, the organization's inward focus on fitting Mexican Americans with the tools and values to aggressively protect their own interests in a hostile society included women as well. Numerous women were present at the founding convention, and although their influence was not officially recognized, doubtless they played a role behind the scenes, perhaps in nudging the men to overcome their petty factionalism. LULAC's push for educational equality assumed that girls as well as boys would use their education to advance all Mexican Americans. Women were still marginalized within the organization, however. At first the male officers limited women to ladies auxiliaries, not unlike the Liga Femenil established at the Primer Congreso Mexicanista in 1911. In 1933, however, women became full voting members. They also played critical and sometimes freely acknowledged leadership roles in local chapters from LULAC's inception. In 1937

Laredo resident Alicia Dickerson Montemayor won election as second vice-president, an office previously held by men.[21]

Much of the reinvigoration of their own people could come from internal efforts, but LULACers knew that wider reform—the end of unequal schooling, the undoing of racial segregation—required political power. Some leaders, such as Perales, still spoke of the old Progressive vision of a party of Mexican Americans becoming the dominant political power in south Texas. Others, such as San Antonio lawyer M. C. Gonzales, ran for political office themselves. At the same time, LULAC as a whole remained wary of partisan politics, preferring to concentrate on issues rather than on parties or campaigns. Tensions over the political ambitions of leaders of OSA led to the group's split in 1927, and some members feared that LULAC might simply become another political machine. LULAC chapters sought to avoid a repeat of such divisions by placing members who were elected to political office on inactive status to maintain their focus on the citizenship rights of Mexican Americans.[22]

This flirtation with electoral politics enraged south Texas's machine, or what remained of it. If Mexican Americans organized themselves to pursue political power in their own interest, then what would become of the machine's already dwindling captive voting bloc? Eduardo Idar recalled that the Laredo machine was very much opposed to the founding of LULAC. Hidalgo County sheriff A. Y. Baker, whose organization continued as a force in county politics through the 1920s, lashed out at LULAC at its inception. "My Mexican-Texan Friends," wrote Baker in the *Hidalgo County Independent* in 1929, "I have been and still consider myself as your Leader or Superior Chief." Baker, who murdered numerous ethnic Mexicans in 1915 and 1916, asserted that "I have always sheltered in my soul the most pure tenderness of the Mexican-Texan race and have watched over your interests to the best of my ability and knowledge." Baker's point in the open letter was to "disapprove the political activity of groups which have no other object than to organize Mexican-Texan voters into political groups for guidance by other leaders."[23]

For its part, LULAC viewed the machine much as the Progressives had, that is, as a corrupt and oppressive organization that relied on their people's greatest vices, passivity and ignorance. "We do not care to be confused with those who are herded," proclaimed one delegate at the 1929 convention. If it appealed to the worst in themselves, the machine was also complicit in denying Mexican Americans their rights as citizens. LULAC condemned the 1920s killings of four Mexican Americans in the Valley by machine-supported sheriffs. "In none of these cases were the murderers punished," wrote Perales, "which demonstrates that the authorities did not grant the unfortunate victims the equal protection of the laws that the fourteenth amendment of the Constitution of the United States of America guarantees us."[24]

LULAC had in a sense resurrected Tejano Progressivism, as Luz, the Idars, and Canales surely recognized. At the same time, there was something profoundly new, perhaps even revolutionarily new, about LULAC. Two decades earlier, Tejanos seeking to check the advances of segregation had looked as much to Mexico as to the United States. If the protections of the U.S. Constitution were appealing, then so too were latter-day Mexican Liberals such as Francisco Madero. If the immigrant symphony of the United States seemed to invite them to join it, then the prospect of rejoining a Mexico redeemed from its corrupt old order possessed an even more powerful pull. Now, however, the most politically active of Tejanos had decisively cast their lot with the United States. The first principle of LULAC's constitution—"To develop within the members of our race the best, purest, and most perfect type of a true and loyal citizen of the United States of America"—indicated that Tejanos had become Mexican Americans.

The founders of LULAC could see that long-term shifts had enabled them to think of themselves in this new way. Even twenty years earlier, they had recognized the differences between them and the hundreds of thousands of refugees from central Mexico who flooded into the United States. They knew that there was something culturally distinct about Texas-Mexicans. Above all, however, they were now Mexican Americans because they had decided to become so, because they had evaluated the situation and concluded that the principles of American democracy had much to offer a people in their position. But they had to be in a position to claim membership in the national community whose ideals they praised. The key decision, the choice that reflected their new commitment, was thus the controversy that nearly wrecked the convention at Harlingen: limiting LULAC membership to U.S. citizens.

The appeal of the United States was, in part, the older Progressive understanding of the differences between American principles and the actual practice of states such as Texas. But this alone was not enough to make them embrace American citizenship so wholeheartedly. After all, they could have maintained the Progressive ambivalence about the United States and continued to hope for as much from Mexican politics. What they had endured during the Plan de San Diego and the subsequent decade of segregation convinced them of the dangers of statelessness and their risk of becoming a people belonging to no nation at all.

The men and women who came together in Harlingen, and then two years later in Corpus Christi, were haunted by the vision of their own history. "Events a thousand times repeated in history," proclaimed the south Texas newspaper *El Popular* shortly before the formation of LULAC, "have made it be that the descendants of three generations born on this piece of earth, would one day find themselves confronted with the sad dilemma of searching for a country, since they had none." Mexican Americans had been betrayed by Mexico—"during the horrors of war, the fratricidal sword of a villain divided that nation in half, and one of its sections was exchanged for a fistful of cursed money"—even as they were "converted from landlords into peons" by Anglos. If the long history of a debased Mexico and a greedy America was an unhappy one, then it had only worsened in the twentieth century. "In 1910 when the Mexican Revolution erupted," wrote Luz, "unfortunately the effects of that disastrous calamity for the Mexican people crossed our borders . . . to embitter our already atrocious civil and political condition in Texas. Innumerable abuses were committed against us . . . more or less this was the time when the abomination of segregated, poorly-equipped, abandoned schools for Mexican children developed."[25]

The result of this sad history was that Mexican Americans were not only oppressed, they also did not know where to turn to fight this oppression. "Like those who have preceded me in this course of deliberation, I see that we form a conglomerate without a country, without prerogatives," said José Gonzáles to heavy applause at the Corpus Christi convention. The Robstown chapter of the League of Latin American Citizens feared that "our children [are] today the vestiges of a great disinherited family and tomorrow, if our apathy permits, they will be begging for a country and even for homes." Mexican Americans had fallen into the crack between the two nations. "We are becoming a new people on the margin of two great and powerful nations," editorialized *El Paladín* in its announcement of the Corpus meeting, "and continue being Americans to religiously fulfill all of our obligations, and Mexicans when it comes to sharing rights, especially in the South of Texas." Even the immigrant diversity of the United States did not make room for those of Mexican descent. "This country is formed or comprised of many lineages, the families of many peoples," wrote Castulo Gutiérrez. "The greater part of the immigrants to this country maintain their original citizenship, but naturally as they make their homes and their children are born, they are henceforth American citizens." Although the Mexican people made up one of these immigrant groups, he said, "IT IS THE ONLY ONE . . . THAT IN ITS TOTALITY IS CONSIDERED AS A FOREIGNER that has nothing to do with the political and economic machinery of this country."[26]

The predicament of Mexican Americans was most clear when segregation reared its ugly head. "How many times, respectable fellow-citizens, do we know that one of our race, here in his own land, in his own country is denied the right of entering certain public establishments in some places in the State of Texas," delegate N. R. Montalvo asked the convention. "This cold demonstration is made to him, which cannot be translated except in the blackest and vilest humiliation. This poor brother of ours in such painful moments he raises his eyes in his turn in search for a fountain which will give him justice but does not find it, and his shame and his pain which disturb his spirit go unnoticed, and the only recourse for him is to bow his head and go out of that place and sob out his shame and sadness on finding himself turned into a new Wandering Jew, condemned to travel, a stranger among stranger[s], and a stranger even in his own land."[27]

If resolving this problem would be difficult, then at least the path was clear: Mexicans in the United States had to grasp the mantle of citizenship, claim all of the rights that were theirs as American citizens. "What should we do to destroy the prejudice of those who would deny our rights as citizens?" asked *El Popular*. "We should decide for our unification confident of being better prepared, in more intimate contact with the system of the country in which we live." "Mexican-Americans," emphasized Gutiérrez, "as long as we do not elevate ourselves to the level of citizens, will be nothing more than the conquered."[28]

The embrace of American citizenship was the most divisive aspect of LULAC's program within the ethnic Mexican community, generating strife long after the controversial conventions. Mexican consuls and immigrants who aspired to return to a redeemed homeland south of the river—especially wealthy exiles in San Antonio—condemned these first Mexican Americans as traitors to their own people and cultural heritage. Mexicans were exiles, refugees, and immigrants; they were not American citizens. "In all times and in all countries political agitators take advantage of the popular discontent created by poverty," wrote Mexican consul Enrique Santaibáñez from San Antonio in 1930. "[A]llow me to say to the Mexicans, my co-nationals, that they should always remember that they live in a foreign nation, that they came by their own choice to the United States and that they have no right to disturb the existing social conditions here." If "luck is bad in one place," he concluded, "they should seek their fortune in another or return to their country." Santaibáñez had his sub-consuls read this missive at meetings across the state.[29]

LULACers had no patience for this counsel. Many "Mexicans" were now part of the United States. They insisted that they were simply recognizing historical necessity, and that their embrace of United States citizenship did not mean that they rejected Mexican culture or Mexicans. Indeed, just two weeks after the new organization was formed, one of its first official actions was to protest to federal authorities about the treatment of detained illegal immigrants, who were often confined with common criminals while awaiting deportation. Moreover, many LULACers openly proclaimed their pride in Mexican culture. "[O]ur efforts to be rightfully recognized as citizens of this country do not imply that we wish to become scattered nor much less abominate our Latin heritage," the organization proclaimed shortly after its founding, "but rather on the contrary, we will always feel for it the most tender love and the most respectful veneration." Those who feared that Texas-Mexicans would lose their culture by deciding to become American citizens, chided Gutiérrez, had too little confidence in their abilities. "[H]ow strong we are to survive the abominable weight of the life of the conquered," he argued, but according to LULAC's opponents, "our heart is very small, since the traditions of two peoples, smelted together in one desire, do not fit."[30]

Smelting together the traditions of two nations was not an easy task. Texas's racial order proved impervious to LULAC's early challenges. The politics of exile continued to appeal to many ethnic Mexicans. Moreover, the challenge that LULACers had created for themselves was steep. They told themselves and all who would listen that Mexican Americans had to transform themselves into a modern, vigorous, well-educated people. They emphasized this so heavily that they risked falling short in their own eyes. Speaking English, for example, was an essential part of this modern self-image, as well as another way of proving the loyalty of Mexican Americans to the United States. But many LULACers did not grow up speaking English. (At a 1930 meeting in San Diego, Canales asked for special permission to speak in Spanish so that all thousand delegates could follow the debate over immigration restrictions.) "You will also excuse my grammatical errors," wrote an embarrassed Eduardo Idar to the head of the OSA, "as I am not very able to write english and I am trying to do things right." Their lack of full fluency made them conscious of just how demanding their political project was.[31]

　　Citizenship politics was not easy, but it was compelling. LULAC spread quickly across south Texas. Membership grew throughout the 1930s, even in the face of the Depression and the federal government's subsequent deportation of hundreds of thousands of ethnic Mexicans. The organization sent an *Escuadrón Volante*, or Flying Squadron, into Valley towns to form new chapters, occasionally confronting roadblocks set up by their old nemesis, the Texas Rangers. By World War II, LULAC had more than eighty councils in five states—Texas, New Mexico, Arizona, California, and Kansas—though the bulk of its membership and power remained in Texas, particularly in south Texas. LULAC used its power to oppose local segregation ordinances, pursue lawsuits against school segregation, and register many Mexican Americans to vote. The end of World War II bolstered such efforts, as returning veterans revitalized LULAC and formed other organizations to defend the civil rights of Mexican Americans. The organization is the oldest surviving and most prominent civil rights organization for Mexican Americans, a counterpart of sorts to the National Association for the Advancement of Colored People.[32]

　　The gospel of citizenship rights appealed to so many Mexican Americans because it gave them hope that their second-rate status could be overturned and also allowed for those with different, even sharply contradictory, political philosophies to join and become active members. Having agreed that their destiny lay within the larger trajectory of American society and politics, LULACers were free to disagree on almost everything else. And disagree they did. In 1930, just a year after the organization's founding, some of its most prominent members came to loggerheads and nearly to blows. A bill sharply restricting immigration was under consideration in Congress. Canales and others strongly opposed it, arguing that it was based on racist assumptions about Mexicans and other immigrants. Canales and LULAC president Ben Garza went to Washington, D.C., to testify against the proposal. Others within LULAC saw it differently, however. M. C. Gonzáles and Clemente Idar, who was working at the time as an organizer for the American Federation of Labor, sided with what they saw as the interests of Mexican American labor in limiting the numbers of desperate immigrants willing to work for very low wages. Gonzáles and Idar, angered that Canales and Garza were speaking on behalf of the organization without a wider internal debate or consensus, sent the congressional committee a telegraph indicating that LULAC had not adopted an official stance on the immigration bill. At the next general LULAC meeting, held in San Diego, Texas, a furious Canales lashed out at the two, railing against "the virus of the American Federation of Labor" in front of the thousand-odd delegates. Although Canales had the upper hand within the organization, internal debates over immigration and the proper relationship between LULAC and organized labor would continue.[33]

LULAC contained a similar diversity of opinions on the subject of race. Some Mexican Americans—especially in parts of the state with significant black populations and thus strict enforcement of Jim Crow provisions—emulated the anti-black racism of local Anglo society. "Recently a group of Negro musician[s]," wrote LULAC member Gregory Salinas in 1936, "have capitalized on the unsuspecting good-nature of our people, who employed them to play at some public dances, with the result that this contact has led to a few cases of illicit relations between these Negroes and certain ignorant and ill-informed Mexican girls." For Salinas, the obvious solution was to police the color line. "Let us tell these Negroes," he urged his fellow LULACers, "that we are not going to permit our manhood and womanhood to mingle with them on an equal social basis." Even those who were not racists had an incentive to distance themselves from African American civil rights agitation, because segregation legally applied only to non-whites.[34]

Many others, however, understood that the real problem was racism. Mexican Americans were not white in any meaningful sense, they believed, and were unlikely in any event to be treated as equals in a society with stark racial hierarchies. At the Corpus Christi convention, Luz damned Anglos for betraying the promises of America by insisting on "SUPREMACY OF RACES ON ACCOUNT OF COLOR." He would consistently maintain his opposition to all racial discrimination and segregation in such declarations as "[t]he colored people has been subjected to accept, by brutal force, the mandates of the unfair Jim Crow Law promulgated by snobbish legislators." Throughout its existence, LULAC would sometimes cooperate with its black counterparts in the assault on racial segregation.[35]

LULACers sometimes even saw their own people in strikingly different ways. On the one hand, some believed that Mexican Americans were a backward people, too much like the rest of Latin America. "Confidentially," Perales wrote to Garza in 1928 from Nicaragua, "I will tell you that I find Managua very hot, dusty, filthy, and backward. However, I will not criticize these people, for I feel that I have no right to. Although I am an American citizen and the United States is the leading country in the world, I belong to the Mexican-American element of our nation, and as a racial entity we Mexican-Americans have accomplished nothing that we can point to with pride . . . our Mexican districts in the United States are just as filthy and backward as Managua."

Others were appalled by such sentiments, proudly invoking what they saw as the finest achievements of Mexican culture. Indeed, despite their embrace of American citizenship, many in LULAC still thought of themselves as the bearers of the culture of Latin America. For somebody like Canales, this meant the more Catholic, elite Hispanic culture; at the Corpus Christi convention in 1929, he delivered the dinner address, "bringing to the imagination of the listeners the birth, development, and the greatest conquests of Latin culture." For somebody like Luz this meant the indigenous, popular culture. "Everybody knows that the majority of the first Europeans to come to the New World engaged in vandalism, pillage, and conquest," he wrote. Mexican Americans, he insisted, should be proud to consider themselves "all of the indo-Americans or Amerindians without regard to whatever other blood that now runs mixed with it in their veins."[36]

The Sediciosos and Postrevolutionary Mexico

The founders of LULAC embraced U.S. citizenship as a means of combating their marginalization, hoping to link their fate to the best of American traditions. Some of the Sediciosos eventually charted a similar course with Mexican citizenship. The Plan de San Diego itself had envisioned such a possibility, providing for the possible joining of the newly freed U.S. Southwest with the Mexican nation. Luis de la Rosa, Aniceto Pizaña, and their cohorts had all been inspired by the hope that Mexicans' violent purge of their corrupt leaders could be repeated in the United States. For a time, their ambitions seemed to be realized. General Emiliano Nafarrate's early support for them confirmed the hope that Mexico would embrace the struggles of those of Mexican descent in the United States. But it was not to be: Venustiano Carranza's efforts to curtail the Texas uprising, motivated by fear of a U.S. invasion, betrayed this promise.

With their movement crushed, the former rebels scattered themselves across Mexico. Within a few years, Luis de la Rosa, once hailed in border towns as a savior and a champion of the oppressed, was a broken man. Now living in Mexico City, he wrote Carranza a series of increasingly desperate and pleading letters. De la Rosa invoked his service to the Constitutionalist cause and requested a job, financial support, or Carranza's agreement to pay him for importing weapons through Matamoros. With no response, and now unable to feed his family, the former Tejano rebel wrote to the head of the Mexican state that "my only remaining recourse is to ask you for a final favor. ... [F]inding myself removed from my homeland, where I have some ability to make an honorable living, in the name of the friendship that you have extended me," he begged only for "a pass for the railroad . . . for me my wife and five children, to the port of Matamoros Tamaulipas."[37]

Not all of the Sediciosos were reduced to such a condition. In 1920, a widespread military rebellion led by General Alvaro Obregón overthrew Carranza, killing him in the process. Some of the more radical agrarian factions, including followers of the assassinated Emiliano Zapata, had joined Obregón's movement and now found themselves a part of the national government. These revolutionaries were kindred spirits to the Sediciosos, men and women who had been stripped of their lands and driven from their homes, but who had refused to accept the judgment of this so-called progress. Having struggled for years, they now seemed to have won a victory of sorts. Once he ascended to the presidency, Obregón ratified many of the land occupations made by these revolutionary forces over the past decade. His government recognized the need for further land redistribution by setting up an agrarian reform program, which established grants of land, *ejidos*, to be communally held by groups of applicants, and provided them with credit and infrastructure support. Its architects intended this system both to address the landlessness that gave rise to much of the revolution in the first place and to provide the new government with a wide base of social support. For a time land redistribution was a significant feature of Mexican economic and political life, ensuring the support of many of those who had fought with Villa, Zapata, and other popular leaders. By 1934 the government redistributed approximately 10 percent of the cultivated land, a figure that rose to 47 percent by 1940, the end of the presidency of the more radical Lázaro Cárdenas.[38] For many of its recipients the ejido system was tangible proof that the Mexican government had finally honored the struggle—for land, liberty, and thus for the redemption of the Mexican nation—to which the revolutionaries had sacrificed so much.

Pizaña and his family eventually got a taste of land redistribution—not in Texas, but in Tamaulipas, under the ejido program. After the defeat of the uprising, Pizaña apparently remained in the border region for at least a decade. The late scholar and Brownsville native Américo Paredes remembered the tumult caused by Pizaña's appearance, gun slung over his hip, at a wedding just south of the Rio Grande in the late 1920s. At some point he headed south, by one account serving as a police officer in Tampico. He may have lived for a time in Mexico City. A 1938 letter addressed to him there made extensive reference to Pizaña's memoirs, which his interlocutor emphasized "would be the greatest capital you could leave to your child." The exiled Tejano did in fact write a detailed memoir of his early life and some of the uprising, filling one hundred and fifty-two pages with handwritten recollections. He titled the work "Biographical Notes of a Revolutionary of the Year 1915," suggesting that he identified with Mexico's revolutionary struggle, if not necessarily with its government.[39]

In early 1945, twenty-eight men and women, the former rebel leader among them, wrote the Mexican government to request that a land grant be made near Llera, Tamaulipas, a small town in the southern portions of the state. The following year, they were provisionally awarded some four hundred and sixty hectares, and in 1950 the Mexican government formalized the grant. Pizaña's daughter Beatríz continued to be a part of the ejido until at least 1970, when she became a recipient of a government irrigation grant. His son Guadalupe, maimed for life by the 1915 raid on his family's ranch, apparently was also involved in the ejido. In 1955 the government issued him a membership card for the Confederation of Revolutionary Veterans of the Division of the North. The postrevolutionary Mexican government sought legitimacy by portraying itself as the heir to the popular struggle of the revolution. That the Division of the North was in fact Pancho Villa's army, with which Pizaña had no dealings, and that Guadalupe was more a victim than a veteran, did not dampen its enthusiasm. The Pizaña family held on to his veteran's card, the land grant declaration, and the numerous petitions and correspondence that preceded it—all kept together with Pizaña's handwritten memoir—perhaps as a tangible reminder that Mexico had finally recognized at least some of their struggles.[40]

If he gained some satisfaction from this recognition, the old Tejano rebel also had abundant reasons to temper it. From its inception, the ejido struggled with a nearby wealthy landowner who used his political influence and his own armed forces to intimidate ejido members and to take away some if its lands for his sugar cane ventures. Perhaps life in Mexico, even after the great revolution, was not so different from life back in south Texas.[41]

But then again, it may have had its rewards, consisting of some of the same things that Pizaña had so loved about his life as a ranchero. Those who knew him from his days in the ejido recalled that he enjoyed raising fruit trees, reading detective novels, and, above all, riding his horse along the river. He died in 1957. A Tampico newspaper painted his death as solitary and tragic. Identifying him as a "veteran of the revolution," it stated that Pizaña died "in the most complete abandonment and in the midst of total poverty" and had been forced by economic necessity to work up until the very day of his death. "His lone death," the article concluded, "has caused deep consternation here and along the coast, where he was well known and regarded."[42]

Memories of the Plan de San Diego

Aniceto Pizaña's decision to write a memoir indicated that he gave some thought to how the events that had so marked his adult life would be remembered by others. In his writing he went to some length to represent himself as an honest, upright man, devoted to his family and to the life of a ranchero. He portrayed himself as forthright in his principles and noted that he did not join the uprising until forced into it by the savagery of his Anglo neighbors.

Pizaña was not the only one to pay attention to the question of memory. The remembrance of things past played a critical role for Tejano Progressives and for many of the founders of LULAC. They knew that segregationists had not always controlled their homeland, that Texas-Mexicans once occupied positions of political authority and social respect in towns now littered with signs reading "No Mexicans Allowed." The Anglo farmers who had overturned this old order told their own version of the past, one in which they arrived in an impoverished and backward corner of the nation dominated by feudal rulers and made it bloom.

Almost everybody who lived through the 1915–19 violence in south Texas had reasons to reflect back on the events, perhaps thanking God for sparing them or thinking of those they had lost. At the same time, some had reasons not to remember or, at least, not to discuss the Plan de San Diego publicly. Many of the founders of LULAC, for example, left virtually no public record of their views of the uprising. Canales, Clemente and Eduardo Idar, and Luz must have had occasion to reflect upon the uprising and its legacy —they had been caught up in the violence, and it had showed them the dangers of being a people without a state. But how would an active remembrance or discussion of these events have contributed to LULAC's politics of citizenship? The organization's strong emphasis on loyalty to the United States, present from its inception and strengthened by the deportation campaigns of the 1930s and postwar anticommunism, provided little incentive for its leaders to dwell on an episode in which some ethnic Mexicans committed treason.

Even those who had less reason to feel ashamed of the Plan de San Diego remembered it with strongly mixed feelings. The *corrido* "Los Sedici-osos," written about the Plan de San Diego shortly after the raids and sung in the border region for many years thereafter, expresses such feelings. On the one hand, the song expresses admiration for the raiders, and especially for their attacks on "those cursed Rangers." The second verse casts the Sedici-osos in the classic role of Mexican border heroes defending their rights with pistol in hand. The narration uses nearly the same language to describe early Plan de San Diego raids as that used in the most popular corridos detailing the exploits of ethnic Mexican folk heroes such as Jacinto Treviño. This verse refers to some of the more successful raids: "Ya con esta van tres veces / que sucede lo bonito / la primera fue in Mercedes, / en Brónsvil y en San Benito" (With this it will be three times that remarkable things have happened; the first time was in Mercedes, then in Brownsville and San Benito). Its listeners would recognize this verse as virtually identical to the first verse of the best-known corrido about a heroic Tejano who had defended his family against brutal Anglo farmers: "Ya con esta van tres veces / que se ha visto lo bonito, / la primera fue en McAllen / en Brónsvil y en San Benito" (With this it will be three times that remarkable things have been seen; the first time was in McAllen, then Brownsville and San Benito).[43]

On the other hand, those responsible for the Plan de San Diego hardly come across as unvarnished heroes. Luis de la Rosa cries "like a baby" during the fight at the Norias house. A more sinister aspect of the uprising also emerges. While the song attributes the raids to Mexican nationals, Texas-Mexicans clearly will pay the price:

Ya la mecha está encendida	Now the fuse is lit
por los puros mexicanos,	by the real Mexicans,
y los que van a pagarla	but the Texas-Mexicans
son los mexicotejanos.	will pay the price.
Ya la mecha está encendida	Now the fuse is lit
con azul y colorado,	in blue and red,
y los que van a pagarla	and those of this side
van a ser los de este lado.	will pay the price.
Ya la mecha está encendida,	Now the fuse is lit,
muy bonita y colorada,	very nice and red,
y la vamos a pagar	and we will pay,
los que no debemos nada.	we who are blameless.

The corrido ends on much the same note:

Ya se van los sediciosos	The Sediciosos left
ya se van de retirada,	they have retreated,
de recuerdos no dejaron	as a remembrance they left
una veta colorada.	a red swathe.
Ya se van los sediciosos	The Sediciosos left
y quedaron de volver,	they said they would return,
pero no dijeron cuando	but didn't say when
porque no podían saber.	because they couldn't know.
Despedida no la doy	I will not give you a farewell,
porque no la traigo aquí,	I did not bring it with me,
se la llevó Luis de la Rosa,	Luis de la Rosa took it with him
para San Luis Potosí.	to San Luis Potosí.[44]

"Los Sediciosos" offers no clear message or explanation of the rebellion, reflecting the divided loyalties and mixed feelings of so many of the Tejanos who lived through the Plan and the vigilantism. Of course, Anglos also remembered the Plan. For decades south Texas newspapers and historical societies produced accounts and recollections of the uprising. Although the authors' perspectives and direct knowledge of the events varied widely, they most often resorted to the term *banditry* to explain the origin of the violence. Anglo discussions of the Plan de San Diego tended to offer a story with a more specific moral than that of "Los Sediciosos": "disorder" and "lawlessness" had become features of the Valley's past, part of a colorful history that no longer troubled a happy and prosperous present. For example, fourth-generation Valley resident Dorothy Pope, writing in 1971, explained the unrest by stating simply that "[e]arly days of the Rainbow Era were darkened by tragic tales of bandits tearing into days of golden sunshine and blissful tranquility." In the 1920s, C. H. Pease, who ran a general store in Mercedes during the uprising, wrote a long series of articles detailing the raids and their defeat by the Rangers and U.S. army. His narration began by noting the presence of "individuals among the Mexican population that were irresponsible and dangerous criminals" and traced the escalation of theft and mayhem that erupted in 1915. Pease used the term *bandits* throughout, as in "the Thrilling Days of 1915 When Bandits Roamed the Border," "Description of Attack When Five Bandits Were Killed," and "Mexican Bandits Terrorize Delta," to name some of the titles of his serialized account. Similarly, Mary Lane's 1936 essay "Bloody, Dangerous Days in the Valley Weren't So Long Ago," which won a newspaper prize as "best article submitted by a representative of a Valley federated women's club," invoked a long string of "bandits," starting with Juan Cortina, included train robberies and bank holdups, and ended with Pancho Villa and other "bandits" of 1915. Not surprisingly, subsequent accounts by Rangers and law enforcement officers also used the rhetoric of order and disorder. Former Ranger and future adjutant general William Sterling noted in his memoir that south Texas had long been plagued by "hard riding centaurs [who] made their living by stealing cattle" and that the violence was explained by the fact that "[t]hese freebooters welcomed the opportunity to engage in any form of outlawry."[45]

By invoking the classic motif of courageous Tejano resistance, "Los Sediciosos," for all of its resentment against the raiders, connected the Plan de San Diego to the larger question of race relations. The Anglo rhetoric of law and criminality, on the other hand, tended to divorce the uprising from any political meaning. In these accounts, the conflict was a simple matter of a few bad men. "So far as the Mexican and American people were concerned, they got along without friction—whatever trouble arose was caused by irresponsible and dangerous criminals such as are usually found in every large community," declared Mary Lane. Nevertheless, all of the "bandits" were Mexican, of course, and thus tales of banditry often hinted at racial conflict. Some openly acknowledged it. Lane, oblivious to the contradiction in her argument, recognized that disputes between Anglos and Mexicans over land ownership planted "the seeds of revolution [that] culminated in bandit raids, the most serious of which were in 1914 and 1915." C. H. Pease wrote that the first several months of raiding "promised to be a Mexican uprising . . . there was a restive feeling among the Mexican population that was different from any they had ever experienced."[46]

Others offered an explicitly racist explanation for the unrest. Virgil Lott, who served as a deputy for Hidalgo County sheriff A. Y. Baker, referred to the Sediciosos as "deluded, duped peons" who paid a high price for challenging the white conquest of south Texas. "It was not down in the cards that this race would stand idly by and see this land of theirs devastated," Lott explained. The corpses of Mexicans testified to might of the Anglo race: "It had fought for all it had ever gained, and it had gained much since its trek from the shores of Albion to the chaparral fringes of the Rio Grande, therefore fighting was not new to it as attested by the gruesome skeletons found even at this late day, twenty years after, in the wilderness, lying in neatly arranged rows, side by side, each with a trim, round hole in the forehead squarely between the empty eye-sockets —'Brands' of the Texas [R]angers' 'irons,' the never-failing 45-Colts." D. P. Gay, who was present at the fight at the Norias ranch house, put the unrest in a similar context in his recollections. "[K]nowing there were 75 or 80 bandits, and being outnumbered seven or eight to one," he later wrote to the historian Walter Prescott Webb, "I could not help from thinking of those immortals, Travis, Bowie, and Crockett, and their memoriable fight at the Alamo, when a hundred and eighty red-blooded Americans fought about five thousand greasers."[47]

The vigilantism unleashed by the Plan de San Diego was horrific enough to leave a note of disquiet in many Anglo accounts, even in the most triumphal stories of the "bandits'" defeat. Although she praised the Rangers for their control of lawlessness, stating that "[n]o new and raw country ever had or was blessed with a finer set of guardians ... of their adventures a second Iliad might be written," Lane nonetheless acknowledged that the Rangers led "a manhunt that resulted in a verified total of 100 Mexicans killed in August 1915." Pease similarly credited the Rangers with "cleaning up the country," but also lamented the fact that "[t]here is little doubt that many innocent Mexican people lost their lives during these terrible times. I knew of one Mexican who had been faithful to his American employer, and who had carried to him information of the bandits ... and who even joined in trying to trail them down. One day his body was found by the roadside riddled with bullets."[48]

Anglos describing the Plan de San Diego in the 1920s and afterward wrote from a position of confidence that such unrest and tumult was far behind them. Miriam Chatelle, who moved to the Valley as a young child just before the uprising, stated in her 1948 memoir that the "bandits'" defeat "led the way to another era of understanding and good fellowship which has restored the old friendliness and the old confidence." High school student Jean Walker concluded in 1960 that despite the "racial clashes" and "summary executions," nonetheless "the raids and the insane Plan de San Diego established a way for later developments and indicated what could be gained at little cost." Lane, so insistent on the "bloody" and "dangerous" times faced by earlier pioneers, opened her essay with the declaration that "[t]oday there is peace along the Rio Grande.... The clutching fear of attack from men in ambush and the din of noisy skirmishes have given way to the rush and hurry of a busy thoroughfare. Lovely farm homes, beautiful citrus groves with their promise of golden harvest, acres on acres of vegetables, thriving cities of the Lower Rio Grande Valley are now fairy-like views along the highways."[49]

This agricultural landscape was not as tranquil as Lane made it out to be. Mexican Americans were flocking to LULAC out of discontent with their second-class status, laying the foundation for the systematic challenge to segregation that would come after World War II. At the same time, in the 1930s and early 1940s agricultural workers, both Mexican and Mexican-American, repeatedly struck the fields near Laredo, the Winter Garden district west and south of San Antonio, and in the Valley itself. They sought better wages, freedom from the unchecked and often cruel whims of their supervisors, and safer working conditions. At times they were successful: the strikes frequently drove up wages and resolved specific grievances, and in a few instances they resulted in formal settlements with farmers and processors. In 1937 the United Cannery,

Agricultural, Packing and Allied Workers of America, a union affiliated with
the Congress of Industrial Organizations, boasted locals in Weslaco, La Feria,
Mercedes, Harlingen, San Benito, and Donna. However, despite a resurgence
of strikes in 1944, agricultural workers were unable to win long-term contracts
and thus to ensure a lasting institutional presence for organized labor in the
Valley, much less to actually threaten racial segregation. Anglo farmers still
ruled the Tejano homeland.[50]

Some Mexican-American intellectuals and activists, seeking to understand
and ultimately change segregated south Texas, saw the need to grapple with
the legacy of the Plan de San Diego. In 1938, the same year that she led a strike
of San Antonio's pecan-shelling plants, labor organizer and Texas Communist
Party secretary Emma Tenayuca argued that the Plan de San Diego was a
critical episode in the process of the border region's economic and political
incorporation into the United States. "In 1916, immediately following the
abortive De la Rosa movement in the Texas lower Rio Grande Valley for an
autonomous Mexican regime," she wrote, "Texas Rangers, in cooperation
with land speculators, came into small Mexican villages in the border country,
massacred hundreds of unarmed, peaceful Mexican villagers and seized their
lands. Sometimes the seizures were accompanied by the formality of signing
bills of sale—at the point of a gun." For Tenayuca this theft was the most important land transfer since the Mexican-American War and set the pattern for
the subsequent oppression of ethnic Mexicans in the Southwest: "[W]here,
until 1916, virtually all of the land was the property of Mexicans, today almost
none of it is Mexican-owned. In many cases farmers who were well-to-do land
owners today barely eke out a living employed as irregular wage workers at
60c to 75c a day on the very lands they once owned. This land-grabbing has
continued under one guise or another throughout the Southwest." As terrible
and brutal as the violence was, it also linked the inhabitants of Mexican descent
of the border region to the larger economic forces of the United States. Although
few in LULAC shared her radical politics, Tenayuca shared their sense that
Mexican Americans had to realize that their destiny lay within the United States.[51]

Américo Paredes, writing at the roughly same time as Tenayuca,
also argued that the Plan de San Diego was a critical chapter in the history of
Mexican Americans. Born in Brownsville in 1915, the very year of the uprising,
Paredes became a prominent academic and public intellectual. His 1958 book
"With His Pistol in His Hand" analyzed the ballad of the folk hero Gregorio
Cortez in the context of south Texas's violent history. It remains one of the
foundational texts of Mexican-American studies and border history. Paredes
taught for decades at the University of Texas at Austin, where he founded the
Center for Mexican American Studies and mentored several generations of
scholars of folklore, the border, and Mexican Americans. Even before launching

his academic career Paredes grappled with the legacy of the Plan de San Diego. In the late 1930s, while working as a reporter for the *Brownsville Herald* and honing his own musical talents, he wrote a historical novel titled *George Washington Gómez*. The book opens with the violence and chaos of the Plan de San Diego, as an uprising led by "Anacleto de la Peña" has prompted Texas Rangers to engage in the wanton murder and dispossession of Tejanos. Into this terror is born Guálinto Gómez, nicknamed "George Washington" by his family in the hope that he will someday be "a leader of his people."[52]

As its title suggests, the novel is the story of Gómez's life and the challenges that he faces growing up as a Mexican American in segregated south Texas. Texas Rangers murder his father, and so Guálinto is raised by his mother and his uncle Feliciano. As he dies, Gómez's father makes Feliciano promise that he will not tell his son that Rangers killed him: "My son. Musn't know. Ever. No hate, no hate." Feliciano honors his promise, though perhaps ultimately with tragic results. His nephew endures hostile school teachers, racist classmates, and other difficulties of growing up on the wrong side of the color line. But when a grown-up Gómez returns to south Texas in the last chapter, he is all too successful at navigating the white world. He is known as "George," has married an Anglo woman (the daughter of a Texas Ranger!), works for the army's intelligence unit, and scorns the LULAC-like Tejanos organizing against the white power structure.[53]

Paredes' fictionalization of the Plan de San Diego reflects aspects of the Tejano folk memory of the uprising. Many of the same ambiguities present in "Los Sediciosos" mark his depiction of the events. On the one hand, Tejanos join the rebellion for the most understandable of reasons. Sediciosos firing on soldiers from an ambush say "For my father," "For my brother," or "For my ranch, you thieving sons-of-bitches!" At the same time, some of the rebels are wantonly cruel. Lupe, Gómez's other uncle, takes pleasure in killing seemingly innocent Anglos and Mexican "collaborators." Paredes based Lupe's character on stories he was told of one Sedicioso. The Carrancistas come across as simple profiteers with little concern for the well-being of average Mexicans on either side of the border. On the other hand, Paredes portrays some Anglos sympathetically. The soldiers sent to quell the rebellion are lonely young men far from home with little idea why others were shooting at them. In his account they have nothing to do with lynchings, also a reflection of the discussion of the Plan that he heard as a child. In Paredes' account, Brownsville Anglos involved with the machine frequently treat Mexicans with kindness and decency.[54]

Ultimately the most admirable character in the book is Feliciano. Though he joins the Sediciosos for a time, Feliciano refuses to participate in brutalities. After he moves with Gómez and his mother to the fictional town of Jonesville,

Feliciano becomes friendly with several of the soldiers he serves while working at a cantina. Whereas Lupe is consumed by bitterness and Guálinto ultimately turns his back on his own people, Feliciano survives as a respected small businessman and farm owner. If the terror during the Plan de San Diego casts a shadow over the lives of George Washington Gómez and his family, then it is nonetheless still possible for Mexicans in Texas to steer a course between consuming resentment of Anglos and abject identification with them.

LULAC was attempting to steer just such a course, but when Paredes was writing *George Washington Gómez* during the 1930s he was not clear whether other Mexican Americans would finally have the chance to do the same. Slowly but surely they did. Just as with European immigrant groups, a wide range of changes in American social and political life—popular music, theatres, shared high schools, the New Deal, labor unions—drew more and more ethnic Mexicans toward thinking of themselves as U.S. citizens.[55] Particularly when so many Mexican-American veterans returned from World War II more intent than ever on fighting for equality, LULAC's political program became more appealing to a greater proportion of the Mexican-American community.

In the 1960s and 1970s, another generation came to the fore, one intent on both continuing the struggle for civil rights and departing from what its adherents perceived as the overly accommodating stance of LULAC and similar organizations. Where many of their parents had gone out of their way to use English and proclaim themselves loyal Americans, Chicano activists embraced Mexican culture and emphasized their ties to other oppressed or "colonized" peoples. Although Mexican Americans might live in the United States, Chicano activists pointed out that their ancestors had lived in "Aztlán," the mythic homeland of the Aztecs, long before the land of the Stars and Stripes had ever existed. The Chicano movement helped give rise to renewed labor organizing—which centered around the figure of César Chávez but included numerous strikes in the fields of south Texas—a cultural renaissance, and local victories for La Raza Unida Party in Texas.

Where LULAC's leaders had no reason to invoke the memory of the Plan de San Diego, Chicano activists took much greater interest in it. The interracial aspects of the Plan's appeal, its Mexican nationalist elements, and its protest of oppressive working conditions seemed to anticipate aspects of their own movement. "In the year 1915, in the town of San Diego in the lower Rio Grande Valley, there was written a document which expresses many of the sentiments of today's militant chicanos," wrote a student leader in 1976. The Plan attracted scholarly attention from Chicano academics for similar reasons. Juan Gomez-Quiñones wrote a brief description of the Plan in the first issue of *Aztlán,* a pioneering journal founded in 1970 to publish articles on the neglected field of Mexican-American history. Rebuking earlier studies that emphasized the role of U.S.-Mexican relations and diplomatic intrigue, his account stressed the social conditions and racism of south Texas. The Plan de San Diego, he insisted, was part of the Chicano experience. In 1975, on the sixtieth anniversary of the Plan, historian Emilio Zamora argued that the uprising demonstrated that early twentieth century Chicano resistance to Anglo domination was more organized and powerful than in his own day.[56] Such accounts, while accurately invoking the terror of racial violence in south Texas, had also lost the ambivalence and sense of division within the Tejano community expressed by Paredes and "Los Sediciosos." No longer a memory handed down directly by those who had lived through it, the Plan had instead become a symbol of Chicano determination to overthrow the brutal racism that had long outlived Aniceto Pizaña, Luis de la Rosa, and their thousands of followers and admirers.

Afterword

Today, some nine decades after the Plan de San Diego, the rebellion and the events surrounding it are barely remembered outside the small group of historians and other scholars who study the history of the border and Mexican Americans. Few residents of south Texas—much less of greater Mexico or the United States—are aware of the uprising or its brutal suppression. Even many descendants of Aniceto Pizaña, Luis de la Rosa, and their followers are unaware of the dramatic events that their grandfathers or great-uncles helped to make. Sprinkled amid the Valley's intensively worked farm fields and its burgeoning cities are city parks named after prominent developers like Lon Hill, plaques commemorating the exploits of José de Escandón and his colonists, and directions to the ruins of old church buildings and colorful cemeteries. But no signs, markers, or monuments note the existence of the architects of the Plan de San Diego or the victims of the vigilantism that their doomed quest provoked. Even the careers and accomplishments of those who managed to forge something noble out of the smoldering remains of so many lives—the Idars, J. Luz Saenz, J. T. Canales, and others—are uncommemorated.

Nations, like individuals, remember only the events and stories that help them to define who they are. And for many years, border stories seemed to have little to say to most Americans. The uprising and its impact on the founders of LULAC may have been a critical chapter in the history of Mexican Americans, but early in the twentieth century they were a tiny minority of the nation's population. The overwhelming majority of Americans had never met anybody of Mexican descent. When Americans thought of race, most argued about slavery, the crucible of the Civil War, the Jim Crow South, or the black ghettos of the north and west. When reflection or world events made them think of another country, they most often looked east, across the Atlantic, to the European nations that most resembled their own and from which most of their ancestors had come, and to whose wars their sons were sent. When they thought about what made them different from other nations, many looked to the American West, where they told themselves that the ruggedness and abundance of the frontier had made earlier Americans fiercely insistent on protecting their democratic right of self-governance.

Now, however, the dramatic growth of the United States' Latino population means that all Americans will have to know border stories to understand who they are now, and who they and their descendants will be in the new century. For many Americans, this new national history will also be family history. In 2000, Latinos surpassed African Americans as the nation's largest minority. Continued migration, the overall youth of the population, and lower Anglo birthrates ensure that the rise of the Latino population will continue for most of the twenty-first century, reaching about 18 percent by 2025 and perhaps a quarter of the national population by 2050.

In Latin America, and particularly in Mexico, the impact of migration to the United States is enormous. Fully half of the population of the Mexican state of Zacatecas, for example, lives in el Norte, prompting gubernatorial candidates to campaign in California and to propose the creation of legislative positions for U.S. residents. Deported Salvadorans have brought Los Angeles gangs and drug trafficking connections with them to San Salvador. The past president of the Dominican Republic grew up in Manhattan and still holds a green card—he returned to the Big Apple after serving his term. So-called migradollars (funds sent home by immigrants) keep rural communities in Mexico and Central America afloat, and they are already more important sources of foreign exchange than are export crops in several Latin American nations. In fifty years, the projected ninety-six million Latino residents of the United States would, if considered a nation, follow only Brazil and Mexico as the most populous country of Latin America. The economic and military power of the United States has cast a long shadow over Latin America for more than a century and a half, but soon the Colossus of the North will itself be a Latin American nation.

Within the United States, this epic demographic shift is most evident in the Southwest. California is now a "majority minority" state for the first time since the Gold Rush, and in twenty-five years those who identify themselves as Hispanic will constitute more than 40 percent of its population. (As one observer quipped, "Southern Californians are more likely to greet each other with "Qué tal?" than with "Hey, dude.") Texas will cross a similar divide, with Anglos predicted to become a minority in less than twenty years. Even beyond the Southwest and the traditional immigrant entrepôts such as New York City, the scope of the change is undeniable. When J. T. Canales moved to Kansas and then to Michigan in the 1890s, he was one of the few ethnic Mexicans in the Midwest. Now Chicago is one-quarter Latino. More than one million Mexican immigrants live in Alabama, Georgia, Tennessee, and the Carolinas. Heretofore nearly all-white cities such as Salt Lake City, Portland (Oregon), and Anchorage now have ethnic Mexican communities of tens of thousands. Latinos outnumber African Americans in both the Pacific Northwest and New England. From 2025 to 2050, according to federal projections, Latinos will account for two-thirds of the national population growth. Shortly after 2050, the United States as a whole will be a "majority minority" nation.[1]

This new nation in the making will look different from the old United States. It will face new problems and opportunities along with old ones, and to meet them its residents will add new stories to their historical memories. When Americans think of race, they will have to grapple with the meaning of such events as the U.S.–Mexico War, the Mexican Revolution, the forced deportations of ethnic Mexicans during the Great Depression, and the North American Free Trade Agreement. When they think of the impact of other countries on their lives, they will need to look south to Mexico and the rest of Latin America, and west to the far side of the Pacific Rim, as much as to England or Germany. When they discuss what distinguishes America from other nations, they will do so in the shadow of their long and permeable southern border, a line that looks much different from the mythic frontier's neat separation of civilization and savagery, the settled and the empty.

The Latinoization of the United States is but one part of the massive exchange of people, culture, goods, and money between nations constituting the complicated process often referred to as *globalization*. Perhaps globalization will weaken the power of nation-states and the allegiance of ordinary people to them, as many academics and commentators have predicted. How can people think of themselves as part of a nation, they ask, when so many of their neighbors remain tied to distant lands, or when so few of the goods in their houses and so little of the food on their tables come from their own country? And how can people have such a mindset if it is easier to send an email to a colleague on the other side of the planet than it is to talk to the janitor in the hallway? Or if so many of the books we read, the languages we speak, the movies we watch, and the songs we sing are from elsewhere? Or if we live far from our native land, making annual pilgrimages for holidays and festivals, then returning to our jobs on foreign soil? Or if multinational corporations employ more people and wield more power than do our own government? Or if being a Hutu or a Tutsi makes so much more difference than being a Rwandan?

Where much of humanity has for centuries thought that being American or Mexican, Chinese or French, was essential to who they were, perhaps these national affiliations will give way to an overlapping mix of identities. As they do, national governments will surrender many of their powers to international organizations and the emerging global market. The nations of western Europe, where modern nationalism was born, have already ceded many of their functions to the European Union. In the wake of the collapse of Soviet-style Communism, some pundits in the West went so far as to declare the "end of history." Traditional ideological and national conflict was drawing to a close, and the only viable path to the future was to fall into the welcoming arms of the global economy.[2]

Those living along the Texas-Tamaulipas border in the early twentieth century inhabited a world that in critical ways resembles what ours is becoming. No one nation could encompass the experiences or capture the aspirations of these ethnic Mexicans living along the border. They owed too much culturally and ideologically to Mexico, but they lived in the United States and were subordinated by Anglo-Americans and the powerful market economy that they controlled. At the same time, many aspects of American political ideals and social freedoms deeply appealed to them.

What many Tejanos discovered during the Plan de San Diego, however, was that it was dangerous to be a people without a state. A people could combine cultural elements of the two nations that served their own interests, but in crises they had to be able to call on the powers of a central state to protect themselves. They needed to be Mexican or American, and it turned out that to be both was impossible and to be neither was unwise. As far as the Mexican government was concerned, they were entirely expendable. For most Americans —particularly their Anglo neighbors—they were at best irrelevant to the U.S. national project, and at worse a barrier to be removed. The Tejano Progressives' turn to the politics of American nationalism, and the Sediciosos' embrace of irredentist Mexican nationalism, provides abundant evidence that globalization and nationalism walk hand in hand. The world may have entered a new era, but history itself has hardly come to an end.

In an ideal world, people would not need to attach so many of their hopes and aspirations to membership in a national community. There is

nothing about being a citizen of a particular country that should entitle one
to better treatment and more rights than those of another. The twentieth century, after all, is littered with the bodies of victims of nationalism. American
nationalism, like that of other nations, has justified naked racism, the conquest
of other peoples, and the brutal suppression of internal dissenters. In the
U.S.–Mexico borderlands, it has often been synonymous with white racial
supremacy. Since 1848, *American* and *Mexican* have often been used as both
racial and national terms to identify the United States with white people and
Mexico with darker people. Even now, some seven decades after the founding
of LULAC, it can be difficult to avoid conflating nation and race in the borderlands. The Mexican presence in the Rio Grande Valley is so heavy—almost
90 percent of the region's populace is of Hispanic descent, a fact reflected in
the ubiquitous use of Spanish in advertisements and casual conversation alike
—that those heading north often declare, "Now we're in the United States,"
upon reaching the Nueces River, as though to reject President James Polk's
rationale for beginning the Mexican War. "The Valley is a great place to live,"
runs a similar joke in current circulation, "it's so close to the United States."
A place with an overwhelming majority of ethnic Mexicans can only be "American" in the most tenuous of senses, such comments assume.[3]

In practice, however, south Texas, like the rest of the north side of the
border, has become American. Even here, where the U.S. army began the process of stealing half of Mexico, and where Tejanos were subjected to countless
indignities and outrages in the decades that followed, the imagined community of the nation has not been strictly vicious and narrow. The founders of
LULAC were able to envision themselves as American citizens in large part
because of the deep strain of racial egalitarianism in American culture. Since
Sherman's march, the most oppressed and marginalized Americans have been
able to carry the banners of nationalism and citizenship the most proudly.
Even in the midst of the terrible violence of the Plan de San Diego and World
War I, the difference between the general evenhandedness of federal soldiers
and the wanton cruelty of local vigilantes and the Texas Rangers proved that
Tejanos could enter this current of American life. There could, in short, be
such a thing as a Mexican American. The state could enter the borderlands not
only as the agent of conquest, but also as the guarantor of basic civil liberties.

This hope would not be realized somewhat until after World War II,
when the civil rights movement's success in overthrowing Jim Crow was repli-
cated by the efforts of Mexican Americans in the Southwest. Mexican Americans
have won victories and opportunities of which J. T. Canales, the Idars, and
J. Luz Saenz could only have dreamed. Racism, most evident in the hysterical
warnings of U.S. presidential candidate Pat Buchanan and others that ethnic
Mexican population growth meant a "reconquest" for Mexico, has hardly dis-

appeared. (One of the many things that these nativists fail to understand is that only their rejection of racial diversity—already eclipsed even in its most powerful base in California—could again make Mexican irredentism appealing.) Instead, Mexican Americans' burgeoning middle class, increasing political power, and growing prominence in education and the arts seem to confirm the old hopes of the Tejano Progressives.[4]

There is no neat end to a history, however. And in south Texas, the rise of Mexican-American citizenship politics has left some basic needs unmet. More than a quarter of Valley residents live in *colonias,* unincorporated developments that lack such amenities as running water or paved streets. While the region ships its crops across North America, the people who pick them often go hungry. The emergence of the border as one of the world's centers of industrial production has not ended the misery of so many of its inhabitants. This continuation of poverty in the face of abundance cheapens the value of legal citizenship, confirming the grim prophecies of the Flores Magón brothers.

As people struggle for survival and dignity, they do so in the shadow of history. "I believe that rather than from claims to Spanish nobility or inherited class background, dignity in south Texas comes with more down-to-earth, practical concerns such as land ownership, however cash-poor the owner of thousands of acres or five-acre *ranchito* may be," writes scholar and south Texas native Leticia Garza-Falcón. "To this day in South Texas," she argues, "whether one is the owner of a *tendajito* [little store] or a chain of them, it is the autonomy and independence of working for oneself rather than as a wage earner or dependent of a patron that bestows prestige."[5] That both Aniceto Pizaña and Clemente Idar would recognize this perspective suggests that many of the dilemmas of their time are with us still.

Appendix

High Tide of the Plan de San Diego, August – September 1915

AUGUST 2
Clash between raiders and soldiers near San Benito; railroad bridge partially burned

AUGUST 6
Raid on Sebastian and killing of the Austins

AUGUST 8
Raid on Norias division of King Ranch

AUGUST 9
Skirmish with U.S. soldiers near Mercedes

AUGUST 16
U.S. troops fired on from across Rio Grande in two separate incidents

AUGUST 17
U.S. troops fired on at Progreso

AUGUST 20
Battle between troops and band near Hidalgo

AUGUST 25
Cross-river gunfire at Progreso; band ambushes troops near Mission

AUGUST 30
Railroad bridge burned near Brownsville

SEPTEMBER 2
Two railroad bridges burned in Cameron County; farmers killed near Los Fresnos pumping station; skirmish near burned rail trestle, Cameron County; battle with soldiers near Harlingen; start of four-day fight at Ojo de Agua (Progreso)

SEPTEMBER 4
Harlingen-San Benito-Brownsville telegraph lines cut; Rangers, rancher fired on near Mission

SEPTEMBER 5
Cross-river gunfire near Mission

SEPTEMBER 9
Raiders kill Tejano near Lyford

SEPTEMBER 10
Separate clashes with soldiers at Nebraska station, Galveston ranch; battle near Lyford

SEPTEMBER 11
Raiders kill two "pro-American" Tejanos near Lyford

SEPTEMBER 13
Cavalry ambushed near Los Indios

SEPTEMBER 16
Skirmish near Harlingen

SEPTEMBER 17
Skirmish near Turner's ranch; firefight near Donna on Rio Grande

SEPTEMBER 24
Attack on Progreso; raid on McAllen ranch

SEPTEMBER 27
Cavalry fired on near La Feria

SEPTEMBER 28
Harlingen farmer attacked; Rangers clash with raiders at Ebenoza, Hidalgo County

Notes

INTRODUCTION

1. Affidavit of Nellie Francis Austin, *Records of the Special Claims Commission, United States and Mexico, Created Under the Claims Convention of September 10, 1923,* Docket #1884.

2. Testimony of W. B. Huckley, in *Investigation of Mexican Affairs* (2 vols.), 66th Cong., 2d sess., 1920, S. Doc 285, serial 7665, 1185.

3. "Exclusion Act Put in Force Along Border," *New York Sun,* Sept. 15, 1915, from clippings file in Secretaria de Relaciones Exteriores (SRE), Archivo de la Embajada Mexicana en Estados Unidos de América (AEMEUA), Leg 685, Exp 3; *San Antonio Express,* Sept. 11, 1915, cited in James Sandos, *Rebellion in the Borderlands: Anarchism and the Plan de San Diego, 1904–1923* (Norman: Oklahoma University Press, 1992), 98; James Sandos, "The Mexican Revolution and the United States, 1915–17: The Impact of Conflict in the Texas-Tamaulipas Frontier upon the Emergence of Revolutionary Government in Mexico" (Ph.D. diss., University of California at Berkeley, 1978), 164; *Proceedings of the Joint Committee of the Senate and House in the Investigation of the Texas State Ranger Force* (Austin, Texas, 1919), 248.

4. *Proceedings of the Joint Committee,* excerpt reprinted in Oscar Martinez, *Fragments of the Mexican Revolution* (Albuquerque: University of New Mexico Press, 1983), 168; Paul Vanderwood and Frank Samponaro, *War Scare on the Rio Grande* (Austin: Texas State Historical Association, 1992), 78.

CHAPTER 1
Conquest

Epigraph: Quoted in David Gutiérrez, *Walls and Mirrors: Mexican Americans, Mexican Immigrants, and the Politics of Ethnicity* (Berkeley: University of California Press, 1995), 16.

1. *Historical Statistics of the United States: Colonial Times to 1970*, vol. 1 (Washington: U.S. Department of Commerce, 1976), 25, 32, 35; Gutiérrez, *Walls and Mirrors*, 20.

2. U.S. Congress. Senate. *The Congressional Globe*, 30th Cong., 1st sess., 1848, 98–99; quoted in Omar Valerio-Jiménez, "Indíos Bárbaros, Divorcées, and Flocks of Vampires: Identity and Nation on the Rio Grande, 1749–1894" (Ph.D. diss., University of California at Los Angeles, 2000), 387.

3. Albert Hurtado, *Intimate Frontiers: Sex, Gender, and Culture in Old California* (Albuquerque: University of New Mexico Press, 1999), 89; Leonard Pitt, *The Decline of the Californios: A Social History of the Spanish-Speaking Californians, 1846–1890* (Berkeley: University of California Press, 1970), 278. See also Albert Camarillo, *Chicanos in a Changing Society: From Mexican Pueblos to American Barrios in Santa Barbara and Southern California, 1848–1930* (Cambridge: Harvard University Press, 1979).

4. Arnoldo de León, *They Called Them Greasers: Anglo Attitudes Toward Mexicans in Texas, 1821–1900* (Austin: University of Texas Press, 1983), 17.

5. Charles M. Robinson III, *The Men Who Wear the Star: The Story of the Texas Rangers* (New York: Random House, 2000), xviii, 286; Robert M. Utley, *Lone Star Justice: The First Century of the Texas Rangers* (New York: Oxford University Press, 2002).

6. N. A. Jennings, in *Foreigners in Their Native Land: Historical Roots of the Mexican Americans*, ed. David Weber (Albuquerque: University of New Mexico Press, 1973), 189–90; Américo Paredes, *"With His Pistol in His Hand": A Border Ballad and Its Hero* (Austin: University of Texas Press, 1958), 10–11, 24; David Montejano, *Anglos and Mexicans in the Making of Texas, 1836–1986* (Austin: University of Texas Press, 1987), 33; Valerio-Jiménez, "Indíos Bárbaros," 217; Montejano, *Anglos and Mexicans*, 28.

7. John Kelsey, "A Statement of Facts Respecting the Reports About Cattle and Hide Stealing upon the Rio Grande by Citizens of Mexico, and Respecting the Report of the U.S. Commissioners to Texas Appointed Under Joint Resolution of Congress Approved May 7, 1872" (n.p., 1875), 2–3; *La Crónica*, Dec. 3, 1910.

8. Montejano, *Anglos and Mexicans*, 35–37; Armando Alonzo, *Tejano Legacy: Rancheros and Settlers in South Texas, 1734–1900* (Albuquerque: University of New Mexico Press, 1998), 130; Jovita González, "Social Life in Cameron, Starr, and Zapata Counties" (master's thesis, University of Texas at Austin, 1930), 27.

9. Montejano, *Anglos and Mexicans*, 43–44; Evan Anders, *Boss Rule in South Texas: The Progressive Era* (Austin: University of Texas Press, 1982), 13–18.

10. Joe S. Graham, *El Rancho in South Texas: Continuity and Change from 1750* (John E. Connor Museum, Texas A & M University-Kingsville, and University of North Texas Press, Denton, Texas, 1994), 25, 28; Emilia Schunior Ramírez, *Ranch Life in Hidalgo County After 1850* (Edinburg, Tex.: New Santander Press, 1971), n.p.

11. Paredes, *"With His Pistol in His Hand,"* 10–11; Emmanuel Domenech, *Missionary Adventures in Texas and Mexico. A Personal Narrative of Six Years' Sojourn in Those Regions*

(London: Longman, Brown, Green, Longmans, and Roberts, 1858), 309; Alonzo, *Tejano Legacy*, 44.

It is surely an overstatement to claim, as does Armando Alonzo, that "[h]istorically, social class was not an important feature of the society." But David Montejano's assertion that the hacienda was the "dominant social and economic institution of the border region" ignores the large number of independent rancheros and other limitations on class stratification that existed not only in the Nueces Strip, but across much of the northeast of Mexico. See Alonzo, *Tejano Legacy*, 43, and Montejano, *Anglos and Mexicans*, 77.

12. Alonzo, *Tejano Legacy*, 55; Ana Cristina Downing De Juana, "Intermarriage in Hidalgo County, 1860 to 1900" (master's thesis, University of Texas Pan-American, 1998), 60; Alan Govenar, "African-American Ranching in Texas," in *Ranching in South Texas: A Symposium*, ed. Joe S. Graham (Texas A & M University-Kingsville, 1994), 80; Ana Cristina Downing De Juana, personal communication; Arnoldo de Leon and Kenneth L. Stewart, "Lost Dreams and Found Fortunes: Mexicans and Anglo Immigrants in South Texas, 1850–1900," *Western Historical Quarterly* 14 (July 1983): 295; Karl Jacoby, "Between North and South: The Alternative Borderlands of William H. Ellis and the African American Colony of 1865," in *Continental Crossroads: Frontiers, Borders and Transnational History in the US-Mexico Borderlands, 1821–1940*, ed. Samuel Truett and Elliott Young (Durham, N.C.: Duke University Press, forthcoming). The census defined "South Texas" as the present-day counties of Webb, Zapata, Starr, Hidalgo, Cameron, Willacy, Kenedy, Brooks, Jim Hogg, Duval, Jim Wells, Kleberg, and Nueces.

13. Paul Taylor, *An American-Mexican Frontier, Nueces County, Texas* (Chapel Hill: University of North Carolina Press, 1934), 231; Elliott Young, "Red Men, Pocahontas, and George Washington: Harmonizing Race Relations in Laredo at the Turn of the Century," *Western Historical Quarterly* 29 (Spring 1998): 50, 65–67.

14. Montejano, *Anglos and Mexicans*, 42. See Juan Gonzalez, *Harvest of Empire: A History of Latinos in America* (New York: Viking, 2000), 45, for a brief discussion of cattle-ranching terminology.

15. Montejano, *Anglos and Mexicans*, 63–64; Tom Lea, *The King Ranch* (Boston: Little, Brown, and Co., 1957).

16. Kelsey, "A Statement of Facts," 3; Montejano, *Anglos and Mexicans*, 54, 56.

17. Montejano, *Anglos and Mexicans*, 66–68; Alonzo, *Tejano Legacy*, 8.

18. Albert Camarillo, *Chicanos in a Changing Society: From Mexican Pueblos to American Barrios in Santa Barbara and Southern California, 1848–1930* (Cambridge, Mass.: Harvard University Press, 1979); Robert J. Rosenbaum, *Mexicano Resistance in the Southwest: "The Sacred Right of Self-Preservation"* (Austin: University of Texas Press, 1981); Sarah Deutsch, *No Separate Refuge: Culture, Class, and Gender on an Anglo-Hispanic Frontier in the American Southwest, 1880–1920* (New York: Oxford University Press, 1987); Deena González, *Refusing the Favor: The Spanish-Mexican Women of Santa Fe, 1820–1880* (New York: Oxford University Press, 1999); María E. Montoya, *Translating Property: The Maxwell Land Grant and the Conflict over Land in the American West, 1840–1900* (Berkeley: University of California Press, 2002).

19. Montejano, *Anglos and Mexicans*, 72.

20. Montejano, *Anglos and Mexicans*, 34.

21. Susan Johnson, *Roaring Camp: The Social World of the California Gold Rush* (New York: W.W. Norton, 2000), 33.

22. Paredes, *"With His Pistol in His Hand,"* 33.

23. Roberto M. Villareal, "The Mexican-American Vaqueros of the Kenedy Ranch: A Social History" (master's thesis, Texas A & I University, 1972), 7; Utley, *Lone Star Justice*, 276–77.

24. Paredes, *"With His Pistol in His Hand,"* 33.

25. The best account of Las Gorras Blancas remains Robert Rosenbaum, *Mexicano Resistance.*

26. Juan Cortina, "Proclamation," Nov. 23, 1859, in U.S. Congress. House. *Difficulties on the Southwestern Frontier,* 36th Cong., 1st sess., 1860. H. Exec. Doc. 52.

27. Quoted in Jerry D. Thompson, *Juan Cortina and the Texas-Mexico Frontier, 1859–1877* (El Paso: Texas Western Press, 1994), 87; Montejano, *Anglos and Mexicans,* 33–35; Charles C. Goldfinch, "Juan N. Cortina, 1824–1892: A re-appraisal" (Chicago: n.p., 1949), 67–69.

28. Elliott Young, "Twilight on the Texas-Mexico Border: Catarino Garza and Identity at the Cross-Roads, 1880–1915" (Ph.D. diss., University of Texas at Austin, 1997), 230, 85, 40, 87, 33; Juan Fidel Zorilla and Carlos González Salas, eds., *Diccionario biográfico de Tamaulipas* (Victoria: Universidad Autónoma de Tamaulipas, Instituto de Investigaciones Históricas, 1984), 106–7.

29. Young, "Twilight," 129, 182, 313; Richard Harding Davis, *The West from a Car-Window* (New York: Harper Brothers, 1892), 47; see also Montejano, *Anglos and Mexicans,* 89; Young, "Twilight," 182, 313.

30. Arnoldo de León, *The Tejano Community* (Albuquerque: University of New Mexico Press, 1982), 36.

31. John G. Bourke, "An American Congo," *Scribner's* (May 1894); Montejano, *Anglos and Mexicans,* 98; Lea, *King Ranch,* 536–37.

32. Lea, *King Ranch,* 541.

33. Ibid.; J. L. Allhands, *Gringo Builders* (Iowa City, Iowa: n.p., 1931), 39. The Hispanic and mixed committee members were F. Yturria, J. Celaya, Valentin Gavito, M. Fernandez, Jr., George Champion, M. Alonzo, S. Cavazos, Manuel Barredo, Adolph Garza, N. Cantu, Frank Champion, J. H. Fernández, E. Cavazos, and E. C. Forto.

34. Dorothy Lee Pope, *Rainbow Era on the Rio Grande* (Brownsville, Tex.: Springman-King, 1971), 13, 8.

35. Progreso Development Company, *Progreso Haciendas* (San Antonio, Tex.: Sigmund Press, n.d.).

36. Frisco Lines, *Irrigation in the Lower Rio Grande Valley* (St. Louis, Mo.: Burton and Skinner, n.d. [1910s]), 18; *San Benito Land and Water Company* (n.p., n.d. [1911]), 21.

37. Edwin J. Foscue, "Agricultural History of the Lower Rio Grande Valley Region," *Agricultural History* 8, no. 3 (July 1934): 124–38; James Sandos, "The Mexican Revolution and the United States, 1915–17: The Impact of Conflict in the Texas-Tamaulipas Frontier upon the Emergence of Revolutionary Government in Mexico" (Ph.D. diss., University of California at Berkeley, 1978), 115, 166; Armando Alonzo, "A History of the Mexicans in the Lower Rio Grande Valley of Texas: Their Role in Land Development and Commercial Agriculture, 1900–1930" (master's thesis, University of Texas Pan-American, 1983), 44; Progreso Development Company, *Progreso Haciendas,* n.d., n.p.

38. Allhands, Gringo Builders, 98; *La Crónica,* April 9, 1910, 2. For population statistics of

Cameron and Hidalgo counties, see Sandos, "The Mexican Revolution and the United States," 119.

39. Emilio Zamora, *The World of the Mexican Worker in Texas* (College Station: Texas A & M University Press, 1993), 33; Anders, *Boss Rule,* 139; *Pilar Villareal v. A. A. Browne et al.,* no. 2935, 28th Judicial District, Cameron County, Texas, 1205 (transcript in Center for American History, University of Texas at Austin) (hereafter cited as *Villareal v. Browne*); Hidalgo County Deed Records, Hidalgo County Courthouse, Edinburg, Texas.

40. *Villareal v. Brown,* 918, 1317, 1332.

41. Tax rolls, Hidalgo and Cameron counties, Texas State Archives, Austin, Texas; *La Crónica,* May 7, 1910, 2.

42. Graham, *El Rancho,* 25. See also Andrés Tijerina, *Tejano Empire: Life on the South Texas Ranches* (College Station: Texas A & M University Press, 1998), 59–64, especially for description of women's work.

43. "Hearings Before the Committee on Immigration and Naturalization, Relating to the Temporary Admission of Illiterate Mexican Laborers," 66th Cong., 2d sess., 1920, 167; see Neil Foley, *The White Scourge: Mexicans, Blacks, and Poor Whites in Texas Cotton Culture* (Berkeley: University of California Press, 1997), for a discussion of the tenancy and labor system in Texas's cotton belt.

44. Roberto M. Villareal, "The Mexican-American Vaqueros," 35. Villareal does not include the Spanish original of the *corrido.* For an analysis of "Las Labores," see Tijerina, *Tejano Empire,* 93.

45. Montejano, *Anglos and Mexicans,* 131.

46. Michael Perman, *Struggle for Mastery: Disfranchisement in the South, 1888–1908* (Chapel Hill: University of North Carolina Press, 2001), 279; Montejano, *Anglos and Mexicans,* 143.

47. *Regeneración,* Jan. 24, 1914; "A los hijos de Cuahtémoc, Hidalgo y Juárez en Texas" (Nov. 26, 1914, proclamation), Archivo Venustiano Carranza (AVC), Centro de Estudios de Historia de México, Departamento Cultural de Condumex, S.A., México, D.F. [Mexico City], Carpeta 39, doc. 4263. Carranza sympathizers in Laredo sent him a copy.

CHAPTER 2
Trouble in Mind

1. Virgil Lott, "The Rio Grande Valley," TS (n.d.), Center for American History, University of Texas at Austin, 32; John Peavey, "Day by Day Stories and History of Our Rio Grande Valley from 1906 till 1941," MS, Lower Rio Grande Valley Historical Collection, University of Texas Pan-American, unpaginated entry for Dec. 25, 1914. For requests for the deployment of additional state forces, see Adjutant General Correspondence (hereafter cited as "AG Correspondence"), Texas State Archives, Box 548.

2. *La Crónica,* Dec. 3, 1910.

3. Tax rolls, Cameron and Hidalgo counties, 1900, 1910; "Francisco Yturria: Historical Information Provided by Frank D. Yturria, June 1998," TS in the possession of author; Daniel Yturria to Texas Adjutant General, April 27, 1917, AG Correspondence, Texas State Archives, Box 562–1.

4. Evan Anders, *Boss Rule in South Texas: The Progressive Era* (Austin: University of Texas Press, 1982), 21; Armando Alonzo, "A History of Mexicans in the Lower Rio Grande Valley of Texas: Their Role in Land Development and Commercial Agriculture, 1900–1930" (master's thesis, University of Texas Pan-American, 1983), 36.

5. *Records of the Special Claims Commission, United States and Mexico, Created Under the Claims Convention of September 10, 1923* (hereafter cited as "Mexican Claims Commission"), Docket #850; *Texas Family Land Heritage Registry,* vol. 6 (Austin, Tex.: Department of Agriculture, 1980), 40–41.

6. Armando Alonzo, "A History of the Mexicans in the Lower Rio Grande Valley of Texas: Their Role in Land Development and Commercial Agriculture, 1900–1930" (master's thesis, University of Texas Pan-American, 1983), 41. For descriptions of Tejano farmers in Eastern Hidalgo and Cameron counties, see *Pilar Villareal v. A. A. Browne et al.,* no. 2935 in the District Court, 28th Judicial District, Cameron County, Texas, passim.

7. Anders, *Boss Rule,* 206–7.

8. I have chosen the term *Tejano Progressive* to describe these Tejanos in order to emphasize the connections between their political program and the Progressive Era ferment of the United States. George Sánchez points to a similar connection in California in George Sánchez, "The 'New Nationalism,' Mexican Style: Race and Progressivism in Chicano Political Development During the 1920s," in *California Progressivism Revisited,* ed. William Deverell and Tom Sitton (Berkeley: University of California Press, 1994).

Many historians view Progressives quite skeptically, emphasizing their fondness for social control and their unwillingness to confront the economic forces behind so many of the social problems that they did address. Others, however, stress the enormous diversity of Progressives and the extremely democratic nature of many of their proposals. See Robert D. Johnston, "Re-Democratizing the Progressive Era: The Politics of Progressive Era Political Historiography," *Journal of the Gilded Age and Progressive Era* 1 (January 2002): 68–92; and Robert D. Johnston, *The Radical Middle Class: Populist Democracy and the Question of Capitalism in Progressive Era Portland, Oregon* (Princeton, N.J.: Princeton University Press, 2003). Although most historians have treated U.S. Progressives as part of only the trajectory of U.S. history, Daniel Rodgers's recent study shows just how much they were in dialogue with European reformers as well. The term *Tejano Progressivism* therefore can help us to see the ways in which American politics during this period were bound up in international developments. See Daniel T. Rodgers, *Atlantic Crossings: Social Politics in a Progressive Age* (Cambridge, Mass.: Harvard University Press, 1998).

9. For discussions of Liberalism, see Alicia Hernández Chávez, *Anenecuilco: Memoria y vida de un pueblo* (México, D.F.: El Colegio de México, 1991); Peter Guardino, *Peasants, Politics, and the Formation of Mexico's National State: Guerrero, 1800–1857* (Stanford, Calif.: Stanford University Press, 1996); Florencia Mallon, *Peasant and Nation: The Making of Postcolonial Mexico and Peru* (Berkeley: University of California Press, 1995); Guy P. C. Thomson with David LaFranca, *Patriotism, Politics, and Popular Liberalism in Mexico* (Wilmington, Del.: Scholarly Resources, 1992); Guy Thomson, "Popular Aspects of Liberalism in Mexico, 1848–1888," *Bulletin of Latin American Research* 10:3 (1991): 265–91; Alan Knight, "El liberalismo mexicano desde la reforma hasta la revolución (una interpretación)," *Historia mexicana* 35 (1985): 59–85; Charles Hale, *The Transformation of*

Liberalism in Late Nineteenth-Century Mexico (Princeton, N.J.: Princeton University Press, 1989); Jennie Purnell, *Popular Movements and State Formation in Revolutionary Mexico* (Durham, N.C.: Duke University Press, 1999).

10. Emilio Zamora, *The World of the Mexican Worker in Texas* (College Station: Texas A & M University Press, 1993), 61; Theresa Paloma Acosta, "Nicasio Idar," in Ron Tyler, general editor, *The New Handbook of Texas* (Austin: Texas State Historical Association, 1996); Nancy Baker Jones, "Jovita Idar," in Tyler, *New Handbook;* Cynthia Orozco, "Clemente Nicasio Idar," in Tyler, *New Handbook;* Cynthia Orozco, "Eduardo Idar," in Tyler, *New Handbook.*

11. "Personal Recollections of J. T. Canales Written at the Request of and for Use by the Honorable Harbert Davenport in Preparing a Historical Sketch of the Lower Rio Grande Valley for the Soil Conservation District, Recently Organized, in Cameron County, Texas," TS, Center for American History, University of Texas at Austin, April 28, 1945, 8–11. For the best discussion of Canales's life and career, see Richard Ribb, "José Tomás Canales and the Texas Rangers: Myth, Identity, and Power, 1910–1930" (Ph.D. diss., University of Texas at Austin, 2001).

12. "Personal Recollections," 12; Anders, *Boss Rule,* 89.

13. "Personal Recollections," 17, 15; *La Crónica,* May 7, 1911, 2; *La Crónica,* March 5, 1910; Anders, *Boss Rule,* 89.

14. *La Crónica,* Nov. 12, 1910, 1.

15. Octavio García Interview, 1975, Lower Rio Grande Valley Historical Collection, University of Texas Pan-American; *La Crónica,* Aug. 6, 1910, 3.

16. *La Crónica,* May 7, 1910. For a discussion of education and modernization in Mexico's north during the same period, see Juan Mora-Torres, *The Making of the Mexican Border: The State, Capitalism, and Society in Nuevo León, 1848–1910* (Austin: University of Texas Press, 2001), 253.

17. *La Crónica,* Oct. 1, 1910, 1; Sept. 21, 1911, 4; Oct. 26, 1911. For a discussion of changing gender roles in the Mexican north, see William French, *A Peaceful and Working People: Manner, Moral and Class Formation in Northern Mexico* (Albuquerque: University of New Mexico Press, 1996), 87–91.

18. *La Crónica,* Jan. 26, 1911, 3.

19. *La Crónica,* May 18, 1911; March 11, 1911; Feb. 23, 1911; Oct. 15, 1910.

20. *La Crónica,* Jan. 26, 1911; Oct. 15, 1910; Jan. 12, 1911, 2.

21. See John Bodnar, *The Transplanted: A History of Immigrants in Urban America* (Bloomington: Indiana University Press, 1985), for a synthetic treatment of this wave of immigration.

22. Matthew Frye Jacobson, *Whiteness of a Different Color: European Immigrants and the Alchemy of Race* (Cambridge, Mass.: Harvard University Press, 1998), 56, 83; Madison Grant, *The Passing of the Great Race* (New York: Charles Scribner's Sons, 1916), xvi, 80, 15; John Higham, *Strangers in the Land: Patterns of American Nativism 1860–1925* (New York: Atheneum, 1973), 323.

23. Horace Kallen, "Democracy Versus the Melting-Pot: A Study of American Nationality," *The Nation* 100, no. 2590 (Feb. 18, 25, 1915): 217, 220; for immigrant versions of Americanization, see James R. Barrett, "Americanization from the Bottom Up: Immigration and the Remaking of the Working Class in the United States, 1880–1930," *Journal of American*

History 79:4 (December 1992): 996–1020. For an interpretation of the twentieth-century United States centered on the clash between an encompassing civic nationalism and a more exclusive racial one, see Gary Gerstle, *American Crucible: Race and Nation in the Twentieth Century* (Princeton, N.J.: Princeton University Press, 2001).

24. *La Crónica,* Jan. 26, 1911. See Lon Kurashige's argument that second-generation Japanese leaders "knew that they could not simply change Little Tokyo for the sake of the Nissei: they had to change the Nissei for the sake of Little Tokyo's survival." Lon Kurashige, "The Problem of Biculturalism: Japanese American Identity and Festival Before World War II," *Journal of American History* 86:4 (March 2000): 1640.

25. *La Crónica,* Aug. 6, 1910, 4; Nov. 26, 1910; March 18, 1911.

26. *La Crónica,* May 7, 1910; "Personal Recollections," 18; *La Crónica,* Sept. 14, 1911, 29; *Commission on Industrial Relations, Final Report and Testimony,* Senate Doc. 415, Testimony of Emeterio Flores, 9204 (Washington, D.C.: U.S. Government Printing Office, 1916).

27. "Primer Congreso Mexicanista, verificado en Laredo, Texas, EE. UU. de la A. Los Días 14 al 22 de septiembre de 1911. Discurso y conferencias. Por la raza y para la raza" (Laredo: N. Idar, 1912), 2; José Limón, "El Primer Congreso Mexicanista de 1911: A Precursor to Contemporary Chicanismo," *Aztlán* 12 (Fall 1981): 211–26.

28. "Primer Congreso Mexicanista," 7, 8.

29. See *La Crónica,* Oct. 26, 1911, 1.

30. Américo Paredes, *A Texas-Mexican Cancionero: Folksongs of the Lower Border* (Austin: University of Texas Press, 1976), 32.

CHAPTER 3
The Promise of the Revolution

1. Francisco Madero, *La sucesión presidencial en 1910: El Partido Nacional Democratico* (Mexico, 1908), 238, quoted in Enrique Krauze, *Mexico: Biography of Power* (New York: Harper Collins, 1997), 235.

2. For seminal works on the Mexican Revolution, see Alan Knight, *The Mexican Revolution,* 2 vols. (New York: Cambridge University Press, 1986); John Womack, Jr., *Zapata and the Mexican Revolution* (New York: Random House, 1968); and Adolfo Gilly, *La revolución interrumpida* (México, D.F.: El Caballito, 1971).

3. See John H. Coatsworth, *Growth Against Development: The Economic Impact of Railroads in Porfirian Mexico* (DeKalb: Northern Illinois University Press, 1981).

4. Friedrich Katz makes the most sustained and persuasive case for Villa as an agrarian radical. See Friedrich Katz, *The Life and Times of Pancho Villa* (Palo Alto, Calif.: Stanford University Press, 1998). For Chihuahua's frontier, see Ana María Alonso, *Thread of Blood: Colonialism, Revolution, and Gender on Mexico's Northern Frontier* (Tucson: University of Arizona Press, 1995); Daniel Nugent, *Spent Cartridges of Revolution: An Anthropological History of Namiquipa, Chihuahua* (Chicago: University of Chicago Press, 1993). For the Terrazas family and the revolution, see Mark Wasserman, *Capitalists, Caciques, and Revolution: The Native Elite and Foreign Enterprise in Chihuahua, Mexico, 1854–1911* (Chapel Hill: University of North Carolina Press, 1984), and Mark Wasserman, *Persistent Oligarchs: Elites and Politics in Chihuahua, Mexico, 1910–1940* (Durham: Duke University Press, 1993).

5. Quoted in Krauze, *Mexico*, 274.

6. David Gutiérrez, *Walls and Mirrors: Mexican Americans, Mexican Immigrants, and the Politics of Ethnicity* (Berkeley: University of California Press, 1995), 57; Alberto Camarillo, *Chicanos in a Changing Society: From Mexican Pueblos to American Barrios in Santa Barbara and Southern California, 1848–1930* (Cambridge: Harvard University Press, 1979), 200; Leonard Pitt and Dale Pitt, *Los Angeles A to Z: An Encyclopedia of the City and County* (Berkeley: University of California Press, 1997), 403; Thomas Boswell, "The Growth and Proportional Distribution of the Mexican Population in the United States, 1910–1970," *The Mississippi Geographer* (Spring 1979): 57–76; John Ramon Martinez, "Mexican Emigration to the United States, 1910–1930" (Ph.D. diss., University of California at Berkeley, 1957), 58, 68; Lawrence Cardoso, *Mexican Immigration to the United States, 1897–1931* (Tucson: University of Arizona Press, 1980), 38.

7. Commission on Industrial Relations, *Final Report and Testimony* (Washington: U.S. Government Printing Office, 1916), S. Doc 415, testimony of Emeterio Flores, p. 9200.

8. James Alex Garza, "On the Edge of a Storm: Laredo and the Mexican Revolution, 1910–1917" (master's thesis, Texas A & M International University, 1996), 66, 31; Jovita Idar to Venustiano Carranza, Nov. 20, 1916, Archivo Venustiano Carranza (AVC), Centro de Estudios de Historia de México, Departamento Cultural de Condumex, S.A., México, D.F. [Mexico City], XXI-107-12265; Leonor Villegas de Magnón, *The Rebel* (Houston: Arte Público Press, 1994); Nancy Baker Jones, "Jovita Idar," in Ron Tyler, general editor, *The New Handbook of Texas*, 6 vols. (Austin: Texas State Historical Association, 1996).

9. James Sandos, *Rebellion in the Borderlands: Anarchism and the Plan de San Diego, 1904–1923* (Norman: Oklahoma University Press, 1992), 1–12.

10. Ibid., 29; Emilio Zamora, *World of the Mexican Worker in Texas* (College Station: Texas A & M University, 1993), 61; *La Crónica*, June 15, 1911; Commission on Industrial Relations, *Final Report and Testimony*, 9201.

11. *Regeneración*, Aug. 5, 1911, 3.

12. Sandos, *Rebellion*, 59; see, for example, *Regeneración*, Aug. 31, 1912.

13. Sandos, *Rebellion*, 74; Emilio Zamora, "Sara Estela Ramírez, una rosa roja en el movimiento," in *Mexican Women in the United States: Struggles Past and Present*, ed. Magdalena Mora and Adelaida R. del Castillo (Los Angeles: UCLA Chicano Studies Research Center Publication, 1980); Vicki Ruiz, *Out of the Shadows: Mexican Women in Twentieth-Century America* (New York: Oxford University Press, 1998), 99. For a critique of PLM gender ideology, see Emma Pérez, *The Decolonial Imaginary: Writing Chicanas into History* (Bloomington: Indiana University Press, 1999).

14. Sandos, *Rebellion*, 73–74; Aniceto Pizaña, "Apuntes biográficas de un revolucionario del año de 1915," (n.p., [1933]).

15. *Regeneración*, July 12, 1912; ibid., Sept. 7, 1912; ibid., Sept. 21, 1912; Pizaña, "Apuntes biográficas," 21, 39–40; Sandos, *Rebellion*, 9; Carlos González Salas, *Acercamiento a la historia del movimiento obrero en tampico, 1887–1983* (Victoria, Tamaulipas: Instituto de Investigaciones Históricas, 1987), 65–67.

16. Zamora, *World*, 65; *Regeneración*, July 12, 1912, and Aug. 10, 1912.

17. Quoted in C. Vann Woodward, *The Strange Career of Jim Crow* (New York: Oxford University Press, 1955), 63.

18. *Rebel,* March 14, 1914. For treatments of Populism and the region's agrarian Socialist tradition, see Lawrence Goodwyn, *Democratic Promise: The Populist Moment in America* (New York: Oxford University Press, 1976); James R. Green, *Grass-Roots Socialism: Radical Movements in the Southwest, 1895-1943* (Baton Rouge: Louisiana State University Press, 1978); Jim Bissett, *Agrarian Socialism in America: Marx, Jefferson, and Jesus in the Oklahoma Countryside, 1904-1920* (Norman: University of Oklahoma Press, 1999). For a discussion of Texas as the meeting ground of the cultures of Mexico and the U.S. South, see José Limón, *American Encounters: Greater Mexico, the United States, and the Erotics of Culture* (Boston: Beacon Press, 1998).

19. Neil Foley, *The White Scourge: Mexicans, Blacks, and Poor Whites in Texas Cotton Culture* (Berkeley: University of California Press, 1997), 35, 93; *Rebel,* April 4, 1914.

20. *Rebel,* Feb. 7, 1914; ibid., Jan. 31, 1914; ibid., March 21, 1914; ibid., Nov. 7, 1914.

21. Sandos, *Rebellion,* 34; Green, *Grass-Roots Socialism,* 330-32; Zamora, *World,* 133, 147; *Regeneración,* May 11, 1912; Foley, *The White Scourge,* 109; *Rebel,* Oct. 23, 1915.

22. *Regeneración,* Oct. 7, 1911, 1; González, 78.

23. Omar Valerio-Jímenez, "Indios Bárbaros, Divorceés, and Flocks of Vampires: Identity and Nation on the Rio Grande, 1749-1894" (Ph.D. diss., University of California at Los Angeles, 2000), 162.

24. Hubert J. Miller, "Mexican Migration to the U.S., 1900-1920, with a Focus on the Texas Rio Grande Valley," *Borderlands* 7, no. 2 (Spring 1984): 182; Jorge Aguilar Mora, *Una muerte sencilla, justa, eterna: Cultura y guerra durante la revolución Mexicana* (México, D.F.: Ediciones Era, 1990), 221; Octavio Herrera Pérez, *Monografía de Reynosa* (Victoria: Instituto Tamaulipeco de Cultura, 1989), 100-3; Octavio Herrera Pérez, "Del senorio a la posrevolución: Evolución histórica de una Hacienda en el noreste de México," *Historia mexicana* 43, no. 1 (1993): 5-47.

25. Aguilar Mora, *Una muerte sencilla,* 221; Juan Fidel Zorrilla, Maribel Miró Flaquer, and Octavio Herrera Pérez, *Tamaulipas: Una historia compartida II, 1810-1921* (Ciudad Victoria: Universidad Autónoma de Tamaulipas, Instituto de Investigaciones Históricas, 1993), 165, 172-73; *La Crónica,* Oct. 26, 1911, 1.

26. Herrera Pérez, *Reynosa,* 104; Aguilar Mora, *Una muerte sencilla,* 224; "Manifiesto a los soldados Constitucionalistsas de los estados de Nuevo León y Tamaulipas," Fondo Lucio Blanco, Archivo General de la Nación (Mexico City). See also Paul Vanderwood and Frank Samponaro, *War Scare on the Rio Grande: Robert Runyon's Photographs of the Border Conflict, 1913-1916* (Austin: Texas State Historical Association, 1992), 50-51.

27. *La Crónica,* June 15, 1911; Zamora, *World of the Mexican Worker,* 61; Commission on Industrial Relations, *Final Report and Testimony,* 9201. The Flores Magón brothers may have had greater influence on the Progressives than their later disputes indicate. When Magonista Sara Estela Ramírez died in 1910, Jovita Idar, who published many of her poems in *La Crónica,* gave the funeral eulogy.

28. *La Crónica,* July 16, 1910, 5.

CHAPTER 4
Rebellion

1. For a description of border crossings in this period see George Sánchez, *Becoming Mexican American: Ethnicity, Culture, and Identity in Chicano Los Angeles, 1900–1945* (New York: Oxford, 1993), 51.

2. Translations of the documents may be found in *U.S. v. Basilio Ramos, Jr., et al.*, Criminal #2152, Southern District of Texas, RG 21, Fort Worth Federal Records Center (FWFRC); "Gray-Lane Files," *Records of International Conferences, Commissions, and Expositions. Records of the United States Commissioners of the American and Mexican Joint Commission, 1916,* RG 43, United States Nation Archives (USNA), Memo #11; in the Walter Prescott Webb Papers, Center for American History, University of Texas at Austin, Box 2R290 (hereafter cited as Webb Papers); and in General Records of the Department of State, "Records of the Department of State Relating to Internal Affairs of Mexico, 1910–1929," RG 59, M 274 (hereafter cited as "Records"), 812.00/23116.

3. Virgil Lott, "The Rio Grande Valley," TS [n.d.], Center for American History, University of Texas at Austin, 28, 31, 32.

4. Deposition of Deodoro Guerra (Feb. 5, 1915) and testimony of A.Y. Baker (Feb. 5, 1915) in *The U.S. v. Basilio Ramos, Jr., et al.* For a description of Deodoro Guerra, see Evan Anders, *Boss Rule in South Texas: The Progressive Era* (Austin: University of Texas Press, 1982), 47–51.

5. "Records," 812.00/14470.

6. Milo Kearney and Anthony Knopp, *Boom and Bust: The Historical Cycles of Matamoros and Brownsville* (Austin, Tex.: Eakin Press, 1991), 215.

7. James Sandos, *Rebellion in the Borderlands: Anarchism and the Plan de San Diego, 1904–1923* (Norman: University of Oklahoma Press, 1992), 85.

8. "Records," 812.00/15517; Affidavit of W. T. Vann, Mexican Claims Commission, RG 76, *Records of the Special Claims Commission, United States and Mexico, Created Under the Claims Convention of September 10, 1923,* Docket #798 (hereafter cited as Mexican Claims Commission).

9. Ibid.

10. H. L. Yates to Frederick Funston, July 8, 1915, and Blocksom to U.S. army, telegram, July 9, 1915; "Records," 812.00/15517.

11. "Records," 812.00/15559 (report on border conditions for the week of July 17, 1915); Sanders to Adjutant General re Valley tumult, July 22, 1915, Adjutant General Correspondence, Texas State Archives, Box 550-14 (hereafter cited as AG Correspondence).

12. Frank Cushman Pierce, *A Brief History of the Rio Grande* (Menasha, Wis.: George Banta, 1917; revised, Edinburg, Tex.: New Santander Press, 1998), 90; John Peavey, "Day by Day Stories and History of Our Rio Grande Valley from 1906 till 1941," MS, Lower Rio Grande Valley Historical Collection, University of Texas Pan-American, unpaginated entry for July 25, 1915; "Records," 812.00/15730; Caesar Kleberg to Adjutant General, telegram, July 26, 1915, AG Correspondence, Box 550-16.

13. "Records" (Aug. 3, 1915, telegram), 812.00/15730; Vann affidavit, Mexican Claims Commission, Docket #798; "Records," 812.00/15730 (Brownsville commanding officer, telegram,

Aug. 4, 1915); captain of Company D to Adjutant General, Aug. 4, 1915, AG Correspondence, Box 550-18.

14. Lott, "Rio Grande Valley," 40; Rodolfo Rocha, "The Influence of the Mexican Revolution on the Mexico-Texas Border, 1910–1916" (Ph.D. diss., Texas Tech University, Lubbock, Texas, 1981), 266; Report of R. L. Barnes, Aug. 17, 1915, Investigative Case Files of the Bureau of Investigation, 1908–1921, case file 232-84, reel # 856 (hereafter cited as Bureau of Investigation).

15. Affidavit of Nellie Francis Austin, Mexican Claims Commission, Docket #1884.

16. "Records," 812.00/15814 (Samuel Spears to Department of Justice, Aug. 6, 1915).

17. See Sandos, *Rebellion,* 82; "Records," 812.00/23116 (Statement of Basilio Ramos, Jr.); Jorge Aguilar Mora, *Una muerte sencilla, justa, eterna: Cultura y guerra durante la revolución mexicana* (México, D.F: Ediciones Era, 1990), 283.

18. A copy of this manifesto can be found in "Records," 812.00/14245. It is not clear how or where it was circulated.

19. Aguilar Mora, *Una muerte sencilla,* 306.

20. Aguilar Mora, *Una muerte sencilla,* 350; William Warren Sterling, *Trails and Trials of a Texas Ranger* (n.p., 1959), 28.

21. Deposition of Deodoro Guerra (Feb. 5, 1915) and testimony of A. Y. Baker (Feb. 5, 1915), in *U.S. v. Basilio Ramos, Jr., et al.* James Sandos points out the flimsiness of Ramos's story of Huertista intrigue, although he accepts the rest of Ramos's story at face value. See Sandos, *Rebellion,* 80.

22. "Two Officers Fatally Shot at a 'Baile'; One Is Dead," *Brownsville Herald,* July 12, 1915, 1; Harbert Davenport to Walter P. Webb, Nov. 13, 1935, Webb Papers, Box 2M260.

23. Rocha, "The Influence of the Mexican Revolution," 262; "Records," 812.00/16890; ibid., 17136.

24. Affidavit of E. R. Jeffords, Mexican Claims Commission, Docket #850.

25. Lott, "Rio Grande Valley," 51.

26. Affidavit of U.S., Mexican Claims Commission, Docket #850.

27. Vann affidavit, Mexican Claims Commission, Docket #798, Peavey, "Day by Day Stories," Sept. 2, 1915, entry.

28. Lott, "Rio Grande Valley," 55-59; Pierce, *Brief History,* 93-94; report of R. L. Barnes, Feb. 1, 1916, Bureau of Investigation.

29. Vann affidavit, Mexican Claims Commission, Docket #798; Mexican Claims Commission, Docket #850; "Records," 812.00/16397, 16306; Pierce, *Brief History,* 95.

30. "Records," 812.00/16256; Pierce, *Brief History,* 94; Lott, "Rio Grande Valley," 61; Peavey, "Day by Day Stories," Sept. 11, 1915, entry; "Records," 812.00/16159.

31. "Records," 812.00/15814 (Samuel Spears to Department of Justice, Aug. 6, 1915); L. H. Bates to Adjutant General, Aug. 4, 1915, AG Correspondence, Box 550-18.

32. Jesse Pérez, "Memoirs of Jesse Pérez, 1870–1927," Center for American History, University of Texas at Austin (n.d.), 57; "Records," 812.00/17186; Pierce, *Brief History,* 90; "Records," 812.00/15730. For the raid on Saenz Store, see U.S. affidavit, Mexican Claims Commission, Docket #850.

33. Testimony of William G. B. Morrison and J. T. Canales, *Proceedings of the Joint Committee of the Senate and the House in the Investigation of the State Ranger Force* (Austin,

Texas, 1919), 28, 859 (hereafter cited as *Proceedings of the Joint Committee*); Pierce, *Brief History,* 90.

34. Testimony of Alba Heywood, *Proceedings of the Joint Committee,* 67–68.

35. "Necktie party," *Lyford Courant* (Aug. 6, 1915), from Harding Collection, Raymondville Public Library.

36. "A Most Dastardly Crime," *Lyford Courant* (Aug. 13, 1915), from Harding Collection, Raymondville Public Library.

37. Américo Paredes, *"With His Pistol in His Hand": A Border Ballad and Its Hero* (Austin: University of Texas Press, 1958), 27; testimony of W. T. Vann, *Proceedings of the Joint Committee,* 561, 568; Pierce, *Brief History,* 91.

38. "Records," 812.00/15814 (Samuel Spears to Department of Justice, Aug. 6, 1915).

39. Report of E. B. Stone, Oct. 17, 1915, Bureau of Investigation; report of Robert Barnes, Nov. 15, 1915, Bureau of Investigation.

40. Senate Committee on Foreign Relations, *Investigation of Mexican Affairs,* 66th Cong., 2d sess., 1920, S. doc. 285, 1263.

41. "Records," 812.00/15730; testimony of J. T. Canales, *Proceedings of the Joint Committee,* 861.

42. "Pizana vs the State," *Texas Criminal Reports 81: March–October 1917* (Austin: Von Boeckman & Sons, 1919), 83.

43. Aniceto Pizaña, "Apuntes biográficos de un revolucionario del año de 1915" (n.p. [1933]), 46; Harbert Davenport to Walter Webb, Dec. 28, 1934, Webb Papers, Box 2M260; Vann affidavit, Mexican Claims Commission, Docket #798; report of R. L. Barnes, Nov. 18, 1915, Mexican Claims Commission, Docket #1313.

44. Report of R. L. Barnes, Nov. 18, 1915, Mexican Claims Commission, Docket #1313; Pierce, *Brief History,* 90; "Records," 812.00/15730.

45. "Records," 812.00/15517; "Records," 812.00/15517; testimony of R. L. Barnes, in *Investigation of Mexican Affairs,* 1233.

46. Pizaña, "Apuntes biográficos," 61.

47. Ibid., 72.

48. Kleberg to Adjutant General, July 26, 1915, AG Correspondence, Box 550–16; Kleberg and Wells to Adjutant General, Aug. 4, 1915, AG Correspondence, Texas State Archives, Box 550–19.

49. Affidavit of D. P. Gay, Mexican Claims Commission, Docket #2745; Vann affidavit, ibid.; D. P. Gay, untitled MS, Jan. 12, 1933, Walter P. Webb Papers, Box 2M275, 4; "Records," 812.00/15814; Pierce, *Brief History,* 91.

50. Gay, untitled MS, 6; Pizaña, "Apuntes biográficos," 65–66.

51. Pierce, *Brief History,* 92–94; "Records," 812.00/15808, 16160; Peavey, "Day by Day Stories," Aug. 17, 1915, entry; Pizaña, "Apuntes biográficos," 66.

52. W. T. Vann to Adjutant General, Sept. 2, 1915, AG Correspondence, Box 551–10; Vann affidavit, Mexican Claims Commission, Docket #798.

53. Vann affidavit, Mexican Claims Commission, Docket #2745.

54. Pizaña, "Apuntes biográficos," 61, 62.

55. "Records," 812.00/15812.

56. "Records," 812.00/15929.

57. Pierce, *Brief History,* 95; report of Department of Justice Special Agent E. B. Stone, Nov. 6, 1915, in Mexican Claims Commission, Docket #2073.

58. Report of Department of Justice Special Agent E. B. Stone, Nov. 6, 1915, in Mexican Claims Commission, Docket #2073.

59. Kirby Warnock, *Texas Cowboy: The Oral Memoirs of Roland A. Warnock and His Life on the Texas Frontier* (Dallas: Trans-Pecos Publications, 1992), 47.

60. "Records," 812.00/15877 and 16054.

61. Mexican Claims Commission, Docket #1313; Pierce, *Brief History,* 93.

62. Mexican Claims Commission, Docket #1313; Pierce, *Brief History,* 93; Miriam Chatelle, *For We Love Our Valley Home* (San Antonio: The Naylor Company, 1948), 68; "Records," 812.00/16199.

63. See, for example, AG Correspondence, Box 551–6; Warnock, *Texas Cowboy,* 44.

64. Mexican Claims Commission, Docket #1113.

65. "Records," 812.00/16054; AG Correspondence, Box 551–11.

66. Mexican Claims Commission, Docket #798, 850.

67. "Records," 812.00/16096.

68. Alan Knight, *The Mexican Revolution,* 2 vols. (New York: Cambridge University Press, 1986); Friedrich Katz, *The Life and Times of Pancho Villa* (Palo Alto, Calif.: Stanford University Press, 1998); Douglas W. Richmond, *Venustiano Carranza's Nationalist Struggle, 1893–1920* (Lincoln: University of Nebraska Press, 1983).

69. Leoncio Reveles to C. Teniente Coronel Z. Vela Ramirez, letter, Aug. 4, 1915, Secretaria de Relaciones Exteriores (SRE), Archivo de la Embajada Mexicana en Estados Unidos de América (AEMEUA), Leg 477, Exp 19; Teniente Coronel Z. Vela Ramirez to Lencio Reveles, letter, Aug. 5, 1915, SRE, AEMEUA, Leg 477, Exp 19; "Records," 812.00/16054; Pierce, *Brief History,* 92. For more general accounts of the diplomatic maneuvering of Carranza's government during this period, see Joseph A. Stout, Jr., *Border Conflict: Villistas, Carrancistas, and the Punitive Expedition, 1915–1920* (Fort Worth: Texas Christian University Press, 1999); Linda B. Hall and Don M. Coerver, *Revolution on the Border: The United States and Mexico, 1910–1920* (Albuquerque: University of New Mexico Press, 1988); and Don M. Coerver and Linda B. Hall, *Texas and the Mexican Revolution: A Study in State and National Border Policy, 1910–1920* (San Antonio: Trinity University Press, 1984).

70. Garza, letter, Dec. 28, 1914, SRE, L-E-868 R, Leg 3.

71. R. Ciro de la Garza, *La revolucion Mexicana en el estado de Tamaulipas* (México, D.F.: Libreria de Manuel Porrua, 1975), 96, 109, 172.

72. Ibid., 62.

73. Pizaña, "Apuntes biográficos," 62; Aguilar Mora, *Una muerte sencilla,* 327.

74. "Records," 812.00/15745.

75. Press bulletin, Aug. 13, 1915, SRE, AEMEUA, Leg 460, Exp 3; report by Pan-American News Service, Aug. 4, 1915, SRE, AEMEUA, Leg 460, Exp 5. See also "Records," 812.00/16041, for another assertion that the perpetrators were Texas residents; "Mexican IWW's Want War, He Says," *New York Sun,* Sept. 28, 1915 (Washington, D.C., Sept. 27 dated), SRE, AEMEUA, Leg 685, Exp 3.

76. Arredondo to Lencio Reveles, Aug. 12, 1915, SRE, AEMEUA, Leg 477, Exp 19; Garza to

Arredondo, telegram, Sept. 25, 1915, SRE, AEMEUA, Leg 477, Exp 1; Arredondo to Carranza, telegram, Sept. 6, 1915, SRE, AEMEUA, Leg 477, Exp 1.

77. Arredondo to Samuel Scott, letter, Sept. 7, 1915, SRE, AEMEUA, Leg 460, Exp 3.

78. "Records," 812.00/16346.5.

79. Pierce, *Brief History*, 96; Peavey, "Day by Day Stories," Oct. 10, 1915, and Oct. 12, 1915 entries; "Records," 812.00/16600.

80. Lott, "Rio Grande Valley," 69; Mexican Claims Commission, Docket #115, #604, #1313; Pierce, *Brief History*, 96–97.

81. Lott, "Rio Grande Valley," 69; Mexican Claims Commission, Docket #115, #604, #1313; Pierce, *Brief History*, 96–97.

82. "Records," 812.00/16667; Pizaña, "Apuntes biográficos," 74.

83. Katz, *Life and Times*, 515, 529.

84. "Records," 812.00/16660.

85. Ibid., 16665; ibid., 16686; ibid., 16755.

86. Garza to Arredondo, telegram, Oct. 21, 1915, SRE, AEMEUA, Leg 477, Exp 19; "Records," 812.00/16667; Ciro R. de la Garza, *El plan de San Diego* (Victoria, Tamaulipas: Universidad Autónama de Tamaulipas, 1970), 42; de la Garza, *La revolucion Mexicana*, 207; Reveles to López, Nov. 1, 1915, Archivo Venustiano Carranza (AVC), Centro de Estudios de Historia de México, Departamento Cultural de Condumex, S.A., México, D.F. [Mexico City], 58, 6528; "Records," 812.00/16803. Luis de la Rosa may actually have been arrested in the first week of November. According to one account, he was seized in Matamoros and sent to Monterrey, where he was to be executed. Other reports placed de la Rosa on the streets of Monterrey a week later, so perhaps the Monterrey authorities were unwilling to execute him. See de la Garza, *El plan de San Diego*, 42; "Records," 812.00/16842.

87. "Records," 812.00/16842.

88. "Records," 812.00/16842.

89. "Records," 812.00/16836; Mission officer to Lansing, letter, Dec. 9, 1915, "Records," 812.00/16936.

90. Pierce, *Brief History*, 100.

CHAPTER 5
Repression

1. "Plot of San Diego," *Lyford Courant* (Aug. 20, 1915), from Harding Collection, Raymondville Library; Testimony of William G. B. Morrison and J. T. Canales, *Proceedings of the Joint Committee of the Senate and the House in the Investigation of the State Ranger Force* (Austin, Texas, 1919), 355 (hereafter cited as *Proceedings of the Joint Committee*).

2. *Proceedings of the Joint Committee*, 307, 315, 1142.

3. "Plot of San Diego," *Lyford Courant* (Aug. 20, 1915), from Harding Collection, Raymondville Library; General Records of the Department of State, "Records of the Department of State Relating to Internal Affairs of Mexico, 1910–1929," RG 59, M 274 (hereafter cited as "Records") 812.00/15559; "Necktie Party," *Lyford Courant* (Aug. 6, 1915), from Harding Collection, Raymondville Library.

4. Report of R. L. Barnes, Aug. 17, 1915, Investigative Case Files of the Bureau of Investigation, 1908–1921, case file 232–84, reel # 856 (hereafter cited as Bureau of Investigation).

5. Report of R. L. Barnes, Nov. 15, 1915, Bureau of Investigation. Forto broke with Wells and mounted an unsuccessful campaign for county sheriff in 1900 in affiliation with anti-machine Republicans, but returned to the machine several years later. Evan Anders, *Boss Rule in South Texas: The Progressive Era* (Austin: University of Texas Press, 1982), 35, 152.

6. Adam Medveckey, interview by Amando Ramos, Pharr, Texas, Aug. 22, 1978 (Lower Rio Grande Valley Historical Collection, University of Texas Pan-American); Lloyd David, interview by Xavier Pérez, Oct. 22, 1972 (South Texas Archives, Texas A & M University-Kingsville).

7. Aug. 13, 1915, press bulletin, Secretaria de Relaciones Exteriores (SRE), Archivo de la Embajada Mexicana en Estados Unidos de América (AEMEUA), Legajo 460, Expediente 3; "Records," 812.00/16175.

8. Samuel Spears to Frederick Funston, Sept. 23, 1915, Bureau of Investigation. For a brief mention of Spears's politics, see Anders, *Boss Rule,* 277–78.

9. J. L. Allhands, *Gringo Builders* (n.p., 1931), 268. Three years later, D. W. Glasscock would break away from Wells and run against state senator Archie Parr in one of the most bitterly contested and fraudulent elections in Texas history. See Anders, *Boss Rule,* 254.

10. "Records," 812.00/16890; Rodolfo Rocha, "The Influence of the Mexican Revolution on the Mexico–Texas Border, 1910–1916" (Ph.D. diss., Texas Tech University, 1981), 262; report of R. L. Barnes, Nov. 4, 1915, Bureau of Investigation; Mexican Claims Commission, RG 76, *Records of the Special Claims Commission, United States and Mexico, Created Under the Claims Convention of September 10, 1923,* Docket #2667 (hereafter cited as "Mexican Claims Commission").

11. Jesse Pérez, "Memoirs of Jesse Pérez, 1870–1927," Center for American History, University of Texas at Austin (n.d.), 58; D. P. Gay, MS, Jan. 12, 1933, Walter P. Webb Papers, Center for American History, University of Texas at Austin, Box 2M275, 9 (hereafter cited as Webb Papers); Fox to Adjutant General, Aug. 21, 1915, Adjutant General Correspondence, Texas State Archives, Box 551–16 (hereafter cited as AG Correspondence); Frank Cushman Pierce, *A Brief History of the Rio Grande* (Menasha, Wis.: George Banta, 1917; revised, Edinburg, Tex.: New Santander Press, 1998), 94. Jesse Pérez, at the time a Texas Ranger, gave the men's names as Alejos Vela, Ignacio Angel, and Jose Angel.

12. *Proceedings of the Joint Committee,* 678, 655.

13. Report of [illegible on film], Jan. 6, 1917, Bureau of Investigation; J. Z. Garza to Secretary of Foreign Relations, May 30, 1918, SRE, 30–16–54. For a detailed account of another effort of Hill's to drive off a ranchero, see *Proceedings of the Joint Committee,* 271.

14. John Peavey, "Day by Day Stories and History of Our Rio Grande Valley from 1906 till 1941," MS, entry for Sept. 28, 1915, Center for American History, University of Texas at Austin; *Proceedings of the Joint Committee,* 646, 677, 356.

15. "Kill Mexican Rebel Head," *Washington Herald,* Oct. 2, 1915, in clippings file, SRE, AEMEUA, Leg 685, Exp 3; Allhands, 268; Pierce, *A Brief History,* 97; "Records," 812/16667. See also Virgil Lott, "The Rio Grande Valley," TS [n.d.], Center for American History, University of Texas at Austin, 69; *Proceedings of the Joint Committee,* 575.

16. Report of E. B. Stone, Oct. 28, 1915, Bureau of Investigation. Also see Pérez, "Memoirs," 57, for a mention of the killing of a man named Robles.

17. Kirby Warnock, *Texas Cowboy: The Oral Memoirs of Roland A. Warnock and His Life on the Texas Frontier* (Dallas: Trans-Pecos, 1992), 49–50.

18. Ibid., 125.

19. Pérez, "Memoirs," 57–58; *Proceedings of the Joint Committee,* 47–48.

20. Dorothy Lee Pope, *Rainbow Era on the Rio Grande* (Brownsville, Tex.: Springman-King, 1971), 121.

21. *Proceedings of the Joint Committee,* 599.

22. "Exclusion Act Put in Force Along Border," *New York Sun,* Sept. 15, 1915, in clippings file, SRE, AEMEUA, Leg 685, Exp 3.

23. Maude T. Gilliland, *Rincon: A Story of Life on a South Texas Ranch at the Turn of the Century* (Brownsville, Tex.: Springman-King, 1964), 93; Francisco Sandoval, interview by Luis B. Gonzalez, June 7, 1973 (Lower Rio Grande Valley Historical Collection, University of Texas Pan-American); Rossington Reynolds, interview by Peggy Canion, April 20, 1973 (South Texas Archives, Texas A & M University-Kingsville), p. 1 of transcript.

24. *San Antonio Express,* Sept. 11, 1915, cited in James Sandos, *Rebellion in the Borderlands* (Norman: Oklahoma University Press, 1992), 98; *Proceedings of the Joint Committee,* 272–73.

25. Pierce, *A Brief History,* 114; *Proceedings of the Joint Committee,* 355; Undated and unsigned memo on reasons for border unrest, AG Correspondence, 573–21, filed with January 1918 correspondence (the letter's language, arguments, and statement of having served as both a Cameron county judge and sheriff overwhelmingly suggest that Emilio Forto is the author); Funston to Secretary of State Lansing, letter, June 9, 1916, "Records," 812.00/18364; Ricardo Flores Magón, "Los Levantamientos en Texas," *Regeneración,* Oct. 2, 1915, 2; "Pro Aniceto Pizaña," *Regeneración,* April 8, 1916.

26. Lott, "The Rio Grande Valley," 85, 41; *New York Sun,* Sept. 28, 1915, in clippings file, SRE, AEMEUA, Leg 685, Exp 3.

27. Walter Prescott Webb, *The Texas Rangers: A Century of Frontier Defense* (Boston: Houghton Mifflin, 1935), 478. For a comparison with Argentina, see Richard Ribb, "José Tomás Canales and the Texas Rangers: Myth, Identity, and Power in South Texas, 1900–1920" (Ph.D. diss., University of Texas at Austin, 2001), 2.

28. "Exclusion Act Put in Force Along Border," *New York Sun,* Sept. 15, 1915, in clippings file, SRE, AEMEUA, Leg 685, Exp 3; "Mexican Suspects Killed on Border," *New York Times,* Sept. 15, 1915, in clippings file, SRE, AEMEUA, Leg 685, Exp 3.

29. "Records," 812.00/16256; *Proceedings of the Joint Committee,* 957.

30. "Records," 812.00/16054, 16175, 16319, 16723, 16803.

31. Telegram from Captain Ransom, Sept. 19, 1915, AG Correspondence, 551–17; Ireneo de la Garza, Jr., to José Z. Garza, Sept. 20, 1915, SRE, AEMEUA, Leg 477, Exp 19; report of Rogers, Nov. 9, 1915, Bureau of Investigation.

32. "Records," 812.00/14526.

33. "Records," 812.00/16256; report of Rogers, Oct. 1, 1915, Bureau of Investigation.

34. Ransom to Adjutant General, Jan. 24, 1916, Aldrich Papers, Center for American History, University of Texas at Austin, Box 3P157, Folder 2.

35. "Border Fighting Worse," *New York Sun,* Sept. 28, 1915, in clippings file, SRE, AEMEUA, Leg 685, Exp 3; "Mexicans Kill U.S. Soldier, Loot Texas City," *New York Tribune,* Sept. 25, 1915, in clippings file, SRE, AEMEUA, Leg 685, Exp 3.

36. "Kleberg Would Clear Bank of Rio of Brush," *Brownsville Herald,* Nov. 27, 1915, 1.

37. Harbert Davenport to Walter P. Webb, Jan. 30, 1935, Webb Papers.

38. *La Crónica,* June 15, 1911, 2.

39. Testimony of J. T. Canales, *Proceedings of the Joint Committee,* 922; "Records," 812.00/16752. For a mention of the potential usefulness of such a system, see L. H. Bates to Adjutant General, Aug. 4, 1915, AG Correspondence, 550–18; *Proceedings of the Joint Committee,* 548–49.

40. "Records," 812.00/16752.

41. *Proceedings of the Joint Committee,* 564, 375, 197–98.

42. Oct. 30, 1915, telegram from Robert Lansing, Mexican Claims Commission, Docket #2745.

43. Funston to Ferguson, Sept. 16, 1915, "Records," 812.00/16198; Sandos, *Rebellion,* 97.

44. Nov. 16, 1915, AG Correspondence, 552–13.

45. "U.S. Soldiers Shoot Mexicans in Hot Fights," *New York Tribune,* Sept. 18, 1915, in clippings file, SRE, AEMEUA, Leg 685, Exp 3; "Records," 812.00/16600.

46. Ibid., 17030.

47. *Proceedings of the Joint Committee,* 950–51.

48. Sept. 4, 1915, telegram from Sheriff W. T. Gardner, AG Correspondence, 551–12; Sept. 6, 1915, AG Correspondence, 551–10.

49. Report of A. L. Barkey, Sept. 8, 1915, Bureau of Investigation; Garrett to Lansing, letter, Sept. 14, 1915, "Records," 812.00/16216; *New York World,* Sept. 26, 1915, in clippings file, SRE, AEMEUA, Leg 685, Exp 3. For a recollection of the searchlight and of growing up in Kingsville during this fear, see Mrs. R. L. Cooper Memoirs, South Texas Oral History and Folklore Collection, Texas A & M University-Kingsville.

50. Alexander Boynton to Governor Ferguson, letter, Sept. 14, 1915, AG Correspondence, 551–15; report of Arthur Barke, Oct. 12, 1915, Bureau of Investigation. For another alarmed message, see Captain Saunders to Adjutant General, letter, Sept. 16, 1915, AG Correspondence, 551–17.

51. "New Plot by Mexicans," *Washington Post,* Sept. 26, 1915, in clippings file, SRE, AEMEUA, Leg 685, Exp 3.

52. Reports of Howard Wright, Sept. 14 and Sept. 17, 1915, Bureau of Investigation.

53. Report of R. L. Barnes, Sept. 18, 1915, Bureau of Investigation; Aug. 28, 1915, "Records," 812.00/16011. For other similar accounts, see report of R. L. Barnes, Aug. 28, 1915, Bureau of Investigation; report of R. L. Barnes, Aug. 30, 1915, ibid.

54. Report of R. L. Barnes, Dec. 28, 1915, Bureau of Investigation; report of Charles Breniman, Jan. 12, 1916, ibid.; General Funston to Adjutant General, letter, Dec. 14, 1915, "Records," 812.00/116999.

55. Feb. 3, 1916, in "Records," 812.00/17260.

56. Antimaco Sax, *Los Mexicanos en el destierro* (San Antonio: [n.p.], 1916), 7, 9; *Regeneración,* Oct. 9, 1915, 3.

57. A clipping of the article is included in a Sept. 4, 1915, letter from San Benito resident J. L. Crawford to Congressman John Nance Garner, "Records," 812.00/16096.

58. *Regeneración,* Oct. 2, 1915, 1; ibid., Oct. 9, 1915, 1; ibid., Oct. 30, 1915, 1.

59. Guy Smith, "The Border Troubles," *Rebel,* Oct. 9, 1915, 1; "Land League Organizer Arrested," *Rebel,* Oct. 23, 1915, 1; "Hernandez Case," *Rebel,* Nov. 6, 1915, 4.

60. Report of A. L. Barkey, Sept. 3, 1916, Bureau of Investigation. Hernández's article is included in Barkey's report as a typewritten translation. I cannot find the original and therefore cannot verify the translation.

61. Peavey, "Day by Day Stories and History," 80.

62. "Records," 812.00/17030.

63. "Records," 812.00/17078 and 17112.

64. Weekly border report based on dispatches from week of March 25, 1916, "Records," 17754.

65. U.S. Memorial, Mexican Claims Commission, Docket #850; Pierce, *A Brief History,* 99; "Records," 812.00/17592; J. J. Sanders to Texas Adjutant General, April 13, 1916, Aldrich Papers, Box 3P157, Folder 2; "Records," 812.00/18976.

66. March 23, 1916, to Adjutant General, AG Correspondence, 553–23; War Secretary to State Secretary, letter, Jan. 6, 1916, AG Correspondence, 17070.

67. Pierce, *A Brief History,* 99; *Proceedings of the Joint Committee,* 865.

68. "Excerpt from Letter from Special Agent Barnes," Dec. 20, 1915, in "Gray-Lane Files," *Records of International Conferences, Commissions, and Expositions. Records of the United States Commissioners of the American and Mexican Joint Commission, 1916,* RG 43, United States Nation Archives (USNA), Memo #11 (hereafter cited as "Gray-Lane Files").

69. Sandos, *Rebellion,* 131; General Frederick Funston to State Department, telegram, Feb. 11, 1916, "Records," 812.00/17266; Ciro R. de la Garza, *El Plan de San Diego* (Victoria, Tamaulipas: Universidad Autónama de Tamaulipas, 1970), 42; Ciro R. de la Garza, *La revolución Mexicana en el estado de Tamaulipas* (México, D.F.: Libreria de Manuel Porrua, 1975), 215. R. Ciro de la Garza also maintains that Pizaña was taken to Querétaro for three days and released by Carranza with the understanding that he would stay away from the U.S. border. See de la Garza, *El Plan de San Diego,* 34.

70. "Por la libertad de Aniceto Pizaña," *Regeneración,* March 4, 1916, 3; Ricardo Flores Magón, "Aniceto Pizaña," *Regeneración,* Feb. 19, 1916, 3; Marcos Mendoza to Venustiano Carranza, March 14, 1916, Archivo Venustiano Carranza (AVC), Centro de Estudios de Historia de México, Departamento Cultural de Condumex, S.A., México, D.F. [Mexico City], Carpeta 69, Legajo 7559; "Pro Aniceto Pizaña," *Regeneración,* April 8, 1916, 3.

71. Sandos, *Rebellion,* 134; "Records," 812.00/17062; Salvador Hernández Padilla, *El magonismo: Historia de una pasión liberaria, 1900–1922* (México, D.F.: Ediciones Era, 1984), 197.

72. Josefina Zoraida Vázquez and Lorenzo Meyer, *México frente a Estados Unidos: Un ensayo histórico, 1776–1993,* 3d ed. (México, D.F: Fondo de Cultura Económica, 1995), 137; Friedrich Katz, *The Life and Times of Pancho Villa* (Palo Alto, Calif.: Stanford University Press, 1999).

73. Carranza to Arredondo, telegram, May 8, 1916, "Records," 812.00/18145.5; Secretary of War to Secretary Lansing, letter, May 17, 1916, "Records," 812.00/18199; State Department to Rogers, telegram, May 22, 1916, ibid.

74. Quoted in Katz, *The Life and Times of Pancho Villa,* 604; Vázquez and Meyer, *México frente a Estados Unidos,* 158.

75. Arredondo to Lansing, May 22, 1916, "Records," 812.00/19450.

76. For Ferguson's statement, see Arredondo to Carranza, telegram, May 23, 1916, SRE, AEMEUA, Leg 484, Exp 5.

77. For these different reports, see Arredondo to Carranza, telegram, May 23, 1916, SRE, AEMEUA, Leg 484, Exp 5; "Records," 812.00/17981, 17112, 17664, 17212; report of J. B. Rogers, Feb. 5, 1916, in "Gray-Lane Files," Memo #11.

78. "Records," 812.00/18431; Arredondo to Carranza, telegram, June 7, 1916, SRE, AEMEUA, Leg 484, Exp 6; Funston to Lansing, June 9, 1916, "Records," 812.00/18364.

79. Arredondo to Carranza, telegram, June 10, 1916, SRE, AEMEUA, Leg 484, Exp 6; "Records," 812.00/18505.

80. "Records," 812.00/18505.

81. Confessions of Simón Solis, Antonio Cuevas, and Norberto Pezzot, in Case No. 5204, *State of Texas v. Norberto Pezzot et al.,* District Court of Webb County, Texas, in Webb Station Raids, "Gray-Lane Files," Memo #11; Sept. 1, 1916, letter from Sebastian Wilcox, "Gray-Lane Files," Memo #11; Sandos, *Rebellion,* 146–47.

82. "Records," 812.00/18473, 18598; Pierce, *Brief History,* 101; Sandos, *Rebellion,* 147–48. See typescript of trial document titled "The State of Texas vs. Jose Antonio Arce et al., No. 5209. In the District Court of Webb County, Texas. April Term, 1916," in "Gray-Lane Files," Memo #1; *Jose Antonio Arce, et al., v. Texas* (District Court of Webb County, No. 4314).

83. Pierce, *Brief History,* 100; Matamoros Consul to State Department, telegram, June 17, 1916, "Records," 812.00/18462.

84. Pershing to War Department, telegram, June 17, 1916, "Records," 812.00/18544; Tampico Consul to State Department, telegram, June 17, 1916, ibid., 18458; Juarez Consul to State Department, telegram, June 17, 1916, ibid., 18472.

85. Pierce, *Brief History,* 103; Rodgers to State Department, telegram, June 18, 1916, "Records," 812.00/18457; Piedras Negras Consul to State Department, telegram, June 18, 1916, ibid., 18452; Lansing to Arredondo, letter, June 20, 1916, "Records," 812.00/19450.

86. Sandos, *Rebellion,* 150–51; "Records," 812.00/18590, 18591.

87. Monterrey Consul General to Lansing, telegram, June 14, 1916, "Records," 812.00/18419; Matamoros consul to Lansing, June 15, 1916, ibid., 18426. For an example of U.S. suspicion of Ricaut, see Randolph Robertson, Monterey Vice-Consul, to State Department, letter, June 9, 1916, ibid., 20165.

88. Weekly border report from week ending July 8, 1916, ibid., 18756; weekly border report from week ending July 15, 1916, ibid., 18801.

CHAPTER 6
Citizenship at War

1. General Records of the Department of State, "Records of the Department of State Relating to Internal Affairs of Mexico, 1910–1929," RG 59, M 274 (hereafter cited as "Records"), 812.00/15813; "Confessions of Simón Solis, Antonio Cuevas, and Norberto Pezzot," in typescript "Webb Station Raids," in "Gray-Lane Files," *Records of International Conferences, Commissions, and Expositions. Records of the United States Commissioners of the American and Mexican Joint Commission, 1916,* RG 43, United States Nation Archives (USNA), Memo #11 (hereafter cited as "Gray-Lane Files"); Seb. S Wilcox, Official Shorthand Re-

porter, 49th District of Texas, Laredo, Texas, to Gray-Lane Commission, letter, Sept. 1, 1916, ibid.; James Sandos, *Rebellion in the Borderlands: Anarchism and the Plan de San Diego, 1904–1923* (Norman: University of Oklahoma Press, 1992), 199n30.

2. John Vals to Texas Governor's Office, letter, July 17, 1916, "Gray-Lane Files," Memo #44.

3. Testimony of Thomas Hook, *Proceedings of the Joint Committee*, 240–41; Charles Warren, Assistant Attorney General, to State Department, Aug. 29, 1916, "Gray-Lane Files," Memo #44.

4. *Proceedings of the Joint Committee of the Senate and the House in the Investigation of the State Ranger Force* (Austin, Texas, 1919), 247–49 (hereafter cited as *Proceedings of the Joint Committee*).

5. Ibid., 1396–97, 1409, 1414.

6. David Kennedy, *Over Here: The First World War and American Society* (New York: Oxford University Press, 1980), 26, 86.

7. Kennedy, *Over Here*, 24.

8. Kennedy, *Over Here*, 14, 26, 27. Wilson is quoted on page 24.

9. Kennedy, *Over Here*, 10.

10. Border report based on dispatches of week of April 21, 1917, "Records," 812.00/20880; border report based on dispatches of week of May 5, 1917, ibid., 20931.

11. Adolph Oosterveen to Governor Ferguson, letter, May 12, 1917, Adjutant General Correspondence, Texas State Archives, 563–5 (hereafter cited as AG Correspondence). For other accounts of fleeing for fear of law enforcement officials, see border report based on dispatches of June 2, 1917, "Records," 812.00/21122; and border report based on dispatches of week of June 9, 1917, "Records," 812.00/21044.

12. Ibid.; border report based on dispatches of week of Aug. 4, 1917, "Records," 812.00/21205; J. Luz Saenz, *Los Mexico-Americanos en la gran guerra* (San Antonio, Tex.: Artes Gráficas, 1933), 13, 60.

13. Nancy Gentile Ford, "'Mindful of the Traditions of His Race': Dual Identity and Foreign-Born Soldiers in the First World War American Army," *Journal of American Ethnic History* (Winter 1997): 37; U.S. Army proclamation to "The Mexican Citizens Residing in the States of New Mexico, Arizona, Oklahoma, and Texas," n.d. [1918], Texas War Records, Box 2J355, Center for American History, University of Texas at Austin.

14. Report of J. M. S. Mennet, July 9, 1917, Investigative Case Files of the Bureau of Investigation, 1908–1921, case file 232–84, reel # 856 (hereafter cited as Bureau of Investigation).

15. Luz Saenz, *Los Mexico-Americanos*, 60; *Proceedings of the Joint Committee*, 924–25.

16. *Proceedings of the Joint Committee*, 309–10; Virginia Corn Yeager to Hobby, letter, Nov. 3, 1917, Texas Ranger Correspondence, 1183–16, Texas State Archives, Austin. For a similar incident, see Luz Saenz, *Los Mexico-Americanos*, 16.

17. *Proceedings of the Joint Committee*, 1010, 1013–14; Luz Saenz, *Los Mexico-Americanos*, 30, 44, 60.

18. *Proceedings of the Joint Committee*, 1513–14.

19. Steven A. Reich, "Soldiers of Democracy: Black Texans and the Fight for Citizenship, 1917–1921," *Journal of American History* 82 (March 1996): 1486.

20. Neil Foley, *The White Scourge* (Berkeley: University of California Press, 1998), 115; James R. Green, *Grass-Roots Socialism* (Baton Rouge: Louisiana State University Press, 1978), 356.

21. "Records," 812.00/21098.

22. Quoted in Ward Albro, *Always a Rebel: Ricardo Flores Magón and the Mexican Revolution* (Fort Worth, Tex.: Texas Christian University Press, 1992), 138.

23. Report of Manuel Sorola, Aug. 16, 1916, Bureau of Investigation.

24. Report from General Funston to Adjutant General, Dec. 7, 1916, "Records," 812.00/20105; War to State Department, letter, Jan. 17, 1917, enclosing copy of report of War Dept. Intelligence Officer, Jan. 10, 1917, "Records," 812.00/20395.

25. Affidavit of W. T. Vann, Mexican Claims Commission, RG 76, *Records of the Special Claims Commission, United States and Mexico, Created Under the Claims Convention of September 10, 1923,* Docket #798 (hereafter cited as Mexican Claims Commission); "Records," 812.00/21123; Affidavit of J. A. Champion, Mexican Claims Commission, Docket #798.

26. "Records," 812.00/21592.

27. *Proceedings of the Joint Committee,* 1170–731; Tom East to Adjutant General, March 11, 1918, Adjutant General Papers, 574-10, Adjutant General's Records, Texas State Archives, Austin, Texas; "Report on the Bandit Raid on the East Ranch," by Ranger captain W. L. Right, March 7, 1918, Walter Prescott Webb Papers, Center for American History, University of Texas at Austin, Box 2R290 (hereafter cited as Webb Papers); Mexican Claims Commission, Docket #1389.

28. Report of J. P. S. Mennet, Dec. 14, 1916, Bureau of Investigation; border report based on dispatches of week of Oct. 7, 1916, "Records," 812.00/19628; report of J. P. S. Mennet, Jan. 17, 1917, Bureau of Investigation.

29. See Mexican Claims Commission, Docket #2774; "Records," 812.00/21044; and Mexican Claims Commission, Docket # 2747; Captain Sanders to Adjutant General, letter, Nov. 27, 1917, AG Correspondence, 572-9; Charles Sterns to Adjutant General, letter, Jan. 11, 1918, ibid., 573-12; Charles Stephens to Adjutant General, Jan. 23, 1918, ibid., 573-20; *Proceedings of the Joint Committee,* 378, 566; Oct. 15, 1917, report of Agent Rogers, Bureau of Investigation.

30. Kennedy, *Over Here,* 39.

31. Reich, "Soldiers of Democracy," 1478, 1503.

32. Texas State Council of Defense, "Bulletin No. 35," July 31, 1918, Texas War Records; "Bulletin No. 27," June 5, 1918, ibid.

33. Nancy Gentile Ford, "'Mindful of the Traditions of His Race': Dual Identity and Foreign-Born Soldiers in the First World War American Army," *Journal of American Ethnic History* (Winter 1997): 37, 38, 40–43.

34. *Proceedings of the Joint Committee,* 606, 1097, 550; Folder titled "Department of Labor," in Texas War Records, Box 2J364; C. N. Idar to Joe Hirsch, June 10, 1918, Box 2J376, Texas War Records.

35. See Carole Christian, "Joining the American Mainstream: Texas' Mexican Americans During World War I," *Southwestern Historical Quarterly* 92 (April 1989): 571, 577; W. H. Duncan to Texas National Guard, June 18, 1917, AG Correspondence, 567-6.

36. Emilio Zamora, "Fighting on Two Fronts: The WWI Diary of José de la Luz Saenz and the Language of the Mexican American Civil Rights Movement," unpublished mss., 6–7. I am grateful to Professor Zamora for sharing this article with me.

37. Luz Saenz, *Los México-Americanos,* 112; original letter dated Aug. 17, 1918.

38. Ibid., 18, 249, 283, 7, 13.

39. Ibid., 98.

40. Ibid., 59, 35, 246–47. See, also, Zamora, "Fighting on Two Fronts," 6–7, for further discussion of Luz Saenz's pan-American identity. Luz Saenz is clearly influenced by Mexican *indigenismo,* the cultural identification with an Indian past, as even a cursory examination of José Vansconcelos's classic *La raza cósmica* will indicate. (The two may actually have met, since Vansoncelos visited Corpus Christi in the late 1920s at the invitation of some of Luz Saenz's fellow LULACers.) But contact with living native people in the distinctly unromantic setting of the American Expeditionary Force prevents his discussion of Indians from being purely cultural or ideational, as the elite Mexican identification with the Aztec past so often was.

41. Luz Saenz, *Los México-Americanos,* 282.

42. Ibid., 250; J. Luz Saenz, "Racial Discrimination," in Alonso S. Perales, *Are We Good Neighbors?* (San Antonio: Artes Gráficas, 1948), 33.

43. *Proceedings of the Joint Committee,* 3, 469, 471, 493, 4, 481, 782.

44. Ibid., 1057, 1309–14, 1367, 4, 486, 501.

45. Ibid., 147, 645, 821–23, 1429.

46. Ibid., 818, 827.

47. William Hanson to Adjutant General Harley, Feb. 11, 1918, AG Correspondence, 573–27.

48. Reich, 1486; John Martínez, "Mexican Emigration to the United States, 1910–1930" (Ph.D. diss., University of California, Berkeley, 1957), 31, 45.

49. May 18, 1917, to Chair of the Texas State Council of Defense, Texas War Records Collection, Box 2J355; Minutes of the May 19, 1917, meeting of State Council of Defense, ibid., 2J358.; June 5, 1917, circular letter from the Council of National Defense to State Councils, ibid., 2J355.

50. Evan Anders, *Boss Rule in South Texas: The Progressive Era* (Austin: University of Texas Press, 1982), 250.

51. Anders, *Boss Rule,* 250–53; William Hanson to Adjutant General, June 27, 1918, AG Correspondence, 576–8.

52. Captain Stevens to Adjutant General, Aug. 2, 1918, AG Correspondence, 576–24.

53. Unsigned report on elections filed on Nov. 5, 1918, from Alice, in Webb Papers, Box 2R290.

54. *Proceedings of the Joint Committee,* 578, 684, 1044.

55. Ibid., 685, 880.

56. "Report from W. H. Hanson to General James A. Hartley, Adjutant General of the State of Texas, re Florencio Garcia" [n.d.], in Mexican Claims Commission, Docket #1389; W. T. Vann to Harry Wallis, April 23, 1918, Webb Papers, Box 2R290; W. T. Vann to William Hanson, April 19, 1918, AG Correspondence, 574–25.

57. Charles Stephens to Adjutant General, April 26, 1918, Webb Papers, Box 2R290; William Hanson to Adjutant General, letter, March 28, 1918, AG Correspondence, 574–13.

58. J. T. Canales to Adjutant General, telegram, Aug. 31, 1918, AG Correspondence, 577–5; William Hanson to Adjutant General, telegram, Aug. 31, 1918, Webb Papers, Box 2R290; W. R. Jones to Adjutant General, Sept. 6, 1918, AG Correspondence, 577–6.

59. *Proceedings of the Joint Committee,* 869.

60. Ibid., 210; Anders, *Boss Rule,* 267–68.

61. For Canales's charges against the Rangers, see *Proceedings of the Joint Committee,* 1–6, 145–54.

62. Anders, *Boss Rule,* 263.

63. Richard Ribb, "José Tomás Canales and the Texas Rangers: Myth, Identity, and Power in South Texas, 1900–1920" (Ph.D. diss., University of Texas at Austin, 2001), 196.

64. *Proceedings of the Joint Committee,* 1010–1019.

65. Ribb, "José Tomás Canales," 297.

66. Charles M. Robinson III, *The Men Who Wear the Star: The Story of the Texas Rangers* (New York: Random House, 2000), 283; Ribb, "José Tomás Canales," 171.

67. *Proceedings of the Joint Committee,* 886–90. Interview of Ann Locascio (J. T.'s granddaughter) by author, February 1998; J. T. Canales to Gerald Mann, May 15, 1941, South Texas Archives, Texas A & M University-Kingsville, J. T. Canales Papers, Box 430–3.

68. *Journal of the Senate,* State of Texas, Regular Session, Thirty-Sixth Legislature (Austin, Texas, 1919), 23; Anders, *Boss Rule,* 271.

69. Hanson to C. J. Blackwell, telegram, Feb. 19, 1919, AG Correspondence, 578–22; Aldrich to Eugene Buck, May 13, 1919, ibid., 579–12; Hudspeth to Adjutant General, May 26, 1919, ibid., 579–23.

70. *Journal of the Senate,* State of Texas, Regular Session, Thirty-Sixth Legislature (Austin, Texas, 1919), 288; Sandos, *Rebellion in the Borderlands,* 207; Ribb, "José Tomás Canales," 261.

CHAPTER 7
Legacies

1. Arnoldo De León, *Mexican Americans in Texas: A Brief History* (Arlington Heights, Ill.: Harlan Davidson, 1993), 113; "La Política en Brownsville," *La Crónica,* Dec. 3, 1910.

2. Armando Alonzo, "A History of the Mexicans in the Lower Rio Grande Valley of Texas: Their Role in Land Development and Commercial Agriculture, 1900–1930" (master's thesis, University of Texas Pan-American, 1983), 44; James Sandos, "The Mexican Revolution and the United States, 1915–1917: The Impact of Conflict in the Tamaulipas-Texas Frontier upon the Emergence of Revolutionary Government in Mexico" (Ph.D. diss., University of California at Berkeley, 1978), 116, 119; and James Sandos, *Rebellion in the Borderlands* (Norman: Oklahoma University Press, 1992), 66, 70.

3. Evan Anders, *Boss Rule in South Texas: The Progressive Era* (Austin: University of Texas Press, 1982), 143; P. E. Montgomery, "Musings of Monty," *Monty's Monthly Review* (February 1935), in Harding Collection, Raymondville, Texas, Public Library (hereafter cited as Harding Collection); A. B. Henry, "Many Soldiers Who Came to Valley in 1916 to Chase Bandits Returned," *Valley Morning Star,* Jan. 20, 1956, B12.

4. Anders, *Boss Rule,* 277–79.

5. David Montejano, *Anglos and Mexicans in the Making of Texas, 1836–1986* (Austin: University of Texas Press, 1986), 129–30, 143, 148.

6. Anders, *Boss Rule,* 279; Montejano, *Anglos and Mexicans,* 160.

7. Montejano, *Anglos and Mexicans,* 162, 167–68; Ozzie G. Simmons, "Anglo Americans and Mexican Americans in South Texas: A study in Dominant-Subordinate Group Relations"

(Ph.D. diss., Harvard University, 1952), 441, 453; Dellos Urban Buckner, "Study of the Lower Rio Grande Valley as a Culture Area" (master's thesis, University of Texas at Austin, 1929), 85.

8. Simmons, "Anglo Americans and Mexican Americans," 130; Buckner, "Study," 86.

9. Montejano, *Anglos and Texans,* 253–54, 169; O. Douglas Weeks, "The League of United Latin-American Citizens: A Texas-Mexican Civic Organization," *Southwestern Political and Social Science Quarterly* 10:31 (1929): 11.

10. David G. Gutiérrez, "Migration, Emergent Ethnicity, and the 'Third Space': The Shifting Politics of Nationalism in Greater Mexico," *Journal of American History* 86:2 (September 1999).

11. Cynthia Orozco, "The Origins of the League of United Latin American Citizens (LULAC) and the Mexican American Civil Rights Movement in Texas with an Analysis of Women's Political Participation in a Gendered Context, 1910–1929" (Ph.D. diss., University of California at Los Angeles, 1992), 175, 179–94; "Order Sons of America," Oliver Douglas Weeks Collection, LULAC Papers, Benson Latin American Collection, University of Texas at Austin, Box 1, Folder 1 (hereafter cited as Weeks Collection).

12. Orozco, "Origins," 201.

13. Eduardo Idar to James Tafolla, letter, Dec. 14, 1927, and James Tafolla to Eduardo Idar, letter, Dec. 17, 1927, Andrés de Luna Collection, LULAC Papers, Benson Latin American Collection, University of Texas at Austin, Box 1, Folder 3 (hereafter cited as de Luna Collection).

14. League of United Latin American Citizens, "History of Lulac," (1977), n.p.; notebook, Weeks Collection, LULAC Papers, Box 1, Folder 4; Orozco, "Origins," 222–39.

15. Weeks, "League," 4, 12.

16. Weeks, "League," 5; Orozco, "Origins," 15, 95; typescript of report of Eagle Pass council No. 19, n.d. [1929], de Luna Collection, Box 1, Folder 3.

17. Orozco, "Origins," 277–80; M. C. Gonzáles to J. T. Canales, Feb. 29, 1932, J. T. Canales Papers, South Texas Archives, Texas A & M University-Kingsville, Box 436.

18. C. N. Idar, "Nuestra liga: Motivos de meditacion," n.d. [1929], newspaper clipping in Album Two, Ben Garza Collection, LULAC papers, Benson Latin American Collection, University of Texas at Austin (hereafter cited as Garza Collection); Orozco, "Origins," 229.

19. Alonso S. Perales, *El México Americano y la política del sur de Texas* (San Antonio, Texas, 1931), 3, 7; Weeks, "League," 4.

20. Undated typescript from Andrés de Luna to McCracken, de Luna Collection, Box 1, Folder 8.

21. Vicki Ruiz, *From Out of the Shadows: Mexican Women in Twentieth-Century America* (New York: Oxford University Press, 1998), 91; Orozco, "Origins," 1.

22. Perales, *El México Americano,* 10; Orozco, "Origins," 201; Richard García, *Rise of the Mexican American Middle Class: San Antonio, 1929–1941* (College Station, Tex.: Texas A & M University Press, 1991), 286; Weeks, "League," 14.

23. Quoted in Orozco, "Origins," 266, 282; Weeks, "League," 16.

24. Weeks, "League," 16; Perales, *El México Americano,* 8.

25. "Nuestra actitud ante la historia," *El Popular,* n.d. [May 14, 1929], Album Two, Garza

Collection, LULAC Papers; J. Luz Saenz, "La Discriminación racial," n.d., n.p., Jose de la Luz Saenz Collection, LULAC Papers, Benson Latin American Collection, University of Texas at Austin, Box 3, Folder 2 (hereafter cited as Luz Collection).

26. José Gonzáles, *El Paladín* [1929], Weeks Collection, Box 1, Folder 10; *El Paladín,* April 31, 1928, de Luna Collection, Box 1, Folder 3; Castulo Gutiérrez, "Para los que no conocen nuestra inst.," n.d. [1929], Album Two, Garza Collection.

27. Transcript, May 24, 1929, Weeks Collection, Box 1, Folder 10.

28. "Nuestra actitud," Garza Collection; Gutiérrez, "Para los que no conocen nuestra inst.," ibid.

29. *La Prensa,* April 24, 1930, Fondo IV, Secretaría de Relaciones Exteriores (SRE), Archivo de la Embajada Mexicana en Estados Unidos de América (AEMEUA), Leg 74, Exp 14.

30. Alonso Perales to Rep. John Nance Garner, May 27, 1929, Album Two, Garza Collection; Guadalupe San Miguel, *"Let All of Them Take Heed": Mexican Americans and the Campaign for Educational Equality in Texas, 1910–1981* (Austin: University of Texas Press, 1987), 71; Gutiérrez, "Para los que no conocen nuestra inst.," Garza Collection.

31. Undated and unsigned description of Feb. 16, 1930, meeting in San Diego, Texas, in Weeks Collection, Box 1, Folder 6; Eduardo Idar to James Tafolla, Dec. 14, 1927, de Luna Collection, Box 1, Folder 3.

32. García, *Rise,* 261; Mario T. Garcia, *Mexican Americans: Leadership, Ideology, and Identity* (New Haven: Yale University Press, 1989), 33.

33. Typescript copy of resolution presented to San Diego Convention, Feb. 16, 1930, Weeks Collection, Box 1, Folder 6.

34. Quoted in Benjamin Márquez, *LULAC: The Evolution of a Mexican American Political Organization* (Austin: University of Texas Press, 1993), 33; see also Neil Foley, "Becoming Hispanic: Mexican Americans and the Faustian Pact with Whiteness," in *Reflexiones 1997: New Directions in Mexican American Studies* (Austin: University of Texas, Center for Mexican American Studies, 1998); Steven Wilson, "Brown over 'Other White': Mexican Americans' Legal Arguments and Litigation Strategy in Desegregation Litigation," *Law and History Review,* forthcoming.

35. Report on convention, May 24, 1929, Weeks Papers, Box 1, Folder 10; J. Luz Saenz, letter, July 23, 1948, Luz Collection, Box 3, Folder 10.

36. May 24, 1929, report on convention, Weeks Collection, Box 1, Folder 10; J. Luz Saenz, "La Discriminación racial," Luz Collection, Box 3, Folder 2.

37. See Luis de la Rosa to Venustiano Carranza, [n.d.], Archivo Venustiano Carranza (AVC), Centro de Estudios de Historia de México, Departamento Cultural de Condumex, S.A., México, D.F. [Mexico City], 136, 15541; de la Rosa to Carranza, July 16, 1919, ibid.; de la Rosa to Carranza, July 28, 1919, ibid.

38. Jean Meyer, "Mexico: Revolution and Reconstruction in the 1920's," in *The Cambridge History of Latin America,* vol. 5, ed. Leslie Bethell (Cambridge: Cambridge University Press, 1986), 187–88; Alan Knight, "Mexico, c. 1930–46," in ibid., vol. 7, 20.

39. Américo Paredes, interview by author, Sept. 29, 1998, Austin, Texas; [Illegible] to Aniceto Pizaña, letter, Aug. 3, 1938, Pizaña papers, Carlos Larralde Collection, Calimesa, California; Ciro R. de la Garza Treviño, *El Plan de San Diego* (Ciudad Victoria, Tamaulipas: Universidad Autónoma de Tamaulipas, Instituto de Investigaciones Históricas, 1970), 44.

40. Petition (Jan. 15, 1945), provisional land grant (Feb. 4, 1946), *Diario Oficial* (Jan. 23, 1950), Agente General de la Secretaria de Recursos Hidrálicos to Beatríz Pizaña (May 2, 1970), all in Aniceto Pizaña Papers, Carlos Larralde Collection, Calimesa, California; Guadalupe Pizaña Papers, Carlos Larralde Collection, Calimesa, California.

41. "Dotación de Ejidos pob. 'Conrado Castillo,' antes El Encino, Llera, Tamps," Archivo Agrario, Liga de Comunidades Agrarios to Jefe del Departamento Agrario, Nov. 22, 1948, 23/19067.

42. Francisco Ramos Aguirre, *Historia del corrido en la frontera Tamaulipeca* (Ciudad Victoria, Tamaulipas: Fondo Nacional para la Cultura y las Artes, 1994), 81; "Murió Solo y abandonado conocido veterano en Encino," *El Sol de Tampico,* March 3, 1957, clipping in Aniceto Pizaña papers, Carlos Larralde Collection, Calimesa, California; Benjamin Johnson and Carlos Larralde, eds., *A Texas Revolutionary of 1915: Aniceto Pizaña's Recollections of Life in the Lower Rio Grande Valley* (The DeGolyer Library and the Clements Center for Southwest Studies, Southern Methodist University, under contract).

43. Ramos Aguirre, *Historia,* 84; translation is altered from Américo Paredes, *A Texas-Mexican Cancionero: Folksongs of the Lower Border* (Urbana: University of Illinois Press, 1976), 71–73.

44. Paredes, *A Texas-Mexican Cancionero;* see also Richard R. Flores, "The Corrido and the Emergence of Texas-Mexican Social Identity," *Journal of American Folklore* 105 (1992): 166–82.

45. Dorothy Lee Pope, *Rainbow Era on the Rio Grande* (Brownsville, Tex.: Springman-King, 1971), 120; C. H. Pease, "Reminiscences of Early Delta," *Gravity Irrigation News,* March 3, 1926, clipping in Harding Collection; Mary E. Lane, "Bloody, Dangerous Days in the Valley Weren't So Long Ago," *Star,* May 10, 1936, clipping in Harding Collection; William Sterling, *Trails and Trials of a Texas Ranger* (Norman: University of Oklahoma, 1968), 28, 23.

46. Lane, "Bloody, Dangerous Days"; C. H. Pease, "Mexican Bandits Terrorize Delta," *Gravity Irrigation News,* March 10, 1926, clipping in Harding Collection.

47. Virgil Lott, "The Rio Grande Valley," TS [n.d.], Center for American History, University of Texas at Austin, 24; D. P. Gay, untitled MS [1933?], Walter Prescott Webb Papers, Center for American History, University of Texas at Austin, Box 2M275.

48. Lane, "Bloody, Dangerous Days"; C. H. Pease, "U.S. Troops End the Bandit Raids of 1915," *Hidalgo County Independent,* June 6, 1930, clipping in Harding Collection; C.H. Pease, "Outlaws Captured, Peace Restored," *Delta Irrigation News,* April 7, 1926, clipping in Harding Collection.

49. Miriam Chatelle, *For We Love Our Valley Home* (San Antonio, Tex.: The Naylor Company, 1948), 21; Jean Walker, "Plan de San Diego," *The Junior Historian* 21 (September 1960): 29, clipping in Harding Collection; Lane, "Bloody, Dangerous Days."

50. Victor Nelson Cisneros, "UCAPAWA Organizing Activities in Texas, 1935–1950," *Aztlán* 9 (Spring and Summer 1978): 73, 75.

51. Emma Tenayuca and Homer Brooks, "The Mexican Question in the Southwest," *The Communist* (March 1939): 259, 263.

52. Américo Paredes, *George Washington Gómez* (Houston, Tex.: Arte Público Press, 1990), 9, 40.

53. Ibid., 21.

54. Ibid., 23; Paredes interview with author, Sept. 29, 1998.

55. George J. Sánchez, *Becoming Mexican American: Ethnicity, Culture and Identity in Chicano Los Angeles, 1900–1945* (New York: Oxford University Press, 1993); Mario T. García, *Mexican Americans.*

56. Adolfo Ramirez, "An Historical Note: 'El Plan de San Diego,'" in *Hojas: A Chicano Journal of Education* (Austin, Tex.: Juarez-Lincoln Press, 1976), 25; Juan Gomez-Quiñones, "Plan de San Diego Revisited," *Aztlán* 1 (Spring 1970): 124–30; Emilio Zamora, "Texas and the History of the Southwest (Plan de San Diego '15)," Feb. 19, 1975, Benson Library rare book collection, cassette 133.

AFTERWORD

1. Mike Davis, *Magical Urbanism: Latinos Reinvent the U.S. Big City* (New York: Verso, 2000), 1, 2, 4, 6, 14.

2. See especially Francis Fukuyama, *The End of History and the Last Man* (New York: Free Press, 1992); Robert D. Kaplan, *An Empire Wilderness: Travels into America's Future* (New York: Vintage, 1998).

3. For a reaffirmation of the place of nationalism even in a universalist moral perspective, see Richard Rorty, *Achieving Our Country: Leftist Thought in Twentieth-Century America* (Cambridge: Harvard University Press, 1998).

4. Patrick J. Buchanan, *The Death of the West: How Dying Populations and Immigrant Invasions Imperil Our Country and Civilization* (New York: St. Martin's, 2002).

5. Leticia Magda Garza-Falcón, *Gente Decente: A Borderlands Response to the Rhetoric of Domination* (Austin: University of Texas Press, 1998), 92. For discussion of agrarian radicalism in postrevolutionary Mexico, see Armando Batra, *Los herederos de Zapata: Movimientos campesinos posrevolucionarios en México* (México, D.F.: Ediciones Era, 1985), and Fernando Salmerón Castro, *Los límites del agrarismo* (Zamora: El Colegio de Michoacán, 1989).

Acknowledgments

Books bear the name of a single author, but they are in fact made possible by a multitude of people and institutions. This one began as a dissertation at Yale University, where Johnny Faragher, Robert Johnston, Gil Joseph, and Steve Pitti supported me with their enthusiasm and (occasionally contradictory) advice. Cesar Rodríguez and George Miles helped with the early stages of bibliographic work. The History Department (through the Mellon Foundation) and the Program in Agrarian Studies provided grants that enabled me to do the necessary fieldwork while a graduate student. Stephen Johnson, Pamela Walker, Walter Isle, Andrew Johnson, and Michelle Nickerson made it possible to get through graduate school and were good company even when I wasn't.

The research necessary to tell this story took me to diverse places in Texas and Mexico. Raymond Craib, Rick López, and Steve Bachelor all provided housing and much-needed guidance in Mexico City. The staff of the Secretaría de Relaciones Exteriores, especially Marta Ramos, went out of their way to be helpful. Andrés Lira at El Colegio de México offered instrumental advice and support about gaining access to the archives of the Mexican military. I am also indebted to the staff at Condumex and the Archivo General de Nación for their assistance. Jesús Ávila guided me through the Archivo General del Estado de Nuevo León. At the Universidad Autónoma de Tamaulipas, Octavio Herrera Pérez shared his thoughts on the Plan de San Diego and some of his vast knowledge on how to research Tamaulipan history.

In California, Tim Isle, Bettina Rubin, and Jimmy Faragher housed me. James Sandos, author of *Rebellion in the Borderlands,* a fine study of the connections between the Flores Magón brothers and the Plan de San Diego uprising, generously shared his insights and leads over one hell of a lunch and through later correspondence. Our approaches to these events differ, as do some of our interpretations, but I am grateful for his generosity. Carlos Larralde went out of his way to open his tremendously rich private collection for my perusal, sharing many of his own memories and much of his own research in the process.

Most of my research, however, took place in Texas. The staff at the Benson Latin American Collection, the Center for American History, and the Texas State Archives (particularly the Benson's Margo Gutiérrez) were tremendously helpful and friendly. Richard Ribb was a model colleague when others would have been consumed by territoriality. My work in Austin would have been much slower and more isolated without his advice and generosity. Readers familiar with his dissertation will particularly recognize the influence of his careful reconstruction of the Canales hearings and the political intrigue surrounding them. Elliott Young also helped with advice and knowledge of the University of Texas and the borderlands. David Montejano provided useful advice early on, and I am grateful for his continued interest in this project. Emilio Zamora endured several long phone calls, sharing his work on J. Luz Saenz and the Plan. Meg Seaholm, Greg Cantrell, David Ulbrich, Ann Moore, Adam Gordon, Stacey Jeffries, and Nathaniel Norton made my time in Austin less lonely than it otherwise would have been.

I was also fortunate to find support in south Texas. Cecilia Aros Hunter and her staff at the South Texas Archives at the University of Texas A & M Kingsville helped me with knowledge of both their collection and the region. Lisa Neely at the King Ranch Archives also pointed me in useful directions. Jerry Thompson at Texas A & M International in Laredo was kind enough to share his knowledge of Juan Cortina and Laredo's history—to say nothing of bearing with my case of Montezuma's (Cortina's?) Revenge. Román Ramos was a gracious host while I was in Laredo.

Numerous people made my time in the Valley itself fun and productive. Selena Solís, Pam Brown, and David Hall hosted me. David and Pam allowed me to return repeatedly even though they really didn't know me, and David's firsthand knowledge of the Valley was awe-inspiring. Cristi de Juana went out of her way to share her research on intermarriage and her experiences of living in the Valley. Finally, George Gause and numerous staff members and student workers at the Lower Rio Grande Valley Historical Collection treated me like a king.

A dissertation and a book are very different things. Nobody was more influential in this journey than my agent, Susan Rabiner, who put me through a sometimes brutal but always effective writing boot camp. It was an ideal experience for a first-time author, and much of whatever grace there is in these pages is because of her. Lara Heimert at Yale University Press helped me greatly in determining how to write a book that could have wide-ranging appeal while retaining its academic rigor. Jeffrey Schier, my manuscript editor at Yale, cleaned up much of my prose and caught numerous errors. The California Institute of Technology supported a research trip to Mexico, and a Baruch-Marshall Grant from the George Marshall Foundation supported additional trips to Mexico and Texas. In southern California, Bill Deverell, Monica McCormick, Roberto Lint-Sagarena, Mark Wild, Daniel Hurewitz, Clark Davis, and Shana Bernstein provided stimulating conversations and useful feedback on my book proposal.

Returning to Texas, where I grew up, was a blessing. My colleagues and students at the University of Texas at San Antonio helped me think about how to fit borderlands stories into the larger sweep of American history. At Southern Methodist University, the history department and Clements Center for the Study of the Southwest provided a supportive and intellectually stimulating environment for the completion of the manuscript. A National Endowment for the Humanities/Social Science Research Council Area Studies Grant from the American Council of Learned Societies enabled me to devote six months of uninterrupted time to this task. My department helped subsidize this time and underwrote the cost of illustrations and permissions. Dick J. Reavis and Roberto Salmón offered close readings of the final manuscript, saving me from numerous factual and writing errors.

Of all the friends that I made in the process of researching and writing this book, none was more dear to me than Clark Davis. Like so many others, I benefited from his kindness, generosity of spirit, and unfailingly good humor. And like so many others, I was devastated by his untimely and tragic death. He was as fine a human being as I will ever know. This book is dedicated to his memory.

Index

"A los Hijos de Cuahtémoc, Hidalgo and
Juárez en Texas" (manifesto), 37
African Americans: Brownsville Affair, 16;
civil rights agitation, 193; conditions
faced by, 16, 50–51; fears of enlisting
in uprising, 130; and immigration,
50–51; military service, 16, 153, 158,
161; and Plan de San Diego, 72, 131;
and PLM, 63; population of compared
to Latinos, 207, 208; school segregation, 180; sexual relationships with
other races, 16, 193; voting, 36, 64.
See also Slavery
Agricultural boom, 29–32; effect on
Tejanos, 177, 178; and local economy,
40–41; and need for laborers, 165;
and Tejano Progressives, 46
Agricultural workers, 34–36, 165, 201–
2, 211; campos de desenraiz, 41;
farmer's use of force to maintain,

164; Mexicans as, 177, 178
Agriculture: aggressive marketing to,
28–29; agrarian radicalism, 63–66, 101,
132; dispossession of small Southern
farmers, 63–64; large-scale, 40, 41.
See also Ranching
Aguilar, Tomas, 113
Alamo, 11, 173, 200
Alema, Octabiana, 118
Allhands, J. L., 115
Anarchism and Flores Magón brothers,
65, 80
"Angel of Death." *See* Hamer, Frank
Anglos: acculturation of, 13; economic
dominance, 17–18, 20; solidarity, 111–
13; in south Texas, 26. *See also* Racial
issues; White supremacy
Arce, José Antonio, 141
Arms. *See* Weapons
Army, U.S. *See* U.S. Army